vegan Bible

Acknowledgements

There are often more people than you think involved in writing a book! A huge thank you to my editor, Laurence, for offering me this somewhat crazy but very exciting project. Endless thanks to my parents who gave me incredible help and support during the creation of this book; without you I would never have achieved it. And tons of thanks to the best friends in the world who were always ready to try my recipes, to lend me a hand with the photos, to give me their opinion as well as their tips; but above all for their unflagging support at all times: Flo, Hervé, Anael, Emma, Wahiba, Laura, Sébastien.

This English language paperback edition published in 2019 by
Grub Street
4 Rainham Close
London
SW11 6SS

Email: food@grubstreet.co.uk
Twitter: @grub_street
Facebook: Grub Street Publishing
Web: www.grubstreet.co.uk

Copyright this English language edition © Grub Street 2019

Copyright © 2014 Éditions La Plage, Paris
Published originally in French under the title *Vegan*
Graphic design: Olivia Design
Copy preparation: Clémentine Bougrat
Page layout: Transparence
Illustrations: Myrtille Couten (with the help of Quitterie Roger)

A CIP record for this title is available from the British Library

ISBN 978-1-911621-32-4

vegan *Bible*

Text and photographs by

Marie Laforêt

With the participation of
Doctor Jérôme Bernard-Pellet

Grub Street · London

SUMMARY

 Quick   *Easy*   ● *Economical*

INTRODUCTION

Vegan. A word almost unheard of by the general public a few years ago but which today is regularly discussed in magazines, on TV programmes and found on the labels of our food and cosmetics. Presented time after time as a new craze or dangerous extreme, the vegan lifestyle, or veganism, although now much more common, is still very poorly understood. Vegan cuisine is, unfortunately, even less understood. It is bland according to some, full of unnatural ingredients and 'fake' foods according to others, of little nutritional value, far from gourmet...stereotypes abound. Yet vegan cuisine is unparalleled with regard to its variety and creativity, and this can be seen every day thanks to the numerous visionary chefs who are making it known around the world. Plant-based food has in fact been the trend in traditional gastronomy for some years now. Chef Jean-Georges Vongerichten, who has three Michelin stars, announced in 2013 that he was going to open a 100% raw, vegan restaurant in New York. A few years ago, the winner of the well-known American baking television programme 'Cupcake Wars' was a young vegan baker who proved that not only could vegan cuisine be as good as 'traditional' cuisine but that it could even be better. One thing is certain, you haven't heard the last of vegan cuisine.

But, how do you cook vegan? Do you have to eat tofu? How do you make cakes without eggs? And barbecues with friends? What to do then? Don't panic! This book will provide you with the gradual means to discover vegan cuisine. It will show you how to cook plant-based proteins, replace eggs and dairy products, cook vegetables and find your way around gourmet, classic and more unusual recipes. You will even learn how to make your own fermented non-dairy cheeses, create impressive desserts for celebrations, and make almost every classic dish in a 100% vegan way. Whether you are a beginner in the kitchen or a well-versed enthusiast, pressed for time or on a budget, you will find recipes to suit your needs, and dishes to enjoy whatever the season or occasion.

The author

Fascinated by plants and vegetables and committed to cooking in an ethical, healthy gourmet way, Marie Laforêt shares her culinary discoveries and experiments on her blog '100% végétal'.
Also a photographer, her photos accompany her recipes. In addition, she is involved in promoting responsible eating through numerous community projects.
She is also the author of books such as *Desserts gourmands sans œufs ni lait* (Eggless and Dairy-Free Desserts) and *Coco* (Coconut) published by La Plage.

A brief glossary of veganism

Vegetarians: Do not eat animal flesh (meat, fish or shellfish) or, in theory, by-products resulting in the death of animals (gelatine, rennet cheeses).

Dietary vegans: Do not eat anything of animal origin (therefore no dairy products, eggs, honey, etc.).

Ethical vegans: Do not eat or use any product involving animal exploitation. This means that these vegans do not wear fur or leather, do not buy cosmetics or household products containing animal substances or which have been tested on animals, and do not go to shows where animals are exploited such as bullfights, zoos, or circuses that use animals.

Anti-speciesism: Anti-racism and anti-sexism are fully recognised concepts today. Anti speciesism works according to the same implacable logical reasoning: the species to which we belong gives us no right, no superiority over other species, just as gender or ethnicity does not make us superior to others.

Abolitionist: This word may sound familiar to you because of the 18th century abolitionist movement that fought for the abolition of slavery. We also talk of abolitionists in the context of the death penalty, torture and even prostitution. Among animal rights defenders, abolitionists are those who campaign for the abolition of all animal exploitation. They are often contrasted with animal *welfarists* who campaign for better living conditions for animals but are not necessarily opposed to their use if they are well treated.

What does it mean to be vegan?

Being vegan is to reject the exploitation of animals. It is a complete lifestyle that goes beyond vegetarianism and simply eating a vegan diet, and it does not only involve food. It is reflected by a different approach to consumption that is both committed and ethical, and which excludes products resulting from animal exploitation.

The origin and definition of the word 'vegan'

The term was coined in 1944 by Donald Watson, co-founder of the Vegan Society, from the word *vegetarian* (VEG-etari-AN), with the aim of distinguishing it from lacto-ovo vegetarianism. Since 1951, the Vegan Society has defined veganism as living without exploiting animals. The term vegan comprises both diet and lifestyle (we talk of *dietary vegans* and *ethical vegans*). In French, for instance, the word *végétalien* only refers to food and is therefore not an exact, complete translation of the word 'vegan'. The word can be spelt in various ways; *vegan*, as it is in English, or *végan* and *végane*. All three are pronounced the same. Some years ago I was personally and openly in favour of a French equivalent for the word. It made sense to introduce a word into our language that allowed for a better understanding of the meaning and a better way to convey the concept. However, I have never managed to get used to spelling it *végane*, and the English spelling of the word is still the most commonly used (on the Internet, in the press or in the few books in which the word appears). So I finally decided to stick with the English spelling. It is the one to which I have naturally gravitated to and which most French vegans also use, but there is disagreement within the vegan community on this matter.

Veganism in the world

Veganism has developed naturally in every country all over the world. Its values are shared by people of all ages, cultures and social groups. Vegans are often told that this lifestyle is the preserve of the elite, but this is not the case as lentils and tofu are a much less expensive source of protein than meat, and there are many vegans in countries with a lower standard of living than our own. There are vegans all over the world, in Europe and across the American continent of course, but also in Africa, India and Asia, and especially in China where there are 50 million vegetarians (vegans included). The number of vegans in the United States doubled between 2009 and 2011 and today there are some 7.5 million of them. In the UK about 2% of the population is vegetarian (including vegans) and in France it is 2% to 3% -- a more modest number than that of our other European neighbours -- but seeing the growth of vegan businesses over these past two years, it is clear that veganism is attracting more and more people here as well.

Why go vegan?

An ethical choice

If we go vegetarian or follow a vegan diet for health reasons or environmental reasons, the decision to adopt a vegan lifestyle encompasses an ethical, moral, even political stance. It is the rejection of animal exploitation and the oppression of animals, of considering ourselves to be 'superior' beings who wield every right over the other living creatures with which we share the planet. The vegan ethos is very simple; animals do not belong to us, their lives are theirs and theirs alone. If it is possible for us to live without exploiting them, we cannot justify disposing with their lives as we currently do. Veganism is a major evolution in our way of viewing the world that surrounds us and the animals within it. Just as the abolition of slavery and colonies -- and more recently, women's rights in Western countries -- have been major social developments which today seem so obvious to us, recognising that animals have the right to life -- and not be exploited -- is the evolution of a mind-set which is already taking place all over the world. It is the logical progression that our agricultural and industrial methods, and our scientific and medical knowledge, have made possible for us today. Given that we are able to meet all our needs and even enjoy our leisure activities without exploiting animals, why not do so?

A more environmentally-friendly lifestyle

Raising livestock, in particular when it is intensively carried out (which is the case for most farms), is a true environmental disaster. It takes over most farmable land, polluting the soil and rivers. On a global level, the raising of livestock produces millions of litres of excrement (generally laced with antibiotics and heavy metal and pesticide residues, etc.) which is not treated but released straight into nature where it seeps into groundwater systems, literally poisoning our drinking water supplies. And because livestock has to be fed, its food has to be grown. As more and more animals are raised to be eaten, more and more land is needed to produce their food. Much of the Amazon rainforest was therefore deforested to plant GMO soy and to raise livestock. This GMO soy is turned into cattle cakes and is, as Fabrice Nicolino explains in his book *Bidoche, l'industrie de la viande menace le monde* (The Meat Industry Threatens the World), imported into Europe to feed livestock (cattle, pigs and chickens). Eating a European steak or chicken therefore contributes to the deforestation of the virgin Amazon rainforest, whose value is incalculable and whose surface area is being dramatically reduced every year. Every seven seconds an area of forest the size of a football pitch is cleared.

Some facts about livestock production:

- 18% of greenhouse gases are the result of livestock production, more than the amount released by all the world's transport put together.

- According to the FAO, livestock production is responsible for 64% of ammonia emissions which contribute to acid rain.

- Approximately 70% of farmable land is taken up by livestock production or the cultivation of cattle feed.

For more information on the effects of livestock production see vegsoc.org and peta.org.uk

Economics and a fairer distribution of resources

A vegan diet requires about 1,000 litres of water a day, compared with the 15,000 litres needed for a diet that includes animal products. An average of 15,500 litres of water are needed to produce 1 kilo of beef, compared with 1,300 litres for 1 kilo of grain. To obtain 1 calorie of animal food (dairy products included), between 4 and 17 calories of plant-based food is required. We could feed the entire planet if we chose a plant-based diet. Meat is not viable from a global perspective, and it seems clear that the current dietary model is reprehensible when we consider that there are nearly 1 billion people in the world who are starving. Malnutrition is not linked to poverty, but to an unfair distribution of food resources. Because it is physically impossible for us to grow all the plant-based food necessary to feed the animals we eat, 'poor' countries now cultivate the food for the cattle in our 'rich' countries.

Several experts have confirmed this: If we want to feed the planet, we are going to have to shift towards a predominantly plant-based diet. It is a fact, a simple matter of the survival of mankind. Many companies are already in the process of addressing the issue and the range of vegetarian and vegan products is growing fast. In the United States, Bill Gates has invested in Beyond Meat, an American 'vegan meat' company. Recently, in France, Laurent Spanghero, whose family is at the helm of the industrial group of the same name, and regarded as a heavyweight in the French meat sector, took everyone by surprise by changing course to launch a company specialising in the production of a range of organic products made from plant-based proteins. Change is already underway.

A healthier diet

Not only is a vegan diet possible, but it would also be beneficial to our health. A reduced risk of obesity, diabetes and high blood pressure, lower cholesterol and less risk of contracting certain types of cancer: In a nutshell, this is what you expose yourself to by opting for a balanced vegan diet. Not to mention a few years added on to your life expectancy. In the Western world, the agri-food industry exerts pressure on our leaders to put financial health before the health of citizens. Not only is the public not informed of the feasibility of a vegan diet -- so that everyone can make an educated decision on the matter of what they eat -- but people are advised to eat more and more animal protein and a large quantity of dairy products, in spite of the fact that current scientific evidence confirms that it would be wiser to drastically reduce their consumption. Fortunately, some countries, perhaps more forward-thinking regarding this issue, have differing policies regarding a vegan diet. In 2011, the benefits of a vegan diet for animals, and also for human health and the environment, were raised before the British Parliament. In 2013, the Australian government recognised that not only is a vegan diet suitable for all ages (including babies, children, pregnant women and the elderly), but that it also offers numerous health benefits. In the United Kingdom, an insurance company even offers a 25% insurance discount for vegetarians and vegans, as they are considered to be in better health and have a longer life expectancy.

Going vegan: everyone does it differently

It is possible go completely vegan overnight, but for some people it takes a little preparation, a period of adaptation or a transitional phase. So how do you start? Are there stages to fulfil in a certain order, or is there a guide to becoming vegan in 10 steps? It actually depends a lot on you. On your personality, your reasons, your habits. Only you can set the pace and your goals, so here are some ways to do it comfortably.

Do some research

Find out all you can! Visit your nearest shop that sells vegan products; learn how to create a balanced, daily vegan diet; find vegan restaurants and eateries in your neighbourhood; learn where to find vitamin B12, etc. Many websites offer 'vegan beginner kits' that are packed with lots of useful information. The Vegetarian Society's web site offers many useful fact sheets on nutrition. The websites www.happycow. net and www.veggieplaces.co.uk help you find vegan restaurants anywhere in the UK and around the world. For vegans in London, the website www.veganlondon.co.uk is 'the' reference for restaurants, shops and vegan products in the capital, and also has a useful blog. Although disturbing to watch, some documentaries or videos -- filmed with hidden cameras -- about animal exploitation, such as those by PETA, *L214* or *Animal Equality*, show the stark reality of raising livestock. *Earthlings* is a documentary about animal exploitation that has converted many people to veganism. What it shows about animal exploitation is upsetting but despite the distressing aspect of the images, I can't help recommending it to anyone who wants to form an opinion on this matter.

Go at your own pace

One step at a time is still the best way forward. If changing everything all of a sudden scares you, do it slowly. Substitute first what is easiest for you such as meat, milk and butter. Then proceed to cheese or leather shoes, etc. Or perhaps start with one vegan meal a day, or a 100% vegan day a week, then go on to two, etc. A practical tip: Replace your non-vegan foods and products with substitutes as you finish them, thus gradually managing your expenses in the process.

But if you decide to do away with everything that is non-vegan in your larder, it is not a problem at all, go for it! The evolution from vegetarianism to veganism is often a logical progression, but is by no means one that has to be followed. The time it takes to adapt to a vegan lifestyle is very different from one person to another and can take anywhere from a few days to sometimes a few years. It is up to you to evaluate your reasons and your goals, as well as to find ways to implement this new lifestyle in a comfortable and lasting way. If you are afraid of finding these changes difficult, bear in mind that I have talked to many vegans about this and they all agree that not only is it much easier than it looks, but that becoming vegan was probably one of the best decisions of their lives.

Meeting other vegans

Don't be shy about becoming a member of a forum, or going to vegan or vegetarian meetings in your area. Many can be found on social networks and they organise regular meetings, carpooling for activist campaigns, or getting together for meals at restaurants. There are many ways of meeting up with people who live near you and with whom you can share your experiences, making friends at the same time. Over the past few years in the UK many vegetarian and vegan social networks have sprung up all over the country. Going it alone can often be difficult, so being able to find like-minded people who share your choice of lifestyle, and to whom you can ask many questions and seek advice, is extremely helpful. Why not sign up for a vegan cooking course where you can meet people while learning to make delicious dishes?

Getting involved

By becoming aware of animal exploitation, we often want to do more than just change the way we eat. Being active in associations, volunteering at a shelter, or providing financial support are all ways of being involved on different levels. The work that associations do is essential. They are often responsible for legislative changes regarding animal rights and protection; they also organise petition signings and are behind decisive actions that have real impact on brands, pressuring them to abandon the use of animal materials such as fur or angora. Taking part in your own way and at your own level to promote veganism will have an impact on other people and on animals. This is perhaps what is most motivating when you become vegan: Knowing that our actions have a direct impact. Each vegan saves the lives of nearly 200 animals every year only because of their diet.

What is vegan cuisine?

Despite the fact that it does not include any ingredient of animal origin, it is not easy to define, in precise terms, what vegan cuisine is. Yet it is as diverse and varied in general as non-vegan cooking as every recipe in the world can poten-

tially be 'veganised'. In fact, there is not just one kind of vegan cuisine, but many. They are shaped by the culinary cultures we have grown up in, by our tastes and our cravings, but also by our concept of food.

When you hear or read the word 'vegan', the image of cooking healthily with organic ingredients and lots of vegetables comes to mind. Although this is not necessarily the case for all vegans, many people do indeed change to a mainly organic diet, to one that is more environmentally friendly and safer for our health, to a healthier way of cooking with homemade food that is rich in fresh fruit and vegetables. Some years ago I also chose to change to this way of eating and it is therefore only natural for me to offer you recipes that go in that direction: dishes that are adapted to the seasons and, on the whole, are prepared with organic vegetables and ingredients.

For this book, we have put together a very wide range of recipes. From very simple ones to more elaborate dishes, from classic recipes to original creations. There are explanations for using a variety of cereals, grains and pulses for everyday meals but also recipes for entertaining, for enjoying on any occasion and in particular for sharing. Isn't good food above all food that is shared? Becoming vegan made me realise that cooking can divide, sideline, and even be a cause for conflict. I hope this book will instead offer recipes that bring people together, that appeal to everyone, a way for family gatherings to no longer be a headache or a worry, but become a time for one and all to enjoy the same dish. I am convinced that new traditions will arise, a leek quiche can become famous and roast seitan with chestnuts can become a Christmas dish that will be requested the following year.

Writing a book about vegan cooking led me to take a more in-depth look at an issue that vegans disagree on: 'Should meat be imitated?' For me, it is not in effect an ethical or philosophical issue, but one of taste...or of aversion. It is a personal matter, to which there is ultimately no 'right' answer. As vegans, we have no moral obligation to ban substitutes that look a little too much like meat and by extension ban all animal products, because if you do that, why drink non-dairy milk or eat vegan cheese? It is perfectly understandable to be disgusted by the idea of eating something that has the appearance, texture and even the taste of meat and not even want to eat those foods or dishes. But replacing meat with plant-based preparations that look like it hardly makes us evil, remorseless 'meat lovers', guilty of wanting to delight in animal flesh by eating substitutes.

Personally, I have never really liked meat. As a child I had something of an obsessive fear about it, and growing up I avoided as much as possible. Today, when I eat seitan chorizo, shepherd's pie or a burger, it is certainly not the idea of eating meat that I seek, but rather the spirit of a dish, the taste of a sauce, a feeling of comfort -- and to be honest, since becoming vegan I eat more burgers, nuggets and roasts than ever! This issue regarding imitation is also often raised by those who eat meat. 'If you don't want to eat meat or cheese, why imitate or recreate them?' I like to reply by saying that I have absolutely nothing against tartiflettes, stews or sausages, as long as they are not produced from the exploitation of animals. And, I do not see why, just because I reject products from this kind of exploitation, I should deprive myself of certain dishes if I can prepare them by finding vegan versions of them. However, these dishes that imitate meat are not the ones I cook on a daily basis. Although 'veganising' traditional recipes by replacing the meat or cheese is great, it is also enjoyable to invent dishes, experiment, create a more personal, original style of cooking; one that is different from what we are familiar with. One that allows us to explore new horizons and create dishes that focus on vegetables rather than giving animal protein a central role. I do not find these two approaches to vegan cuisine at all contradictory, but rather, complementary.

It is this diversity in approaches to vegan cuisine that makes it so varied and interesting and it will, I am sure, become ever more appealing to more and more people over the years. In particular to those who still view it as a rather limited cuisine, a cuisine that is 'missing' something, one that is paltry and sad; attractive for those who choose to adopt it for ethical reasons but not because of what it tastes like. Vegan cuisine is not just a cuisine for vegans; it is for everybody, and it is suitable for people with different spiritual sensitivities and those with various allergies, making it the perfect cuisine for meals and large receptions where everyone can eat everything without concern. It is a sort of universal cuisine.

A closer look at vegan ingredients

Good news: More and more vegan products are becoming available. Some are 100% vegan brands and sometimes labelled as such, others are organic. But how can you find them?

Organic produce

Although organic farming is not directly linked to a vegan lifestyle, it is its continuity or logical starting point. Not harming smaller forms of life, not polluting the soil and rivers, not harming biodiversity and the natural habitats of animals, and in the process not poisoning with pesticides is simply common sense. From a purely vegan perspective, eating organic food -- which is healthier -- is a long-term assurance of better health, and it also reduces the need for medicines and treatments for whose manufacture the pharmaceutical industry tortures many animals.

Approved products

Several organisations offer a vegan certification; the best-known one in Europe is that of the Vegan Society. As with any certification it is the brand that carries out the process of certifying its products, and certifying products entails a cost. Uncertified products, but whose composition does not include any product of animal origin or which states it is 'vegan' can be just as vegan as one that has been approved. As for organic produce, a certification ensures that it is the real thing and that the product and its production process were monitored by a certifying body with strict specifications.

What about palm oil?

As pointed out later in the book, vegan products that include non-organic palm oil -- whose production is of great concern for the survival of wild animals and their natural habitat -- seems incoherent. Putting pressure on brands that offer products for vegans and asking them to use only organically produced palm oil -- or even no palm oil at all whenever possible -- is a direct way to act on this issue and tip the scales in our favour. As consumers we have power, we should not hesitate to use it.

Do vegans eat 'fake' foods?

'Tofurkey', 'mock-meat' or 'soyghurt' are strange words you may have already come across. There are myriad recipes based on 'fake chicken' and if you search, you can even find 'soysauges'. So do vegans truly eat 'real food'? Some vegans find using words like 'cheese' or 'sausage' unacceptable because they refer directly to the animal product and give the idea that they are acceptable foods. Hence the avalanche of wacky new words that make it clear that it is not really cheese or sausages that are being eaten, leaving no room for confusion. I personally have a problem with these neologisms (and I'm not the only one, as other vegans share this view), because many of them use the word 'mock'. Not only does it seem strange to me to associate the word to a food product, but it goes beyond the clichés about vegans and their way of cooking. Giving food names like this is not conducive to endearing vegan food and products to non-vegans. To me it seems better to use terms that are simple and easily understood by everyone. 'Non-dairy cheese' or 'vegan sausage' for example, and even more specific names such as 'seitan chorizo' or 'cashew cheese'. These kinds of coinage make perfect sense in English. In French, the word 'fromage' derives from the Latin word *formaticus'*, meaning 'something made in a mould'. It is therefore not correct to talk about 'non-dairy cheese' or 'vegan cheese'. In English the word 'sausage' derives from the Latin word *'salsicius'* meaning 'salted', while in French, the word for meat 'viande' comes from the Latin word *'vivanda'*, meaning 'things that served to live', and its meaning originally applied to all kinds of food, not just meat. By readapting these words it also -- in terms of communication -- shows that other possibilities exist, that sausages and cheese are not necessarily of animal origin and consumers can therefore choose between a product that is animal or plant-based rather than between a food and a 'mock' food. Using simple adjectives such as 'non-dairy', plant-based' or 'vegan' has the added advantage of clearly explaining what it is.

The products used in this book

For this book, I have chosen not to use processed vegan-type cheeses, sausages, meat-free mince, etc., that can be bought in the shops and I have used simpler, easier to find basic ingredients that are also less expensive. These can be used to make your own non-dairy cheese, chorizo or roast seitan, burgers, etc. Obviously, I have nothing against these products and you are free to use them in these recipes if you wish. They will often allow you to save valuable time.

What to look out for: hidden animal ingredients

Some ingredients have a tendency to sneak into almost everything and in particular where you wouldn't expect them. Here is a list of the most common traps to avoid.

Additives and food colouring

E120 and E471 to name a couple are the typical kinds of additives that we would rather avoid. The former is a completely natural dye that is also called 'carminic acid' or 'carmine' ... but that is obtained from crushed insects, cochineal. The latter is more insidious and is an emulsi-fier widely used in processed foods including breads and is called 'mono- and diglycerides of fatty acids'. It is sometimes vegan but sometimes not at all.

Many additives with strange names that hide behind these Es are not vegan or even vegetarian, so how can you find out what they are?

- On the Internet it is easy to find lists that identify vegan and non-vegan additives.
- The best way to get information is still by asking, so don't think twice about e-mailing the consumer service department of brands and asking them. A look at a vegan forum, however, can often give you the answer as someone may have asked the same question before you.
- Choose organic products! This is because organic regulations allow far fewer additives than conventional processed products and many organic processed products are vegan.
- Choose raw and homemade produce over others whenever possible but the best way to be sure of what you are eating is still to prepare it yourself.
- Look for products labelled 'vegan' or stating 'suitable for vegetarians', as the latter are becoming more and more common.

Beware of the words 'vegetable' and 'meat-free'

These are usually written in bold letters on the packaging to attract us (the words are reassuring and help sales), yet the products still contain ingredients of animal origin. 'Meat-free' steaks or mince may contain egg. Some brands do not hesitate to use the word 'vegetable' or 'meat-free' erroneously. Similarly, honey is often considered to be a horticultural product. Beware also of the names of animal by-products that are not always clearly identifiable such as 'albumin', 'casein' or 'whey'.

Drinks

Fruit juices and alcoholic drinks are often clarified with animal products such as gelatine, casein (milk protein) or egg whites (albumin). Most of the time, it is impossible to know this just by reading the label. To avoid worrying about this, buy juices that state they are '100% juice' and avoid those made from concentrates. Choose a good but cloudy organic apple juice that has not been clarified or abbey-type craft beers. Take a look at www.barnivore.com or veggiewines.co.uk to check if an alcoholic drink is vegan or not.

Wine

Wines are very often clarified with products of animal

origin, even organic wines. Since 2013, winemakers must indicate the presence of any type of egg or milk allergen on their bottles, but as gelatine is not an allergen, there is no way of knowing if a wine has been clarified with it just by reading the label. Fortunately, there are several options available for finding vegan wines: Contact producers and ask them directly; buy 'natural wines' -- the specifications for them are stricter than for organic wines (natural wines are also organic) and exclude animal products -- such as Ampelidae wines that are certified by the Vegan Society. Some websites offer vegan wines: in the UK www.vegan-winesonline.co.uk. is a good option, while in France www.meilleursvinsbio.com has a 'vegan wine' section.

Tips and techniques for cooking

Cooking can be simple but it sometimes requires specific equipment, very precise quantities and cooking times which leave no room for inaccuracy. Here are my tips for making all the recipes in this book successfully.

Cooking

Unless otherwise stated, the temperatures indicated are for a fan-assisted oven setting. If your oven does not have this setting, cooking times will be slightly longer and will vary from oven to oven. Simply keep an eye on the food towards the end of the cooking time and then jot down your oven's correct cooking time for that recipe. Stove-top recipes have been done on a ceramic hob. Induction and gas hobs heat up faster. Always watch what is being cooked and if you feel that the temperature or the cooking time needs adjusting with regard to the recipe, follow your cooking instinct!

Portions

You will see that the recipes often indicate that they serve 2-4 people. Recipes can be made as a first course or side dish for four, but also make a perfect main course for two.

Measurements

Teaspoons and tablespoons are measured flat, using measuring spoons. Spoons for eating often vary considerably in size and are not reliable for measuring precise quantities such as ¼ tsp. I strongly recommend buying a set of measuring spoons; they do not cost a lot and you will find them very useful. For your information: 1 tsp = 5 ml and 1 tbsp = 15 ml.

Essential equipment

As well as a set of measuring spoons, a good knife and a wooden chopping board, here is a list of equipment used throughout the book which you will need frequently:

- An immersion blender is very useful. Inexpensive and very practical, I use it for most of my recipes: it is much more practical than a blender for small quantities and for somewhat thick mixtures.
- A measuring jug.
- Kitchen scales.
- Basic baking tins: cake tins, tart tin, spring form cake tin and muffin tin.
- Saucepans, frying pans and oven-proof dishes.

Expert equipment

Not essential for everyday cooking or for simple recipes but pretty cool to have in the cupboard to make more elaborate recipes.

- Metal ring moulds.
- Ice lolly moulds.
- A mini-chopper.
- Food processor
  (a basic machine with its famous 'S' blade).
- A waffle iron.
- A pasta machine for making fresh pasta.
- A mini-blowtorch is essential for making crème brûlée (inexpensive ones are easy to find).
- A tofu press.
- A syphon.
- A log mould.
- An electric whisk.
- A crêpe pan.
- A tagine.

Preferred materials

Healthier, more environmentally-friendly and longer-lasting, here are some materials which have everything going for them, and which are also great value for money:

- Wood: chopping boards and spoons for cooking (definitely avoid plastic for these uses).
- Glass, terracotta and ceramics: dishes, cocottes, casserole dishes, cake moulds. Not only do they ensure even cooking, but they are also very hard-wearing and easy to look after. The only drawback is that they can break.
- Steel, tin, cast iron, stainless steel: for frying pans, cake tins, saucepans. Avoid non-stick pans coated with PFTE and PFOA, and throw away any baking pans, frying pans or saucepans that are scratched: this is when they become dangerous as the toxic components can pass into the food. Enamelled steel is making a comeback: make the most of it to stock up on baking dishes as they last forever and are very pretty.

Avoid as much as possible: silicon and plastics containing BPA.

Essentials for vegan cooking

My short list of products to always keep on hand, from the most basic to the lesser known. These are used throughout the book and will soon become your best friends in the kitchen!

Tofu. The ultimate versatile ingredient, there's nothing it can't do. There are two types: silken and firm. Silken tofu, which is soft in texture, is used for mousses, puddings, and as a replacement for eggs. Firm tofu can be found in natural or flavoured forms (smoked, herbed, curried, etc.). It is most often used diced and pan-fried, but it can also be glazed, grilled, in quiches, to make non-dairy cheeses and cheesecakes. Tip: Avoid buying 'long-life' tofus from the organic section of the supermarket as these are not fresh. Try various brands to find the ones you like the best. Tofu is like cheese as the taste, appearance and texture is extremely different from one variety to the next. Some are very firm while others are very soft.
Where to find it? Shops that sell organic products.

Non-dairy creams. Soy, oat, rice, almond or even thick, lacto-fermented cream can not only replace crème fraîche and normal cream, but also eggs for cakes, and these ingredients are found in numerous recipes. To replace thick (double) cream, soy is the best option and if you want to make your own crème fraîche from scratch, the recipe is waiting for you on page 143 of this book!
Where to find them? Health food shops and the organic section in the supermarket.

Nut and seed butters. True plant-based 'butters' that can be found 'white/blanched', 'whole' and even 'toasted'. Almond and sesame are the most commonly used in organic cooking, but cashew butter, hazelnut butter and black sesame butter are also types to try for a great gourmet experience. My favourite is white cashew butter as its slightly 'cheesy' taste makes it perfect for savoury dishes, non-dairy cheese, sauces, soups and risotto.
Where to find them? Shops selling organic products or with organic sections.

Agar-agar. This is a magical ingredient that replaces gelatine, but unlike the latter, it needs to be prepared hot. It is a seaweed that is most often found in powdered form. It allows you to make not only a wobbly panna-cotta or a pudding which holds its shape, but also well-set jellies and non-dairy cheeses. The amount used makes all the difference in terms of texture. It can be bought in sachets or in a container. Go for the container as it is more economical, is easier to measure and will avoid you having half-used sachets lost in the back of the larder.
Where to find it? Shops selling organic products or with organic sections.

Starches. Corn, potato and arrowroot starches are used to thicken sauces and they allow you to create light, creamy textures. They can even replace eggs for cakes and crêpes, and they are great for holding burgers and rissoles together.
Where to find them? Shops selling organic products or with organic sections.

Raw (unroasted) cashew nuts. These are worlds away from the roasted kind that are served with pre-dinner drinks. When they have been soaked for a few hours and whizzed in a food processor, they can become cream, mascarpone and even non-dairy cheese. Perfect for spreads and pesto, they are also one of the ingredients used to make fabulous vegan Parmesan.
Where to find them? Shops selling organic products.

Flaxseeds and chia seeds. Flaxseeds (buy the golden ones as they won't alter the colour of your dishes) and chia seeds (don't worry, it's pronounced 'tchia') have a particular quality: They are mucilaginous seeds, and when they are combined with a liquid they release a sticky, gelatinous substance. They are therefore the perfect replacement for eggs in certain recipes, mainly because they bind the ingredients. In addition, they are both rich in omega-3. Flaxseeds however need to be soaked or ground to be digested. Delicious uncooked puddings and porridges can be made with chia seeds.
Where to find them? Shops selling organic products.

Liquid smoke. A natural flavouring made from wood smoke that has been condensed and mixed with water. It is used to give a smoky flavour to dishes, to make homemade smoked tofu, smoked seitan, for BBQ sauce and to give dishes a bit of zing. A few drops are all you need. It is not the easiest ingredient to find and you may well have to order it online, but it's not wildly expensive and it would be a shame to miss out on it.
Where to find it? Vegan shops or online.

Textured vegetable protein (TVP). This can be found 'minced', in 'chunks', in small or large 'nuggets', strips, and even dark brown in colour to convincingly replace beef. The golden rule is that it must be rehydrated in a well-seasoned liquid (or even lightly spiced) to infuse it with flavour before cooking it. Remember that the quality varies from one brand to the next.
Where to find it? Health food shops and vegan shops. Where possible buy brands from vegan shops as they are generally better and not more expensive.

Tamari, shoyu and miso. Well known by fans of organic, macrobiotic and Japanese cooking, these different soy sauces and misos are used widely throughout this book to salt, flavour and season dishes, to make marinades and sauces, and for stocks that replace meat stock. I always have white miso (shiro miso) and brown barley miso in my fridge. They keep in the fridge for a long time and let you make delicious soups and sauces in just a few minutes.
Where to find them? Health food shops or Asian grocery shops. Where possible buy organic brands, some are even produced in the UK!

Non-dairy creams

Nut and seed butters

r-agar

Starches

Cashew nuts

seeds and chia seeds

Textured soy protein

Tamari, shoyu and miso

NUTRITION TIPS FOR A BALANCED VEGAN DIET

Dr Jérôme Bernard-Pellet

Reasons for following a vegan diet

Improving one's health and preventing general health problems such as cardiovascular disease or cancer are good reasons for becoming vegan. This is the main purpose of this chapter.

Unquestionably, veganism is the food trend that preserves more of the Earth's resources as well as being the one that pollutes the least. In fact, it takes an average of 10 grams of vegetable protein to produce a single gram of animal protein. Consuming animal protein therefore leads to a huge waste of resources as it requires much more water, electricity, and petrol in particular, to produce the same amount of food. In other words, a vegan diet is one that allows more food to be produced for a given amount of resources. This can be illustrated by this very significant story. In June 2005, the European Space Agency announced a way of feeding six astronauts who would go to Mars using conventional propulsion systems. They would have to take 30 tonnes of food, obviously impossible using conventional propulsion methods. So they came up with the idea of growing food in the spacecraft itself and recycling the organic materials generated. In this case, the resources for producing food on board would of course be very limited as this is a scenario where waste must be avoided at all costs. In this context, the only rational way to eat would be a strictly vegan diet. The French Society of Gastronomy thus developed a 100% plant-based menu for the European Space Agency. Why should what is good for astronauts, who need to be at their best physically and mentally, be bad for the general population?

Another reason for promoting a vegan diet and its energy efficiency is the desire to fight against world hunger. By eating meat and other animal products, we waste much of the grains and pulses that could be eaten by humans. Thanks to this consumption of meat, we are helping to increase the cost of the global food supply as well as reducing it, resulting in starvation for the most vulnerable populations.

Finally, one of the most common reasons for going vegan is the desire to not inflict great suffering on animals. We are kept in ignorance of the meat industry's true practices. Many people would stop eating meat if they knew about the farming conditions of animals, of their transportation and slaughter, and would consider these practices unworthy of a society that claims to be civilised. The castration of live piglets and the scalding of live chickens are part of the sad truth that few people are aware of.

The increase in life expectancy or proof of the benefits of a vegan diet

The year 2013 was a turning point in the history of the study of vegan diets. For the first time, there was irrefutable proof that a well-designed vegan diet lowered overall mortality from all causes.[1] Several studies had shown this among lacto-ovo-vegetarians[2], but the number of participating vegans was insufficient in previous studies to highlight anything in the latter population. The study published in 2013 by Dr. Michael J. Orlich was the first in the world to be conducted to include such a high number of vegans: 5,548 vegans out of 73,308 participants, which also included omnivores, semi-vegetarians and lacto-ovo-vegetarians. The primary goal of the study was overall mortality from all causes. This criterion is the most difficult to study in medicine because it requires significant investment both in financial and human terms. It is one of the most reliable because it provides a global vision of health based on a specific factor: the death or survival of an individual. In fact, eating habits can be good in the context of one illness yet bad for another and it is difficult to know if they do more harm than good. It is therefore crucial to study overall mortality from all causes. This study showed that over a period of 6 years, the risk of dying was 15% lower in vegans than in omnivores, and 9% lower in lacto-ovo-vegetarians than omnivores. This proves that a vegan diet is better from a health perspective than a vegetarian diet, which in turn is better than an omnivorous diet. In a nutshell, a vegan diet extends life expectancy.

Other benefits of a vegan diet

A vegan diet has myriad health benefits. An increase in life expectancy is only a reflection of the preventive effect on many public health problems such as cardiovascular diseases (including ischemic heart disease), colon and prostate cancer, and type 2 diabetes. Furthermore, a vegan diet positively affects many risk factors such as high cholesterol, high blood pressure and obesity. These benefits are described in an international reference document published in a peer-reviewed journal and is the official position of the American Dietetic Association (renamed the Academy of Nutrition and Dietetics)[3].

Other innovative discoveries have been made following the latest update of this reference document. Since 2011, we know that a strictly vegan diet protects against cataracts[4]. In fact, there is a 40% lower risk of getting cataracts among vegans than among people who consume a lot of meat. Vegetarians have a 30% reduced risk of getting cataracts. This is just another case where veganism is better for health than vegetarianism.

How do you design and balance a vegan diet?

It is easy to balance a vegan diet by principally including six main food groups: vegetables, whole fruits, whole grains, pulses (i.e. lentils, dried beans, soy beans, split peas, chickpeas, broad beans, etc.), nuts (walnuts, almonds, hazelnuts, cashews, pistachios, etc.) and sprouted and non-sprouted seeds (flaxseeds, sesame seeds, sunflower, etc.). These food groups have been proven to prevent a number of very common diseases that have been mentioned above. For example, nuts -- and in particular walnuts -- are known to reduce mortality from cardiovascular disease[5]. Pulses, which are somewhat neglected today, should hold as prominent a place in our diet as they did before the Second World War. In fact, pulses are rich in protein but they are also a good source of iron, zinc, calcium and dietary fibre. In addition, they have more power to prevent type 2 diabetes than

1- Orlich, M. J., et al., Vegetarian Dietary Patterns and Mortality in Adventist Health Study 2, JAMA Internal Medicine, 2013, vol. 173, n° 13, p. 1230-1238.

2- Appleby, P. N., et al., The Oxford Vegetarian Study: An Overview, The American Journal of Clinical Nutrition, 1999, vol. 70, n° 3, p. 525S-531S ; Key, T. J., et al., Mortality in Vegetarians and Nonvegetarians: Detailed Findings from a Collaborative Analysis of 5 Prospective Studies, The American Journal of Clinical Nutrition, 1999, vol. 70, n° 3, p. 516S-524S ; Key, T. J., et al., Mortality in British Vegetarians: Review and Preliminary Results from EPIC-Oxford, The American Journal of Clinical Nutrition, 2003, vol. 78, n° 3, p. 532S-538S.

3- Craig, W. J., and Mangels, A. R., Position of the American Dietetic Association: Vegetarian Diets, Journal of the American Dietetic Association, 2009, vol. 109, n° 7, p. 1266-1282.

4- Appleby, P. N., Allen, N. E., and Key, T. J., Diet, Vegetarianism, and Cataract Risk, The American Journal of Clinical Nutrition, 2011, vol. 93, n° 5, p. 1128-1135.

5- Bao, Y., et al., Association of Nut Consumption with Total and Cause-Specific Mortality, The New England Journal of Medicine, 2013, vol. 369, n° 21, p. 2001-2011 ; Fraser, G. E., Associations Between Diet and Cancer, Ischemic Heart Disease, and All-Cause Mortality in Non-Hispanic White California Seventh-Day Adventists, The American Journal of Clinical Nutrition, 1999, vol. 70, n° 3, p. 532S-538S.

cereals and grains, even whole grains[6]. Pulses have been almost abandoned in favour of cereals and grains due to the implementation of public agricultural policies. In hindsight, this has been a big mistake. They should form the backbone of a vegan diet and even that of an omnivorous diet.

In addition, pulses have agronomical benefits. As these plants are able to fix nitrogen from the air, they do not need fertilisers.

While this may seem surprising at first, a compositional look at this diet by uninformed vegans who compare it to that of omnivores (who are also, it should be pointed out, uninformed with regard to dietetics) highlights the following interesting phenomenon: a vegan diet is, on average, closer to official recommendations that that of their omnivorous counterparts. The intake of complex carbohydrates and polyunsaturated fats are, for example, on average, closer to official recommendations in vegans. This is one reason why people wishing to reduce the consumption of meat, milk and eggs, or stop eating them altogether, should not worry too much. A few simple tips in this chapter will easily help you have a balanced vegan diet. Omnivores need to be informed and educated with regard to nutrition as much as vegetarians do. In fact, one must keep in mind that the diet of Westerners is of mediocre quality and is an example of what not to do. Everyone should be concerned about having a balanced diet, not only vegans. The main principles outlined in this chapter are, in general, equally applicable for omnivores wanting to take care of their health. If you want to find out more about the nutritional balance of a vegan diet, visit www.vegansociety.com. Their friendly website is full of useful information on nutrition and health, offers resources and fact sheets, and even promotes events and competitions. For additional information on the health benefits of a vegan diet, read the official position of the American Dietetic Association available on their website http://www.eatright.org.

Where to find proteins?

The three main sources of proteins in plants are pulses, cereals and grains, and nuts and oily seeds. Of these three sources, the consumption of pulses, nuts and oily seeds

The author

A doctor in nutrition, Dr Jérôme Bernard-Pellet trained at Paris-V medical university and has carried out research on vegetarianism and veganism for over ten years. With a Master's Degree in biostatistics and clinical research, he is passionate about evidence-based medicine -- quality healthcare based on using the best, currently available scientific data. He is also co-founder of APSARes, the Association of Health Professionals for Responsible Diet which promotes a better diet for health as well as aiming to reduce people's environmental footprint as much as possible.

should be particularly encouraged due to the specific health benefits they provide. Among pulses, soy has particular properties and should almost be considered on its own. Its composition of essential amino acids is so similar to that of meat that it is rightly regarded as the perfect substitute. The same can be said of quinoa.

The World Health Organisation (WHO) estimates that humans need about 0.6 grams of protein per kilo of body-weight per day. If you weigh 50 kilos, you therefore need about 30 grams of protein a day. By eating your fill, that figure is quickly reached. People without health problems, and that are not anorexic, run almost no risk of lacking protein; the most common problem is an excess and not a lack of it, even for vegans. If your protein intake is insufficient, you will see particularly visible muscle wasting at the root of your arms and thighs. In fact, the body uses its own muscles as a source of amino acids in the rare cases when dietary intake is insufficient, but this phenomenon is reversible if you return to an adequate intake, although there is little risk of that happening.

6- Jenkins, D. J., et al., *Effect of Legumes as Part of a Low Glycemic Index Diet on Glycemic Control and Cardiovascular Risk Factors in Type 2 Diabetes Mellitus: A Randomized Controlled Trial*, Archives of Internal Medicine, 2012, vol. 172, n° 21, p. 1653-1660.

Scientific evidence

Most of the information contained in this chapter is not from secondary sources such as websites, books, opinions of various experts, official government recommendations, or other sources. It comes from what are called 'primary' sources, in other words, scientific articles published in international peer-reviewed medical journals. The information from these reviews is popularised and other authors write books as well as articles for mainstream newspapers and appear on radio and television programmes. The further away from the source of the initial information, the more the message risks being distorted; it is definitely deformed in practice. Bibliographic research of medical databases such as MEDLINE was undertaken to write this chapter. The methodology for this project was inspired by the book *How to Read a Paper: The Basics of Evidence-Based Medicine* by Trisha Greenhalgh, in addition to working tools used by the French magazine *Prescrire*.

Is it true that animal protein is better?

It all depends on what is meant by 'quality' of protein. If we understand that animal proteins afford us better health than vegetable proteins, the statement is false. The epidemiological studies cited above show that it is beneficial for health to eat mainly plant protein. On the other hand, if we believe that the proportion of essential amino acids in animal proteins is generally closer to the theoretical optimum, it is most often true.

All proteins, whether animal or from plants, are an assembly of blocks formed by the 20 basic amino acids. Proteins contain all of the nine essential amino acids that synthesise the necessary 11 non-essential amino acids. In fact, we do not need the proteins themselves, but the amino acids contained within them. The digestive process breaks down the proteins derived from our diet into amino acids. We need enough of each of the nine essential amino acids, but not the proteins themselves, which we are unable to use as they are. The proportion of essential amino acids varies depending on the nature of each protein. However, amino acids are exactly the same in all proteins, whether plant or animal. For example, protein from red meat does not have the same proportion of different amino acids that wheat or lentils have. This is why it has long been advised that pulses and grains be eaten together. This advice is sensible, but it is not necessary to do so in the same meal. Moreover, even if it is not recommendable, it is possible to ensure a supply of essential amino acids by eating only cereals and grains for example, known to be limited in an essential amino acid, lysine. It would be enough to increase this theoretical protein intake from cereals and grains by about 30% to supply lysine in sufficient quantities. But this is not recommendable because pulses are superior to cereals and grains on many levels and the exclusive consumption of the latter is senseless except, for instance, in a situation of survival. In practice, most Westerners eat too much of everything and have an excessive intake of all essential amino acids. In short, excess protein is more worrying that this idea of 'quality' protein, which really is not very important. In fact, to date, and contrary to popular belief, there is no evidence that animal protein is superior to plant protein, as has been demonstrated by Dr. Young[7], an internationally renowned researcher specialising in proteins.

On the contrary, plant proteins have special properties that animal proteins do not. For example, they are rich in arginine, a non-essential amino acid that allows the body to synthesise nitric oxide, an essential compound for good cardiovascular health and the proper functioning of the immune system. In addition, plant-based lipids are usually lower in saturated fat than those in animal protein. In fact, we rarely eat protein in an isolated way, but rather whole foods containing many nutrients. These properties, particular to plant protein, partially explain the lower incidence of cardiovascular disease among vegetarians. In a nutshell, it would be fair to say that plant protein is generally better than animal protein, and those who claim otherwise are unable to produce scientific studies to prove it.

7- Young, V. R., and Pellett, P. L., *Plant Proteins in Relation to Human Protein and Amino Acid Nutrition*, *The American Journal of Clinical Nutrition*, 1994, vol. 59, n° 5, p. 532S-538S.

Where to find iron?

Iron is easily found in sources of food that are also the above-mentioned sources of protein, i.e. whole grains, pulses and nuts. Lentils and beans, for example, are excellent sources of iron. In addition, there are significant amounts of iron in some fruits such as apricots, figs, plums, and in many vegetables such as parsley, broccoli, green beans, kale and Chinese cabbage.

This list is far from exhaustive and in practical terms, iron is rarely a problem. In fact, epidemiological studies show that there are not more cases of anaemia from iron deficiency in vegans than in omnivores[8]. Iron deficiency is common among women and 20% of them have had, have or will face this problem during their life. However, this is not a problem specific to those who eat a vegan diet.

Is it true that iron from meat is absorbed better than that from plants?

Yes, it is. The bioavailability of haeme iron (contained in red meat, white meat and fish) is more important than the non-haeme iron content of plants. But again, as with protein, it does not lead to better health, which is the aim of optimal nutrition. Any absorption of non-haeme iron is offset by the fact that it is very common in plants, while haeme iron causes health problems. In fact, it has been found that colon cancer is less common in people following a vegan diet than an omnivorous one. We have reason to believe that this difference is in part due to the fact that haeme iron contains an oxidising power that contributes to colon cancer. The intake of haeme iron from meat is therefore probably not the most advisable, and recommending this source of iron is not medically consistent. Furthermore, it should be noted that vitamin C enhances the absorption of non-haeme iron and its consumption should be encouraged.

Should we fear deficiencies of any nutrients?

Some nutrients are harder to find in plants than in animal products. While protein and iron are false problems for those on a vegan diet, other nutrients encompass legitimate concerns. However, we must put these deficiencies into perspective. It is indeed easier to find some nutrients in a 100% vegan diet, such as vitamin B9, vitamin C, and dietary fibre. To give just one example, there is roughly a 30% vitamin C deficiency and a 10% vitamin B9 deficiency in the general population that does not follow a vegan diet. These deficiencies are much rarer in those following a vegan diet as they consume more fruit and vegetables. In fact, a fear of deficiency is a matter that should concern us all; omnivores, vegetarians and vegans. This fear comes primarily from the fact that veganism is a minority diet, representing less than 1% of the population in the UK (and 0.1% of the population in France). Belonging to a majority makes us feel that we do not have to ask this question. It is not logical to 'fear' a vegan diet over an omnivorous diet, given that life expectancy for vegans is higher. With just a modest knowledge of nutrition, it is very easy to eat as healthily, or better, than most omnivores. And if our knowledge about it is broader, it can even improve our health.

Mistakes to avoid

Overeating is the main mistake to avoid in the belief that the possible risk of protein or iron deficiency will be mitigated. By doing this, you will consume too many calories and too much protein. Excess protein intake increases the work done by the liver and kidneys, contributing to long-term kidney failure. It also contributes to osteoporosis by resulting in acidosis. Few people know that, on average, even vegans eat too much protein, although there are considerable variations between individuals.

The other pitfall is excessive anxiety when becoming vegan. Admittedly, the unknown can sometimes be anxiety-provoking. Moreover, health professionals themselves may be worried about the issue, as they too are human beings who fear the unknown just like everyone else. In France it is an almost unknown topic for doctors because there is no honest, quality education about the vegan diet, and the readily available information is unreliable and alarming. In the UK there is increasingly more serious and trustworthy

8- Ball, M. J., and Bartlett, M. A., *Dietary Intake and Iron Status of Australian Vegetarian Women*, The American Journal of Clinical Nutrition, 1999, vol. 70, n° 3, p. 353-358.

information available. A vegan diet is a way of life that requires some knowledge in order for it to be understood. This quest for knowledge should not become an obsession. One goal of this chapter is precisely to offer you information that will save you from worrying excessively.

Another mistake is to think that being vegan means eating only vegetables. We must of course include other food groups such as pulses and nuts and oily seeds to ensure a sufficient intake of the three vital macro-nutrients: proteins, carbohydrates and lipids. Vegetables are poor in these and eating them exclusively is unreasonable given what we know.

In fact, the only major mistake not to commit by being vegan is to omit supplementing vitamin B12 to your diet. This is an essential supplement, in particular for women who are pregnant or breastfeeding. Often people are reluctant to take it, but a vitamin B12 deficiency can contribute to anaemia, neurological disorders, memory loss and even depression.

Vitamin B12

It is very difficult to find vitamin B12 in the plant kingdom. Much false information is given on the subject on the Internet and this creates great confusion. Vitamin B12 is needed to produce red blood cells, platelets and white blood cells, and to maintain a healthy nervous system. It is also needed for many other metabolic processes.

Mammals are not able to generate their own vitamin B12, while in nature, it is produced by bacteria. Too difficult to synthesise in the body, it is industrially produced by using fermentation processes involving bringing together bacteria and plants, thus reproducing what exists in nature. Over 90% of vitamin B12 produced in factories is used for livestock feed. In fact, today's livestock feed is highly deficient in vitamin B12, which was not the case when intensive farming did not exist and quality food that was not lacking in cobalt was given to animals. Cobalt is a component of vitamin B12. Whenever we eat meat or animal products, that animal becomes a link between the vitamin B12-producing factories and us. People following a vegan diet choose to take this vitamin directly in the form of supplements or foods fortified with vitamin B12, such as some breakfast cereals. The diet of animals living in the wild or on traditional farms does not need to be supplemented with vitamin B12.

Specifically, vitamin B12 supplements are now essential for anyone following a vegan diet. Perhaps in the future a plant source to supply us with vitamin B12 will be discovered, but for the moment, research is not advanced enough to provide us with a reliable and readily available plant-based source. People following a vegan diet can take 1,000 mcg vitamin B12 per week (Holland & Barrett, VegLife, etc.) or 10 mcg daily (some types sold on the Internet or in organic shops offer this dosage as does VEG 1 found at www.vegansociety.com/shop/supplements). These products can be bought without a prescription. You will notice that the dose to be taken once a week is much higher than seven times the daily dose. This is not an error of the author: it is related to the maximum daily capacity of active absorption of vitamin B12 by the mucosa of the intestines. Beyond a certain amount, vitamin B12 is absorbed by passive diffusion through the intestinal wall and is much less effective than the active mechanism of absorption. This phenomenon thus requires taking a massive dose if it is not taken every day.

Vitamin D

Vitamin D deficiency is a major general health problem affecting both omnivores and vegans. It is estimated that well over half of the UK population is deficient in vitamin D in winter. This vitamin is essential for the intestines to absorb dietary calcium and for bones to fix it once it has passed into the blood. It also plays a major role on the immune system and probably has a preventive effect against breast, colon and prostate cancer. Optimal vitamin D levels can limit the risk of catching the flu in winter. It is also possible that vitamin D deficiency contributes to depression[9]. It is important to pay attention to optimal vitamin D levels over those for calcium, as this is the way for the body to effectively use the calcium we consume. Our skin produces vitamin D precursors, which are converted into vitamin D in the presence of ultraviolet B (UVB) rays. Diet affords little vitamin D, and most of its supply is carried out by the action of the sun. In practice, few people expose themselves enough and so I advise taking between 3,000 and 5,000 IU of vitamin D a day. Although these doses seem very high compared to official recommendations of 200 IU per day for adults, official doses are insufficient for

9- Murphy, P. K., and Wagner, C. L., *Vitamin D and Mood Disorders Among Women: An Integrative Review*, Journal of Midwifery & Women's Health, 2008, vol. 53, n° 5, p. 440-446.

reaching optimal blood levels. There are many preparations containing vitamin D. Some require a prescription, others do not. For practical reasons, I have given here the name of a preparation found at every chemist's, and that does not require a prescription: Sterogyl oral drops (10 drops per day, corresponding to a daily intake of 4,000 IU). Be aware that vitamin D2 is always of plant origin, whereas vitamin D3 is almost always of animal origin. Vegans will of course tend to favour vitamin D2. However, there are a few preparations that contain vitamin D3 of plant origin. With regard to these, the excellent supplement Vitashine D3 has the big advantage of containing 2,500 IU of vitamin D3 in a single tablet, making it particularly innovative and practical (it can be found at www.vitashine-d3.com).

Calcium

Even though you need to be mainly aware of vitamin D as explained above, calcium intakes are a legitimate concern and vegans can sometimes be lacking in it. This is not a false problem as that regarding protein and iron. There are many plant sources of calcium, and these include soy milk fortified with calcium, tofu, dried beans, almonds, sesame seeds, figs, oranges, Chinese cabbage, collards and broccoli. The nutritional properties of broccoli should be particularly highlighted as, in addition to being an excellent source of calcium, it is also rich in antioxidants that play a role in preventing cancer, which is not the case for dairy products. Water also contains calcium. Information on the calcium content of tap water can be obtained from your Town Hall. If you prefer drinking mineral water, its calcium content is indicated on the label. In the West, calcium requirements are deliberately over-estimated because of the power of the dairy industry, which is present in almost all nutrition decision-making bodies. The WHO believes that 550 mg of calcium per day is sufficient to cover people's needs in most cases. If we go into more depth, calcium requirements are dependent on the consumption of salt and protein. The more we eat the more our calcium requirements increase. Therefore, limiting our consumption of salt and eating an optimal amount of protein is an excellent strategy to ensure our optimal calcium intake.

Omega-3 fatty acids

Omega-3 fatty acids are a particular type of lipid. An omega-3 deficiency is very prevalent and is common to both omnivores and vegans, which shows, once again, the importance of nutritional education for everyone. in general, we tend to over-consume omega-6 and not get enough omega-3. There is a lot of omega-6 in processed food as well as in sunflower, grapeseed and other common commercial oils (except those listed below). Walnuts and flaxseeds are a great source of short-chain omega-3. Its consumption, uncommon even among some vegans, should be promoted. Other good sources of short-chain omega-3 are tofu, rapeseed, linseed, soy bean and nut oils. Short-chain omega-3 (ALA) is converted to long-chain omega-3 (EPA and DHA) by the body.

This conversion varies from person to person and sometimes results in blood levels that are too low in long-chain omega-3. People following a vegan diet, which by definition does not include fish, can take direct sources of long-chain omega-3 in the form of capsules made from microalgae rich in DHA and EPA (brands include Opti3, Nuique, and Dr. Fuhrman's DHA Purity). The supplement Opti3 can be found at www.opti3omega.com, and seems to be the best on the market at the moment. There is no absolute proof of the usefulness of taking supplements with long-chain omega-3, but it is most likely beneficial. This kind of supplement is highly recommended for pregnant and breastfeeding women, whether vegan or omnivorous, as the baby's growing brain uses a large amount of DHA. For adults, omega-3 in general has a beneficial effect on the cardiovascular and central nervous systems. There are arguments to suggest that the optimised properties of omega-3 protect against Alzheimer's disease. Remember that some oily fish are also good sources of long-chain omega-3. They are, in fact, unable to produce it themselves and obtain it by eating microalgae (for vegetarian fish), other fish (for carnivorous fish), or microalgae supplements (for those that are farmed). Fish, whether wild or farmed, have the disadvantage of often being contaminated with heavy metals such as mercury or other toxic elements such as dioxins or PCBs. Overfishing has also led to a depletion of fish stocks that is challenging the long-term consumption of fish as a possible source of EPA and DHA. Supplements of microalgae, also called 'microscopic algae', do not have these disadvantages and therefore are a very good source of long-chain omega-3, in particular because their cost is very low compared to that of eating fish every day. The farming of microscopic algae for long-chain omega-3 is therefore a solution for the future.

During pregnancy

There is no problem for women to follow a vegan diet throughout their pregnancy. A study shows that pre-eclampsia, a disease specific to pregnant woman and which results in hypertension, is less common in women who follow a vegan diet than an omnivorous one[10]. The weight and length of babies at birth are comparable to those of their omnivore counterparts. Pregnant women should pay particular attention to their vitamin B12, vitamin D, calcium and long-chain omega-3 levels. I would advise women who follow a vegan diet to optimise their diet -- in the interest of the unborn child -- as soon as they wish to become pregnant and not wait until they are. Unborn children begin to get used to different flavours by swallowing amniotic fluid. Taste begins to form very early in life, hence the need to make a special effort on the quality of their diet during pregnancy. Children will thus also find it easier later on to enjoy food that is good for their health.

The advice we give to omnivorous pregnant women is the same as that for women who follow a vegan diet. Only minor adjustments need to be made to take into account the specificities of a vegan diet. If only one is to be taken into account, we would stress the great importance of a daily supplement with 10 mcg of vitamin B12 and more for pregnant women following a vegan diet. One can take a supplement containing only vitamin B12, or a supplement containing multiple nutrients specific for pregnant women, such as Vegan Prenatal Multivitamin & Mineral, manufactured by Deva.

Children

Studies published in scientific journals,[11] the most important by far being the Farm Study[12], show that the growth of children who are given a vegan diet from birth is not significantly different from that of omnivorous children and their psychomotor development was normal. They are living proof that it is possible for children who eat no meat or animal products to enjoy good growth. The idea that children cannot be vegan is a myth that is not supported by medical papers published in international peer-reviewed journals.

The elderly

Advanced age does not mean one cannot follow a vegan diet. We find the same risk of vitamin B12 and vitamin D deficiency in the omnivorous elderly as among those who follow a vegan diet. In fact, the production of vitamin D by the skin thanks to the action of the sun decreases with age. In addition, the omnivorous elderly may have difficulty absorbing the vitamin B12 contained in meat due to frequent atrophic gastritis. They risk vitamin B12 deficiency by absorption, while the elderly who follow a vegan diet may risk it due to a deficiency of their properties. Both elderly omnivores and those who follow a vegan diet are therefore advised to take supplements with vitamin B12 and vitamin D.

Furthermore, as the digestive system ages, the need for protein increases as amino acids are less well absorbed from the gastrointestinal tract, which increasingly uses them for its own consumption. The elderly should increase their protein intake to about 1 gram per kilo of bodyweight per day. Thus, a person who weighs 50 kilos should consume about 50 grams a day. A vegan diet can quite easily provide this amount of protein. If unprocessed pulses, cereals and grains, and nuts and oily seeds are not enough, eating plant-based soy (tofu) or wheat (seitan) 'meat' may be more palatable for older people who have appetite problems.

Conclusion

A vegan diet is a promise of a bright future. And, it is undoubtedly the most environmentally friendly way to eat. It is easy to balance by using vegetables, pulses, whole grains, whole fruit, nuts and oily seeds. It offers undeniable health benefits that lead to longer life expectancy, but also to improving quality of life by preventing many chronic diseases.

This cookbook will show you that it is also a lifestyle that will delight the taste buds of children and adults alike, while reducing their environmental footprint as well as saving the lives of animals.

10- Carter, J. P., Furman, T., Hutcheson, H. R., *Pre-eclampsia and Reproductive Performance in a Community of Vegans*, Southern Medical Journal, 1987, vol. 80, n° 6, p. 692-697.

11- Sanders, T. A., *Growth and Development of British Vegan Children*, The American Journal of Clinical Nutrition, 1988, vol. 48, n° 3, p. 822-825 ; Sanders, T. A., and Reddy, S., *Vegetarian Diets and Children*, The American Journal of Clinical Nutrition, 1994, vol. 59, n° 5, p. 1176S-1181S.

12- O'Connell, J. M., *et al.*, *Growth of Vegetarian Children: The Farm Study*, Pediatrics, 1989, vol. 84, n° 3, p. 475-481.

DISCOVERING
PLANT-BASED
PROTEINS

-- GRAINS AND PULSES --

-- SOY, AN ANCIENT ALLY --

-- SEITAN --

-- FLAVOURS FROM THE SEA --

VEGETABLE PÂTÉS AND DIPS

'Hot' dip

Serves 4

450 g cooked red beans
2-3 tsp chilli spice mix
1 garlic clove
½ red onion
3 sun-dried tomatoes, marinated in oil, finely chopped
1 tsp tamari
chilli sauce
½ red pepper, finely diced
½ fresh chilli, finely sliced

Put the beans, spices, garlic, onion, the sun-dried tomatoes and the tamari in a food processor. Whiz to a thick purée. Season to taste with the chilli sauce and add the red pepper. Add the fresh chilli to taste, depending on how hot you want it to be.

Serve with corn chips or toasted bread.

White bean, fresh coriander and lemon dip

Serves 2

300 g cooked white beans
2 tbsp lemon juice
1 tbsp olive oil
½ tsp salt
2 tbsp chopped fresh coriander
pepper

Put the beans, lemon juice, olive oil, salt and freshly ground pepper in a food processor. Whiz until smooth. Transfer to a bowl and add the chopped fresh coriander. Refrigerate.

Winter lentil pâté

Serves 4

150 g green lentils
1 large leek, finely sliced
1 large onion, finely sliced
2 garlic cloves, finely sliced
3 tbsp olive oil
1 tbsp hazelnut butter
3 tbsp tamari
200 ml non-dairy milk
2 tsp agar-agar powder
1 tbsp chopped parsley
pepper

Cook the lentils in boiling water for about 30 minutes. Sauté the leek, onion and garlic in 2 tbsp of the olive oil while the lentils are cooking. They should be well browned and tender. Drain the lentils. Put them in a food processor with the cooked vegetables. Add the hazelnut butter, the remaining tablespoon of olive oil and the tamari. Whiz to a coarse texture. Whisk the non-dairy milk and the agar-agar in a small saucepan and bring to the boil for 1 minute. Pour into the bowl of the food processor. Whiz to a thick, coarse pâté that still contains small chunks. Season with parsley and pepper to taste. Put into jars or a small terrine. Leave to cool and refrigerate for 12 hours before using.

Black olive pâté

Serves 2-4

125 g firm tofu
80 g Greek style black olives, pitted
50 g sunflower seeds
2 tbsp freshly squeezed lemon juice
1 tbsp olive oil
salt and pepper

Whiz all the ingredients in a food processor to obtain a thick pâté. Season to taste and put in a bowl or jar. Keeps for several days in the fridge.

te bean dip, 'hot' dip, and black olive pâté

Black bean hummus

Makes 1 bowl

300 g cooked black beans
4 tbsp black sesame paste
3 tbsp olive oil
1 garlic clove
½ tsp salt
6 tbsp freshly squeezed lemon juice

Whiz the black beans with the black sesame paste and the olive oil. Add the garlic and the salt, and pour in the lemon juice a little at a time while blending so that it emulsifies and becomes creamy in texture.

Sprinkle with black sesame seeds and serve with tomato and lemon wedges.

- -

Red kuri squash and tofu pâté

Serves 2-4

250 g red kuri squash, unpeeled, cut into small dice
2 garlic cloves, finely sliced
2 tbsp olive oil
½ tsp curry powder
½ tsp dried sage
½ tsp dried basil
125 g smoked tofu, crumbled
10 walnuts, shelled and roughly chopped
1 tsp tamari

Sauté the red kuri squash and sliced garlic in a pan with the olive oil over medium heat. Add the curry powder and the dried herbs. Cook for 10 minutes, stirring from time to time. Add the tofu, walnuts and tamari. Mix well. Put into the bowl of a food processor and whiz to a coarse consistency. This pâté tastes even better if it is a little chunky. Press it down well into a small terrine, a jar or bowl. Leave to cool and then refrigerate.

Italian dip

Serves 2-4

5 sun-dried tomatoes in oil and herbs
230 g cooked large white beans
  or borlotti beans
2 garlic cloves
2 tbsp pine nuts
2 tbsp olive oil
2 tbsp freshly squeezed lemon juice
1 tsp dried oregano
½ tsp salt
pepper
1 tbsp chopped fresh basil

Cut the sun-dried tomatoes into very small pieces. Whiz all the ingredients (except the fresh basil) in a food processor until smooth and creamy. Transfer to a bowl. Add the chopped basil and mix well. Refrigerate.

- -

Red lentil dip

Serves 2

100 g cooked red lentils
4 tbsp coconut milk
2 tsp tahini
1 tsp freshly squeezed lemon juice
½ tsp ground cardamom
chilli sauce
salt and pepper

Whiz all the ingredients in a food processor until smooth. Season with salt and pepper. Add a few drops of chilli sauce to taste and to give it a little zing. Keeps for two days in the fridge.

Creamy split pea dip

Makes 1 bowl

100 g split peas
3 tbsp freshly squeezed lemon juice
2 tbsp cashew butter
2 tbsp chopped fresh mint
1 tbsp olive oil
salt and pepper

Soak the split peas for 1 hour, then cook for 45 minutes over medium heat in 2½ times their volume of water. Drain. Blend the split peas with the other ingredients and season. Refrigerate before eating.

Hummus with za'atar and sun-dried tomatoes

Serves 2-4

200 g cooked chickpeas
4-5 sun-dried tomatoes, finely chopped
1 garlic clove
3 tbsp water
2 tbsp tahini
2 tbsp freshly squeezed lemon juice
1 tbsp olive oil
1 tbsp za'atar
salt and pepper

Whiz all the ingredients in a food processor until smooth and thick.

Serve, drizzled with olive oil, a pinch of za'atar, lemon wedges and toasted bread or flatbread.

Black bean hummus

Indian burger

GALETTES, BURGERS, RISSOLES, ETC

Seitan burgers

Makes 6 burgers

500 g red seitan (see p. 101)
2 tbsp dried onion
1 tbsp ground flaxseeds
1 tbsp carob flour
1 tbsp chopped parsley
1 tbsp chopped chives
2 tsp chipotle chilli sauce
1 tsp garlic powder
1 tsp ground coriander
100 g chickpea flour
salt and pepper

Whiz the seitan in a food processor, then mix it in a bowl with the other ingredients (except the chickpea flour). Add the chickpea flour and knead with your hands. The mixture will be very sticky. Flour your hands with chickpea flour and make 6 balls. With your well-floured hands, flatten them a little to make patties. Cook for a few minutes each side in an oiled frying pan over high heat.

Enjoy them classic burger-style with lettuce, topped with slices of vegan cheese, a thin slice of tomato, gherkins and ketchup.

Indian burgers

Makes 4-6 burgers

250 g red lentils
30 g chickpea flour
3 tbsp gluten
3 tbsp dessicated coconut
2 tbsp cornflour
1 tbsp chopped fresh basil
¼ tsp garlic powder
¼ tsp ground cardamom
vegetable oil for cooking
versatile cream cheese (see p. 133)
buns (see p. 37)
lettuce leaves
cherry tomato chutney (see p. 220)

Cook the red lentils in 500 ml of boiling water for 5 minutes. Refresh under cold water and drain. Mix all the ingredients for the burgers together in a bowl and shape into patties. Cook for a few minutes on each side in a very hot pan with a little olive oil until golden. Remove and place on a plate covered with kitchen paper to absorb any excess oil. Spread some cream cheese on the bottom half of each bun. Place a few lettuce leaves and the burgers on them, and top with the cherry tomato chutney. Cover with the other half of the bun.

Tip: To ensure the burgers stay nice and hot, warm the buns in the oven for a few minutes before filling them.

Chickpea burgers

Makes 6 burgers

500 g cooked chickpeas
100 g breadcrumbs
2 garlic cloves, crushed to a paste
2 tbsp chopped parsley
2 tbsp chopped fresh chives
4 tbsp water
salt and pepper
vegetable oil for cooking

Whiz the chickpeas in a food processor or with an immersion blender to a coarse consistency. Put in a mixing bowl. Add the breadcrumbs, garlic paste and herbs. Season to taste. Add the water and knead with your hands until firm and compact. Shape the burgers and cook them for 5 minutes each side in a lightly oiled frying pan over medium-high heat.

Idea: Enjoy a burger inspired by Middle Eastern cuisine! Spread some vegetable caviar (see p. 295) on the buns, add lettuce leaves and the chickpea burgers. Top with a slice of tomato, a thin slice of raw onion, mint leaves and a little hummus (see p. 33).

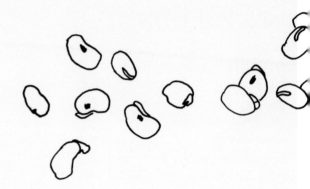

Azuki bean and brown rice galettes

Makes 4-6 galettes

150 g azuki beans, soaked overnight
100 g brown rice
2 tbsp chopped fresh coriander
2 tbsp vegan Worcestershire sauce
2 tsp dried wild garlic
2 tsp ground coriander
1 tsp ground cumin
salt and pepper
olive oil

Cook the soaked beans for 1½ hours. Drain. Cook the rice and drain it. Mix the rice and the beans in a small bowl, mashing them with a fork to make a sticky mixture. Add all the seasoning ingredients and season with salt and pepper to taste. With moistened hands, shape 4–6 galettes. Cook them in a frying pan with a little olive oil.

- -

Polenta and petit pois rounds

Makes 6-8 rounds

400 ml soy milk
½ tsp salt
½ tsp herbs de Provence
½ tsp dried basil
¼ tsp garlic powder
100 g pre-cooked polenta
75 g fresh or frozen petits pois
freshly ground pepper

Bring the soy milk and the seasoning ingredients to the boil. Sprinkle in the polenta, turn the heat to low and stir. Add the petits pois and cook for 5 minutes, stirring. Line a baking tray with parchment paper. Place three oiled ring moulds on the tray and pour in the polenta, pressing down well. Leave to cool and refrigerate for at least 1 hour. Remove the ring moulds. Cut circles 1.5 cm thick.

Fry and enjoy them as they are, like a burger, with a salad, etc.

Herbed quinoa burgers

Makes 6 burgers

125 g red quinoa
75 g peeled potatoes, cut into cubes
1 small onion, finely sliced
1 garlic clove, finely sliced
3 tbsp chickpea flour
1 tbsp chopped parsley
1 tbsp chopped fresh coriander
½ tsp salt
pepper
vegetable oil for cooking

Bring the quinoa to the boil then simmer for about 15 minutes. Bring the potatoes to the boil then simmer until tender. Sauté the onion and garlic in a frying pan for a few minutes. Drain the quinoa well and put it in a bowl. Drain the potatoes then mash them and add them to the bowl together with the onion and garlic, chickpea flour, herbs, salt and pepper. Mix everything well with a fork. Shape into little balls and then flatten to make patties. Cook for 5 minutes each side in a large, well-oiled frying pan. Line a baking tray with parchment paper then cook the burgers for 10 minutes in the oven at 180°C (Gas mark 4).

Buns

Makes 8 buns

1 sachet dried baker's yeast

75 ml soy milk, plus an extra 2 tbsp for glazing

200 ml water

500 g plain flour

2 tbsp light brown sugar

1 tsp salt

3 tbsp vegetable oil (olive, rapeseed, grape seed or
   safflower oil, etc.)

white sesame seeds

Warm the milk and the water and mix with the yeast in a measuring cup. Leave to stand for 5 minutes. Mix the flour with the salt and the sugar in a mixing bowl. Pour in the yeast mixture and mix in with a spoon. Then knead just until the dough comes together. Add the oil and knead again. If the dough is too sticky, add a little flour. It should be elastic and soft. Knead on a work surface for a few minutes, folding the dough over itself. Place it in a bowl, cover with a clean tea towel and leave to rise for 1½ to 2 hours at 25°C minimum (an oven preheated to 30-40°C then turned off is ideal). Knead for a few seconds, then shape into 8 balls. Place them on a baking tray lined with parchment paper and leave to rise again for 1 hour, covered with a tea towel. Brush the buns with soy milk and sprinkle with sesame seeds. Bake for about 15 minutes at 180°C (Gas mark 4). Cool before using.

Tip: *To make the burgers even more gourmet, warm the buns in the oven for a few minutes before filling them.*

White bean rissoles with tomato and basil

Makes a dozen rissoles

1 garlic clove, finely sliced

1 small onion, finely sliced

olive oil

225 g cooked white beans

50 g breadcrumbs, crumbled

1 tbsp white miso

5 herb-scented sun-dried tomatoes, finely chopped

2 tbsp breadcrumbs

1 tbsp chopped basil

salt and pepper

Sauté the onion and garlic in a frying pan for a few minutes with a little olive oil. Put the beans, breadcrumbs, miso, chopped sun-dried tomatoes, breadcrumbs, garlic, onion and basil in a food processor. Whiz and season to taste. Shape a dozen round rissoles. Heat 2 tbsp of olive oil in a large frying pan. Put the rissoles in and, over high heat, swirl the pan so that they roll around and brown evenly. This will help them keep their shape. Heat the oven to 160°C (Gas mark 3). When the rissoles are well browned and crispy, take them out and put them on a plate lined with parchment paper and finish cooking them in the oven for 10 minutes.

Mini petits pois and mint galettes

Makes 10 mini-galettes

200 g fresh or frozen petits pois

200 ml non-dairy cream

5 tbsp plain flour

3 tbsp arrowroot

3 tbsp chopped fresh mint

vegetable oil for cooking

salt and pepper

Mix all the ingredients together in a large bowl. Heat a little oil in a frying pan over high heat and cook the mini-galettes for a few minutes each side.

Variation: *For an extra burst of flavour, substitute the non-dairy cream with coconut milk.*

Autumn burgers

Makes 4 burgers

40 g textured soy protein

3 tbsp tamari

1 tbsp vegan Worcestershire sauce

100 g red kuri squash or mushrooms, cut into small dice

1 tsp olive oil

300 g fresh chestnuts

1 tbsp chopped parsley

1 tbsp chopped chives

2 tbsp chia seeds

vegetable oil for cooking

Combine the soy protein with the tamari and Worcestershire sauce. Cover with boiling water and leave to hydrate for 30 minutes. Sauté the diced red kuri squash or mushrooms in the olive oil until tender. Combine the soy protein and the red kuri squash or mushrooms in a bowl and add the chestnuts and herbs. Process briefly with an immersion blender, add the chia seeds and mix with a fork. Shape into 4 balls and flatten a little to make patties. Cook the burgers for a few minutes each side in a lightly oiled frying pan over high heat.

Tex-Mex burgers

Makes 4 burgers

1 onion, finely sliced

2 garlic cloves, finely sliced

1 tbsp olive oil

500 g cooked red beans

1 tbsp chopped fresh coriander

2 tsp ground cumin

1-2 tsp chipotle chilli sauce

1 tsp paprika

1 tsp dried oregano

1 tbsp maize flour

½ tsp salt

pepper

Brown the onion and garlic in a frying pan with the olive oil over high heat.. Mash the beans by hand with a fork in a mixing bowl. Add the browned onion and garlic, the seasoning ingredients and the maize flour. Season with salt and pepper and mix well. Shape into 4 balls and flatten a little to make patties. Cook for a few minutes each side in an oiled frying pan.

Tofu and carrot burgers

Makes 2 burgers

125 g firm tofu, crumbled

50 g grated carrot

1 pinch ground cumin

1 tsp chopped fresh coriander

½ tsp ground coriander

20 g maize flour

1 tbsp arrowroot

1 tbsp non-dairy milk

salt and pepper

olive oil

Put the tofu and carrot in the bowl of a food processor and whiz to obtain a coarse mixture that is still a little chunky. Put this mixture in a large bowl and add the cumin, chopped fresh coriander and ground coriander. Add the arrowroot and mix well. Add the non-dairy milk, season to taste and mix well with your hands. Shape into 2 balls and gently flatten a little to make 2 patties. Cook in a frying pan with a little olive oil over high heat for a few minutes each side until well browned.

Delicious with rocket leaves, pink beetroot ketchup (see p. 275), finely sliced gherkins and a few slices of grated cheese (see p. 135).

Cumin and mint semolina galettes

Serves 4-8

320 g medium grain semolina
80 ml olive oil
2 tbsp chopped fresh mint
1 tsp ground cumin
1 tsp salt
250 ml water
50 g flour

Mix the semolina and the olive oil in a mixing bowl with your hands. Add the mint, cumin, salt and a third of the water. Continue mixing with your hands for a few minutes. Add the flour. Knead and add the rest of the water. Knead for a few minutes to obtain a dough. Shape 2 balls. Roll them out on parchment paper and neaten the edges so that they are nice and circular. Cut the parchment paper around the galettes. Heat a frying pan over high heat and place one galette in the pan, paper side down. Cook for about 5 minutes then turn it over. Remove the paper and cook the other side for a few minutes. Place the galette on a plate and cut into quarters. Cook the second galette in the same way.

Green lentil, onion and curry croquettes

Makes about 15 croquettes

125 g green lentils
1 large onion, chopped
olive oil
5 tbsp plain flour
200 ml water
1 tsp curry powder
½ tsp salt
vegetable oil for cooking

Bring the lentils to the boil and then simmer until tender. Heat a little olive oil in a frying pan and brown the onion. Drain the lentils. Put them back in the saucepan and add the flour, water, curry powder, salt and onion. Turn the heat to high and stir continuously until the mixture becomes thick and sticky. It is important that the texture is just right. If it is not thick enough, the croquettes will not hold their shape. Remove from the heat and leave to cool. Heat a little oil in a frying pan. Shape the mixture into balls and put into the frying pan, pressing gently to flatten them a little. Cook for 1-2 minutes each side. Be careful not to use too much oil or the croquettes will absorb it and will not become crispy. Drain on kitchen paper.

Broad bean falafels

Makes 10-12 falafels

350 g broad beans, cooked and peeled
2 garlic cloves
2 tbsp chopped parsley
2 tbsp chopped fresh chives
2 tbsp chopped fresh coriander
1 tsp ground coriander
¼ tsp ground nutmeg
¼ tsp ground cinnamon
salt and pepper
vegetable oil for cooking

Whiz the broad beans with the garlic and herbs in a food processor. (Do not process the bean mixture too much. It must not become a purée.) Put the mixture in a bowl, add the spices and mix in with a fork. Season to taste. Shape 10-12 little balls, then flatten them gently. Pan-fry with a little olive oil over high heat, or fry in a deep fryer. When the falafels are done, place them on kitchen paper to drain off any excess oil.

broad bean falafels, semolina galettes, and green lentil croquettes

Indian-style couscous

COOKING GRAINS

Indian-style couscous

Serves 6

3 tbsp olive oil
4 tsp curry powder
1 large onion, finely sliced
4 garlic cloves, finely sliced
3 carrots, peeled and cut into medium-sized pieces
2 turnips, peeled and cut into medium-sized pieces
4 potatoes, peeled and cut into medium-sized pieces
2 courgettes, diced
1 litre water
1 tsp vindaloo curry paste
200 g cooked chickpeas
125 g curried tofu
600 g medium grain couscous
fresh coriander
salt and pepper

Heat the olive oil over high heat in a large saucepan or casserole. Add the curry powder, onion, garlic, carrots and turnips. Cook over high heat for a few minutes, stirring. Lower the heat to medium and add the potatoes and courgettes. Cook, stirring, for at least 5 minutes. Add the water and the vindaloo curry paste. Season to taste and cook for 20 minutes. Add the chickpeas and the tofu. Cook for a further 5 minutes. Serve with steamed couscous and sprinkled with chopped fresh coriander.

Courgette and coconut risotto

Serves 2

2 tbsp olive oil
½ onion, finely sliced
2 garlic cloves, finely sliced
1 large courgette, cut into small dice
2 tsp ground coriander
3 tsp ground cardamom
1½ tbsp coconut oil
200 g arborio rice
100 ml white wine

600 ml vegetable stock
100 ml coconut milk

In a small frying pan, sauté the onion, garlic and courgette in the olive oil over high heat for a few minutes. Lower the heat to medium and add 1 tsp each of the coriander and cardamom. Cook for 5 minutes. Heat the coconut oil in a large casserole over medium-high heat. Add the rice and stir. When the rice is translucent, add the white wine and allow it to be absorbed. Cover with stock and stir until the rice has absorbed the liquid. Repeat the process until all the stock has been used up. Add the vegetable mixture and the coconut milk and stir to mix. Add the remaining coriander and cardamom. Stir and cook for 1-2 minutes for the rice to become creamy. Serve immediately.

Grilled einkorn with aubergine

Serves 2-4

200 g husked einkorn
400 ml water
1 medium aubergine, washed and cut into cubes
1 onion, cut into large dice
3 tbsp olive oil
2 garlic cloves, finely sliced
herb salt, pepper

Wash the einkorn. Cook it in the water over medium heat until it has absorbed it all (about 40 minutes). Heat 2 tbsp of the olive oil in a frying pan. Add the onion and aubergine and cook for a few minutes. Generously season with pepper. Lower the heat to medium, add the garlic and the remaining tablespoon of olive oil and cook, stirring occasionally, until the aubergine is tender (about 30 minutes). Drain the einkorn and add it to the pan. Season with salt and pepper to taste, and turn up the heat to high. Leave to 'grill' for 5 minutes, stirring often. Enjoy this dish hot or cold, as a salad dressed with a little lemon juice.

Provençale galettes

Makes 4-6 galettes

100 g rice flakes
200 ml water
30 g lupin flour, plus extra for dusting
20 g amaranth flour
4 tbsp tomato passata
1 tsp arrowroot
1 tsp herbs de Provence
1 garlic clove, crushed
salt and pepper
olive oil

Put all the ingredients in a casserole and mix. Cook over medium heat, stirring continuously, until the mixture is like a thick porridge. Remove from the heat and leave to cool for a few minutes. Flour your hands with lupin flour and shape the mixture into 4 balls. Dust them with flour and flatten them. Cook over medium heat in a frying pan with a little olive oil, flattening well in the pan with a spatula. Turn them over often until they are well browned on both sides.

Olive and pumpkin seed crackers

Makes about 35-40 crackers

170 g spelt flour
¼ tsp salt
½ tsp dried oregano
30 g pumpkin seeds, chopped
30 g Greek style black olives, pitted and chopped
2 tbsp olive oil
75 ml water
pepper

Put the flour in a mixing bowl. Mix with the salt and dried oregano. Season with pepper. Add the pumpkin seeds and olives. Pour in the oil and mix with a spoon. Add the water and knead for a few minutes. Roll out between two sheets of parchment paper until you have a fine sheet of dough. Line a baking tray with parchment paper. Cut the dough into squares, diamond shapes or triangles and place on the baking tray. Bake at 180°C (Gas mark 4) for 15-20 minutes.

Cinnamon-scented chocolate and hazelnut porridge

Makes 1 large bowlful or 2 small ones

350 ml chestnut-hazelnut milk
90 g rolled oats
2 tbsp cane sugar
1 tbsp cocoa powder
¼ tsp ground cinnamon
1 handful hazelnuts, roughly chopped
1 tbsp dark chocolate chips

Put the milk, the rolled oats, sugar, cocoa and cinnamon in a medium-sized saucepan and mix well. Cook over high heat, stirring continuously when the oats begin to thicken. Cook for a few minutes. Remove from the heat. Add the hazelnuts and the chocolate chips to the porridge. Mix well and serve.

Pan-fried Brussels sprouts and pearl barley salad

Serves 4

185 g pearl barley
750 ml water
3 tbsp olive oil
200 g Brussels sprouts, cut into quarters
¼ tsp ground turmeric
1 garlic clove, crushed to a paste
salt and pepper
1 bowl sesame cream (see p. 144) or 1 lemon

Bring the pearl barley and the water to the boil in a large saucepan, then turn down the heat to low. Cook for about 1 hour. After 45 minutes, check to see if it is cooked. Remove from the heat as soon as the grains are tender. Refresh under cold water and drain. Heat 2 tbsp of the olive oil in a large frying pan and sauté the Brussels sprouts for at least 5 minutes over high heat. Lower the heat to medium and add the barley, the remaining tablespoon of olive oil, turmeric and garlic. Season with salt and pepper. Cook for 5 minutes for all the flavours to come together. Transfer to a bowl or plate and leave to cool. Serve with sesame cream or wedges of lemon.

and pumpkin seed crackers

Amaranth and raisin cookies

Makes about 12 cookies

125 g amaranth
250 ml boiling water
75 ml neutral vegetable oil
50 g light brown sugar
60 g maize flour
1 tbsp carob flour
½ tsp spice mix for spiced bread
40 g raisins
2 tbsp pre-cooked soy flour

Combine the amaranth and the boiling water in a bowl. Cover and leave for 25 minutes to swell. Drain through a very fine sieve. Mix the oil and sugar in a mixing bowl. Add the maize and carob flours. Add the amaranth and mix well. Add the mixed spices, raisins and pre-cooked soy flour. Mix together with a fork. Line a baking tray with parchment paper. Shape a little ball of the dough with your hands, pressing well to make a compact cookie. Gently place on the parchment paper. Repeat the process with the rest of the dough. Be careful as the dough is very crumbly. Bake for 30 minutes at 180°C (Gas mark 4).

Green millet tabbouleh

Serves 2-4

150 g cooked millet
½ cucumber, finely diced
½ green pepper, finely diced
100 g flat-leaf parsley, finely chopped
20 mint leaves, finely chopped
2 tbsp olive oil
1 lemon, freshly squeezed
salt and pepper

Mix the millet with the cucumber and green pepper in a bowl. Add the chopped parsley and mint, olive oil and lemon juice. Season to taste. Refrigerate before serving.

Lebanese-style sautéed bulgur

Serves 2

150 g einkorn bulgur
5 tbsp olive oil
4 small garlic cloves, finely sliced
1 onion, finely sliced
1 medium aubergine, washed
½ tsp ground cumin
½ tsp ground coriander
¼ tsp ground nutmeg
¼ tsp ground pepper
½ tsp salt
3 tbsp tomato passata
a few mint sprigs
1 lemon, quartered
black pepper

Cook the bulgur for 10 minutes in twice its volume of water. Heat 3 tbsp of the olive oil in a large frying pan and sauté the garlic and onion over high heat. Peel the aubergine and coarsely grate it directly into the pan. Drain the bulgur and add it to the pan together with the remaining olive oil and the spices. Cook for a few minutes, stirring often. Lower the heat to medium and add the tomato passata. Stir and cook for a few minutes. Transfer to a plate. Chop the mint leaves and sprinkle over the dish and serve with the lemon wedges. Can be eaten warm or cold.

Idea: *When entertaining, put together some creative vegan mezze for 6-8 people. Accompany this dish with broad bean falafel (see p. 40), hummus with coriander (see p. 262), vegetable caviar (see p. 295) and raw cauliflower tabbouleh (see p. 210). Serve with Lebanese flatbread.*

Oat groats with petit pois

Serves 4

250 ml oat groats, soaked overnight in plenty of water

2 tbsp olive oil

1 onion, finely sliced

1 garlic clove, finely sliced

80 g fresh or frozen petits pois

1 tbsp tamari

salt and pepper

Cook the groats for 45 minutes in a large saucepan of water. Drain and set aside. Heat the olive oil in a frying pan over high heat. Sauté the onion and garlic in the oil. Add the groats and the petit pois, lower the heat a little and cook for 5 minutes. Add the tamari, season to taste and serve.

Oat groats are whole grains, not to be confused with rolled oats which are used to make porridge.

Polenta purée with tomato

Makes 2 small portions

500 ml water

1 vegetable stock cube

2 tsp shoyu

125 g pre-cooked polenta

200 ml tomato passata

2 tsp malted yeast

2 tsp chopped basil

Combine the water and stock cube in a saucepan and bring to the boil. Add the shoyu and sprinkle in the polenta. Lower the heat to medium. Stir in the tomato passata and stir continuously for 5 minutes. Mix in the malted yeast and basil. Remove from the heat and serve immediately.

Pan-fried barley and fennel with mint

Serves 2

240 g pearl barley

900 ml water

2 small fennel bulbs, finely sliced

1 garlic clove, finely sliced

1 small onion, finely sliced

1 tbsp olive oil

1 handful mint leaves

salt and pepper

Bring the pearl barley and the water to the boil in a large saucepan, then turn down the heat to low and cook for about 1 hour. Refresh under cold water and drain. Heat the oil in a large frying pan and add the barley, fennel, garlic and onion. Pepper generously and sauté over high heat for about 15 minutes, stirring often, until it all begins to brown. Season with salt and sprinkle with the chopped mint.

MAKE GREAT PASTA DISHES

Fresh pasta

Serves 4

150 g plain flour
150 g fine durum wheat semolina
½ tsp salt
150 ml water

Mix the flour and semolina, add the salt and then the water and knead to a very compact, dry dough. It is very important to get the consistency of the dough right. If it is too dry, add a little water; if it is too sticky, add a little flour. Shape the dough into 2 balls and cut each one into 4 pieces. Keep them under a tea towel while you roll out a pasta ball. Set the pasta machine on the work surface. Set the rollers to the widest setting and pass the first piece of dough through the machine. Lightly flour it, fold it in half and pass it through again. Decrease the roller setting to the next grade and pass the dough through the machine again. Eventually, decrease the setting to obtain a very fine sheet of pasta. Put onto a dry tea towel. Repeat the process with the second ball of dough. When you have finished rolling the dough, cut the pasta to the desired width and length (lasagne, spaghetti, tagliatelle, etc.) using the appropriate implement. You could even try making ravioli.

Conchiglioni au gratin

Serves 4

200 g conchiglioni (pasta shells)
300 g seitan stuffing (see p. 102)
3 tbsp olive oil
1 onion, finely sliced
1 garlic clove, finely sliced
2 tbsp chopped flat-leaf parsley
2 tbsp chopped basil
1 tbsp chopped chives
600 ml tomato passata
250 ml soy cream

200 ml almond milk
2 tbsp malted yeast
breadcrumbs
olive oil or margarine
salt and pepper

Stuff the uncooked conchiglioni with the seitan stuffing and arrange them in an oven-proof dish. They should be nice and snug. Heat the olive oil over high heat in a medium-sized saucepan. Sauté the onion and garlic. Add the herbs and tomato passata. Season and cook for a few minutes. Pour over stuffed conchiglioni. Mix the soy cream and the almond milk with the malted yeast. Season to taste. Carefully pour into the dish, ensuring the two sauces don't mix. Sprinkle with breadcrumbs, drizzle with olive oil and dot with little pieces of margarine. Bake at 180°C (Gas mark 4) for 30 minutes.

Tagliatelle alla 'carbonara'

Serves 2

250 g egg-free tagliatelle, or homemade tagliatelle (see recipe above)
1 tbsp olive oil, plus a little extra for cooking the pasta
125 g smoked tofu, cut into slices
200 ml soy cream (or other non-dairy cream)
1 tbsp cashew butter
4 tbsp non-dairy Parmesan (see p. 136)
salt and pepper

Cook the tagliatelle in boiling water with a drizzle of olive oil and a pinch of salt. In a frying pan, sauté the smoked tofu slices in the olive oil for a few minutes. Drain the pasta and add it into the frying pan. Pour in the soy cream and add the cashew butter. Season to taste and mix well. Sprinkle with non-dairy Parmesan and serve immediately.

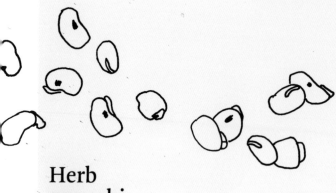

Herb gnocchi

Serves 2-4

500 g firm-fleshed potatoes
175 g T70 spelt flour
2 tbsp chopped chives
1 tbsp chopped basil
salt

Peel the potatoes and cut them into even-sized pieces. Steam until cooked. Press through a potato ricer and leave to cool. On a work surface, use your hands to combine the mashed potato with half of the flour. Next, immediately add half of the remaining flour. Then add the rest of the flour together with the herbs and some salt. Knead well. If the mixture is too sticky, add a little more flour. Take a small amount of the mixture. Roll it between your hands and shape into a sausage. Cut into gnocchi lengths. Repeat with all the dough. Roll each gnocco over the tines of a fork to make ridges, then place on a tea towel. Leave to dry, uncovered, for 15-30 minutes. Bring a large saucepan of water to the boil. Add salt and gently put the gnocchi into the boiling water. When they rise to the surface, remove with a slotted spoon.

Serve with tomato sauce or toss them in a pan with a little olive oil.

- -

Butternut gnocchi

Serves 6

650 g potatoes, peeled and cut into cubes
200 g butternut squash, peeled and cut into cubes
500 g plain flour, plus extra for dusting
1 tsp salt

Steam the potatoes until tender. Simmer the squash until tender. When both are cooked, press through a potato ricer and leave to cool. Add half of the flour and all of the salt. Knead the mixture with your hands. Add the rest of the flour and knead again. Shape into 4 balls and dust them with flour. On a floured work surface, shape each one into a sausage. Cut into gnocchi lengths. Repeat with all the dough. Roll each gnocco over the tines of a fork to make ridges, then place on a tea towel to dry, uncovered, for 30 minutes. Next, bring a large saucepan of water to the boil and gently put the gnocchi into the boiling water. When they rise to the surface, remove with a slotted spoon.

Serve, drizzled with olive oil, pepper and a pinch of dried sage, or the sauce of your choice.

- -

Summer ravioli stuffed with tofu

Serves 4

50 g red pepper, finely chopped
100 g firm tofu, crumbled
5 sun-dried tomatoes, chopped
2 tbsp olive oil
1 tbsp chopped basil
salt and pepper
strips of fresh pasta for 4
  (see p. 48)

Sauté the red pepper, tofu and sun-dried tomatoes in a little olive oil with the basil. Season with salt and pepper, then cook over high heat until the red pepper is tender. Leave to cool. Place teaspoonfuls of the stuffing evenly along a strip of pasta, leaving enough space in between to cut out the ravioli. Cover with another strip of pasta (if necessary, dampen using a wet brush) and cut out the ravioli with a circular ravioli cutter. Repeat the process with the rest of the pasta and stuffing. Cook the ravioli in a large saucepan of boiling, salted water.

Serve, drizzled with a little olive oil or tomato sauce.

Lasagne with summer vegetables, ricotta and pesto

Serves 4-6

2 aubergines, cut into small dice
1 large courgette, cut into small dice
2 small red peppers, cut into small dice
4 garlic cloves, finely sliced
4 tbsp olive oil
3 tsp herbs de Provence
200 ml tomato passata
400 g chopped tomatoes
2 bowls soy ricotta (see p. 128)
9-12 sheets spelt lasagne
salt and pepper

For the pesto
2 bunches basil
65 ml olive oil
2 handfuls cashew nuts
salt

Heat the olive oil in a frying pan and sauté the vegetables with the herbs de Provence for 10-15 minutes until tender. Add the tomato passata and the chopped tomatoes. Season. Cook at least for another 5 minutes.

Prepare the pesto: Whiz the basil leaves with the olive oil and cashew nuts. Season with salt. Mix the pesto with the ricotta. Pour half of the vegetable sauce into an oven-proof dish. Cover with sheets of lasagne and pour half of the pesto and ricotta sauce over them. Cover again with sheets of lasagne, then the vegetable sauce, more sheets of lasagne and finish with the rest of the pesto and ricotta sauce. Bake at 180°C (Gas mark 4) for 30 minutes.

Ricotta and spinach cannelloni

Serves 3-4

10-12 cannelloni
For the stuffing
70-80 g baby spinach leaves
2 garlic cloves, finely sliced
1 tsp olive oil
1 bowl soy ricotta (see p. 128)

For the quick béchamel
300 ml soy cream
1 tbsp cornflour
salt and pepper
ground nutmeg

For the sauce
1 tbsp olive oil
2 shallots, finely sliced
2 garlic cloves, finely sliced
300 ml tomato passata
½ bunch basil, chopped
salt and pepper

Prepare the stuffing: Sauté the spinach and garlic for a few minutes in the olive oil, then mix with the ricotta. Prepare the quick béchamel: Combine the cream and cornflour in a small saucepan. Season with salt, pepper and nutmeg. Turn the heat to high and cook, stirring continuously, for 3 minutes to thicken the sauce. Pour half of the béchamel into the bottom of an oven-proof dish. Stuff the cannelloni and arrange on the béchamel. Prepare the sauce: Heat the olive oil in a frying pan and sauté the shallots and the garlic for a few minutes. Add the tomato passata and the basil. Season and cook for 5 minutes, stirring continuously. Pour the sauce over the cannelloni. Top with the remaining béchamel. Bake for 20-30 minutes at 180°C (Gas mark 4).

Pad Thai

Serves 2

125 g rice noodles or vermicelli
2 tbsp neutral vegetable oil
1 shallot, finely sliced
4 garlic cloves, chopped
1 tsp chopped ginger
½ red chilli, fresh or dried, finely chopped
125 g firm tofu, crumbled
100 g mung bean sprouts

For the sauce
60 ml vegetable stock
2 tbsp tamari
2 tbsp freshly squeezed lime juice
2 tbsp agave syrup
1 tbsp peanut butter
1 tsp red chilli paste
pepper

For the garnish
1 lime, quartered
1 small bunch fresh coriander, chopped
1 handful peanuts or cashew nuts, chopped

Put the rice noodles or vermicelli in a bowl and cover with boiling water. Drain after 5 minutes. For the sauce, mix all the ingredients in a bowl with a fork. Heat the oil in a wok or frying pan and sauté the shallot, garlic, ginger and chilli over high heat for a few minutes. Add the tofu and cook for a few minutes, stirring continuously, to brown it a little. Add the rice noodles or vermicelli and the sauce. Stir gently so as not to break the noodles. Mix in two thirds of the mung bean sprouts. Divide between two bowls or plates and top with lime wedges, chopped fresh coriander and the remaining mung bean sprouts. Sprinkle with the nuts. Serve immediately.

FYI: Mung bean sprouts are often wrongly sold as 'soy bean sprouts'. They are easy to grow at home; simply buy dried mung beans, soak and rinse and in a few days they will germinate.

Penne with seitan, spinach, and red pepper coulis

Serves 2-3

150 g penne rigate
1 tbsp olive oil, plus a little extra for cooking the pasta
100 g baby spinach leaves
150 g gourmet seitan, cut into pieces
1 tbsp chopped parsley
1 tbsp chopped chives
1 tbsp pine nuts
salt and pepper

For the coulis
1 large red pepper, diced
2 tbsp olive oil
2 garlic cloves, finely sliced
75 ml water
1 tbsp cane sugar
salt and pepper

Cook the penne in boiling water with a drizzle of olive oil and a pinch of salt. Prepare the coulis: Heat the olive oil in a small saucepan and sauté the red pepper and garlic. Season with salt and pepper and cook for 5 minutes or until the red pepper is tender. Whiz together with the water and the sugar. Heat the 1 tbsp of olive oil in a large frying pan and quickly sauté the spinach leaves for 2 minutes. Add the penne, the seitan, the herbs and pine nuts. Season to taste. Sauté for 5 minutes and serve with the coulis.

Thai

Millet-stuffed oni

GETTING TO KNOW GLUTEN-FREE GRAINS

Millet with almond milk and orange blossom

Serves 4

150 g husked millet
700 ml almond milk
100 g light brown sugar
¼ tsp vanilla extract
1½ tbsp orange blossom water
chopped pistachios
fresh fruit of your choice

Cook the millet with the milk, sugar and vanilla in a saucepan over medium heat for 20-30 minutes, stirring occasionally. Mix in the orange blossom water and divide among 4 ramekins. Sprinkle with chopped pistachios and diced fresh fruit.

Delicious with apricots, raspberries, peaches, etc.

Gluten-free bread

Makes 1 loaf

140 g maize flour
250 g brown rice flour
50 g soy flour
30 g buckwheat flour
½ tsp salt
1 tsp gluten-free baking powder
500 ml warm water
2 tsp baker's yeast
2 tbsp agave syrup
3 tbsp vegetable oil

Combine the flours, salt and baking powder in a bowl. Mix the yeast with the agave syrup and add to the bowl. Whisk the mixture and add the oil. Line a 25 cm/10 inch cake tin with parchment paper and pour in the batter. Cook at 200°C (Gas mark 6) for 30 minutes. Leave to cool. Unmould and slice as needed.

Oregano-scented cornbread

Serves 4-6

450 ml soy milk
1 tbsp apple cider vinegar
4 tbsp olive oil
125 g maize flour
125 g plain flour
100 g polenta or cornmeal
1 sachet (7 g) baking powder
2 tsp dried oregano
½ tsp salt
pepper

Whisk together the liquid ingredients in a bowl until just foamy. Mix together all the dry ingredients and add them to the liquids. Oil a rectangular dish or line it with parchment paper and pour in the batter. Bake at 180°C (Gas mark 4) for 35-40 minutes. Leave to cool, then cut into little squares.

Serve instead of bread.

Millet-stuffed onions

Serves 3-4

150 g millet
2 garlic cloves, finely sliced
3 tbsp olive oil
1 tsp ground cumin
1 tsp ground coriander
ground nutmeg
2 tbsp chopped fresh chives
2 tbsp tamari
6 large onions
pepper

Cook the millet in twice its volume of water. Sauté the garlic and the cooked millet in a frying pan with a little olive oil. Add the spices and chives and cook for 5 minutes. Add the tamari and season with pepper. Cut the tops off the onions and hollow them out with a melon baller. Fill the onions with the millet mixture and press down well. Put the tops back on the onions and put them in an oven-proof dish. Bake at 220°C (Gas mark 7) for 20-30 minutes. Peel the onions before eating them.

Delicious with tomato sauce and herbed tofu.

Quinoa flake and vegetable croquettes

Makes 12 croquettes

150 g quinoa flakes
50 g brown rice flour
50 g raw, grated vegetables (carrot, courgette, sweet potato, red kuri squash, etc.)
400 ml non-dairy milk
1 tbsp sesame oil
1 tbsp chopped chives
1 tsp dried wild garlic
salt and pepper
gluten-free breadcrumbs
vegetable oil for cooking

Put the flakes, flour, grated vegetables, milk, sesame oil and spices in a saucepan and mix together. Turn the heat to high and cook, stirring continuously, until the mixture becomes very thick and is difficult to mix. Remove from the heat. Spread the breadcrumbs on a plate. Take a small amount of the mixture. Roll it between your hands and shape into a ball. Roll between your hands again to make a cylindrical shape and flatten the ends. Roll each croquette in the breadcrumbs. When all the croquettes are ready, heat enough oil to cover the bottom of a frying pan and brown them. When they are done, place them on kitchen paper to drain off any excess oil.

Tip: To make gluten-free breadcrumbs, whiz crispy gluten-free bread (made with buckwheat, maize flour, chestnut flour, etc.) in a food processor.

Amaranth tabbouleh with grilled peppers

Serves 4

300 g amaranth
600 ml water
olive oil
2 red peppers, finely diced
300 g cucumber, finely diced
4 tomatoes, finely diced
2 handfuls mint leaves, finely chopped
a handful flat-leaf leaves, finely chopped
1 lemon
salt and pepper

Bring the amaranth and the water to the boil in a large saucepan, then turn down the heat to medium and cook for 10 minutes, stirring often. The amaranth will absorb all of the water. Drain through a fine sieve and rise under cold water until the amaranth has cooled and no longer sticks together. Put the amaranth in a bowl and mix with 2 tbsp of olive oil. Sauté the diced red peppers in a frying pan with 1 tbsp of olive oil over high heat. Leave to cool on a plate. Add the diced cucumber, cooled red pepper and tomatoes to the bowl together with the chopped mint and parsley. Refrigerate. Dress with salt, pepper and lemon juice just before serving.

Polenta and chive chips

Serves 2-4

750 ml water
1 vegetable stock cube
150 g pre-cooked polenta
1 tbsp chopped chives
olive oil
wheat flour
pepper

Bring the water with the stock cube to the boil, then sprinkle in the polenta and begin to whisk. Season with pepper. Lower the heat to medium and cook for 10 minutes, whisking continuously. When almost cooked, add the chives. Oil a rectangular dish and pour in the polenta to an even thickness. Refrigerate for 30 minutes. Turn out the polenta and cut it into large chips. Dredge them in the flour. Heat enough olive oil over high heat to cover the bottom of a frying pan and brown the polenta chips all over. When they are done, place them on kitchen paper to drain off any excess oil. Serve immediately; they lose their crispiness as they cool.

inoa flake and vegetable croquettes

Brown rice flour béchamel

Serves 2-4

3 tbsp neutral vegetable oil
5 tbsp brown rice flour
300 ml soy milk, warmed
ground nutmeg
salt and pepper

In a saucepan, heat the oil to medium. Whisk in the flour to make a roux and cook for 1 minute. Gradually add the warm milk, whisking well to avoid lumps. Season and add nutmeg to taste. Keep whisking constantly a few moments longer until thick.

If the béchamel becomes too thick or lumpy, remove it from the heat, add a little soy milk and whisk vigorously. Use it immediately.

Puffed quinoa and chocolate rochers

Makes about 20 rochers

200 g dark chocolate
20 g puffed quinoa
25 g fine coconut sugar
5 tbsp white almond butter

Melt the chocolate in a bain-marie. Mix the puffed quinoa and coconut sugar in a large bowl. Add the almond butter and mix in with a spoon. Shape into little, compact balls, and place on a sheet of parchment paper on a work surface. Line a tray with parchment paper and place it next to the rochers. Use a spoon to pour melted chocolate over a rocher of puffed quinoa and gently roll it so that it is completely covered in chocolate. Very gently place it on the tray.

When all the rochers have been made, put the tray in the freezer for at least 5 minutes. Put each rocher in a little fluted paper case and place in an airtight container.

Sweetcorn tempura

Serves 2

120 g maize flour
65 ml ice-cold water
1 tbsp arrowroot
1 tbsp pre-cooked polenta
½ courgette, finely sliced
½ carrot, finely sliced
vegetable oil for cooking

Whisk the flour and the iced water together. Add the arrowroot and the polenta. If the mixture is too thick, add 1 tbsp of water. Heat the oil in a small saucepan; it should reach 180°C. To check the temperature, put a drop of the batter in the oil; it should rise to the surface immediately. One by one, dip the vegetable slices in the batter and then fry two slices at a time in the oil. Remove when done and place on kitchen paper to absorb the excess oil. Serve at once.

Use other vegetables of your choice if you prefer.

Gluten-free pancakes

Makes 10-12 pancakes

145 g brown rice flour
50 g pre-cooked soy flour
1 tsp arrowroot
1 tsp toasted, ground flaxseeds
1 tsp gluten-free baking powder
¼ tsp ground vanilla
⅛ tsp ground cinnamon
4 tbsp light brown sugar
300 ml soy milk
2 tbsp neutral vegetable oil

Combine all the dry ingredients in a mixing bowl. Whisk in the soy milk. Add the olive oil. Leave to stand for 10 minutes. Cook the pancakes by pouring a spoonful of the batter into a lightly-oiled, hot frying pan. Flip over when little bubbles form and burst, and the surface is almost dry.

Savoury, rice-flake crumble

Serves 2-4

200 g rice flakes
6 tbsp ground almonds
4 tbsp water
4 tbsp olive oil
2 tbsp malted yeast flakes
1 garlic clove, crushed to a paste
½ tsp salt
pepper

Mix all the ingredients together. Spread on a baking tray, pressing down well, and leave to rest for 20 minutes. Bake at 180°C (Gas mark 4) for 25 minutes.

Sprinkle over a bowl of sautéed or steamed vegetables, or to give dishes a crunchy, gourmet touch.

Quick rice, chocolate and almond cream

Serves 4

5 tbsp brown rice flour
4 tbsp light brown sugar
3 tbsp dessicated coconut
500 ml rice milk
2 tbsp white almond butter

Combine the rice flour with the sugar and the dessicated coconut in a medium-sized saucepan. Whisk in the rice milk and melt the almond butter in the mixture. Turn the heat to high and whisk until thick and creamy. Divide among 4 ramekins and leave to cool.

Tip: *This sweet cream is great for children, but it can also be used as a quick pastry cream for filling cakes, as a pancake stuffing, or when making verrines.*

Gluten-free granola

Makes 1 large jar

150 g rice flakes
100 g quinoa flakes
20 g shelled walnuts, chopped with a knife
40 g hazelnuts, chopped with a knife
40 g cashew nuts, chopped with a knife
40 ml neutral vegetable oil
50 ml maple syrup
5 tbsp coconut sugar
500 ml water
¼ tsp vanilla extract
½ tsp ground cinnamon

Combine both flakes. Mix the flakes with the chopped nuts in a bowl. Whisk together all the other ingredients for a few minutes in a small saucepan to heat them well. Pour onto the flakes and nuts. Mix well and spread out on a baking tray lined with parchment paper. Bake at 180°C (Gas mark 4) for 20 minutes. The granola should be golden and crunchy. Leave to cool and store in a large jar or airtight container.

Gluten-free shortcrust pastry

Makes 1 tart crust

100 g pre-cooked polenta
2 tbsp ground flaxseeds
2 tbsp arrowroot
½ tsp salt
50 g chickpea flour
50 g soy flour
4 tbsp olive oil
60 ml water
2 tbsp agave syrup

In a mixing bowl, combine all the dry ingredients. Add the oil and mix with your fingertips, as if making a crumble. Add the water and knead. Pour in the agave syrup and knead again. Roll out between two sheets of parchment paper. Place in a tart tin and remove the top sheet of parchment paper. Bake as any normal dough.

ten-free granola

GOURMET PULSE RECIPES

Black bean burritos

Makes 4-6 burritos

150 g black beans
2 tbsp olive oil
2 shallots, finely sliced
1 tomato, diced
1 tsp ground cumin
1 tsp garlic powder, plus an extra ½ tsp
½ tsp ground coriander
½ tsp dried oregano
¼ tsp paprika
2 tsp chipotle chilli sauce
1 small bowl thick cashew cream
1 tbsp lime juice
1 tbsp malted yeast
½ tsp garlic powder
4-6 wheat or corn tortillas
lettuce leaves, sliced red pepper, sliced avocado (optional)
salt and pepper

Cook the black beans in water for about 1 hour. Heat the olive oil in a frying pan and sauté the shallots. Add the tomato and spices and cook for 5 minutes over high heat. Season well. Drain the beans and add them to the pan. Combine the cashew cream with the lime juice, malted yeast and the ½ tsp garlic powder. Spread a spoonful of the cream on a tortilla and top with some cooked beans and the raw vegetables if you wish. Fold in the sides, then roll the tortilla up from the side closest to you.

Variation: *To prepare delicious enchiladas, simply fold the tortilla over itself (without folding in edges). Arrange the tortillas on a plate, top with a little spicy homemade tomato sauce and vegetable cream. Season, add some gratable cheese (see p. 135) and heat for 10-15 minutes in the oven.*

Sweet, azuki bean paste

Makes 2 jars

200 g azuki beans, soaked overnight
200 g light brown sugar
1 tsp vanilla extract

Soak the beans in water overnight. Put the beans and the soaking water in a saucepan and bring to the boil. Drain, throw away the water and cover the beans with fresh water. Simmer for about 1½ hours. The azuki beans should be tender and easy to mash. Add the sugar and vanilla and mix well. Cook for a few minutes and then whiz with an immersion blender. Add a little water if necessary to give the paste a smooth consistency. Pour into the jars and close. Keeps for 1 week in the fridge.

Use as you would chestnut purée or to make delicious dorayakis, stuffed Japanese pancakes (spread a layer of sweet azuki paste between two small, plain pancakes).

Curried chickpea salad

Serves 4

olive oil
3 tbsp curry powder
1 onion, finely sliced
1 garlic clove, finely sliced
1 green pepper, thickly sliced
250 g cooked chickpeas
3 tomatoes, cut into thin wedges
1 lemon, quartered
salt

Heat 2 tbsp of olive oil and the curry powder in a frying pan over high heat. Add the onion, chickpeas, green pepper and garlic, and sauté for 5-10 minutes, stirring often. Season lightly with salt. Leave to cool in a dish. Top with the tomatoes. Drizzle with a little olive oil and serve with the lemon wedges. Squeeze the lemon juice over the salad just before eating.

k bean burritos

Tomato pan

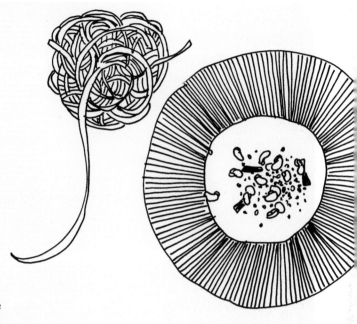

Lisbon-style black-eyed bean salad

Serves 4-6

400 g cooked black-eyed beans
1 onion, sliced
½ red pepper, sliced
1 garlic clove, sliced
1 small bunch flat-leaf parsley, stems removed, finely
    chopped by hand or with a mini-chopper
1 pinch ground pepper
4 tbsp olive oil
1 lemon, juiced
salt and pepper

Drain the beans and combine in a bowl with the onion, the red pepper and the garlic. Add the chopped parsley leaves. Season, add pepper and refrigerate. Pour the lemon juice over the dish when about to serve.

FYI: This delicious salad – and its many variations – can be found everywhere in Portugal and it is not uncommon to come across versions made without animal products; a boon for vegan travellers! In Europe, as well as all over the world, pulses have always been a highly appreciated ingredient for preparing nourishing meat- and fish-free dishes.

Tomato panisse

Serves 2-4

400 ml water
100 ml tomato passata
1 tbsp olive oil
1 tsp salt
½ tsp garlic powder
½ tsp herbs de Provence
150 g chickpea flour

Combine the tomato passata and the water, olive oil, salt, garlic and herbs de Provence in a saucepan and bring to the boil. Whisk in the chickpea flour a little at a time. Continue to mix over high heat until the consistency is thick and sticky. Pour into an oiled dish (or two ring moulds on a flat plate) and press down well with a spatula. Leave to cool and then refrigerate for 1-2 hours. Cut into pieces and sauté for a few minutes before serving.

Broad bean risotto

Serves 2

100 g broad beans, peeled
2 shallots, finely sliced
2 garlic cloves, finely sliced
2 tbsp olive oil
200 g arborio rice
80 ml white wine
1 litre vegetable stock
2 tsp tamari
2 tbsp soy cream
2 tsp cashew butter
2 tsp chopped fresh coriander
1 tbsp non-dairy Parmesan (see p. 136)

Steam the beans for 5-10 minutes. Heat the olive oil in a large frying pan and lightly brown the shallots and garlic. Add the rice and mix well. When the rice is translucent, pour in the white wine and allow it to be absorbed. Cover with stock and stir from time to time until the rice has absorbed the liquid. Repeat the process until the rice is fully cooked. Add the broad beans. Stir in the tamari, soy cream and cashew butter, and remove from the heat. Divide between 2 plates. Sprinkle with the fresh coriander and non-dairy Parmesan.

Chilli sin carne

Serves 6

50 g textured soy protein (small pieces)
1 vegetable stock cube
1 tsp brown barley miso
1½ tsp garlic powder
3½ tsp ground cumin
3 tbsp olive oil
1 onion, finely sliced
3 garlic cloves, finely sliced
1 carrot, finely diced
2 tsp ground coriander
1 tsp dried oregano
1½ tsp paprika
Cayenne pepper
2 tbsp tamari
800 g chopped tomatoes
500 g cooked red beans
100 g sweetcorn

Mix the soy protein, vegetable stock cube, miso, ½ tsp of the garlic powder and ½ tsp of the ground cumin in a bowl. Cover with water and leave to hydrate for 15-30 minutes. Heat the olive oil in a frying pan and sauté the onion and the garlic. Add the carrot, the remaining spices, the soy protein and its liquid, and the tamari. Mix well and cook for a few minutes. Add the tomatoes. Cook for another few minutes. Turn the heat down and add the red beans and sweetcorn. Cook over low heat for a further 20 minutes.

Sprinkle with fresh coriander leaves and serve with wheat or corn tortillas, or plain rice.

Warm broad bean, rocket, lime and sesame seed salad

Serves 4

200 g fresh broad beans, peeled
100 g rocket
½ bunch fresh coriander, chopped
2 tbsp sesame seeds
4 limes, quartered
olive oil
salt and pepper

Steam the beans for 5-10 minutes until cooked but still firm. Combine with the rocket in a bowl. Add the fresh coriander and the sesame seeds. Drizzle with olive oil and season with salt and pepper. Serve with the lime wedges to squeeze at the table.

Split pea and coconut milk soup

Serves 4

200 g split peas, soaked for 1 hour
1 large onion, finely sliced
2 small potatoes, peeled and cut into cubes
2 tbsp olive oil
750 ml water
2 tbsp white miso
200 ml coconut milk
1 garlic clove
salt and pepper

Sauté the onion and the potatoes in the olive oil over high heat in a large saucepan. Cover with the water, dissolve the miso and cook over high heat for 5 minutes and then turn down to medium. Add the split peas and cook for 25 minutes. Add the coconut milk and garlic, and whiz. If the soup is too thick, add a little water until the consistency is like a velouté. Season to taste.

rm broad bean, rocket, lime and sesame seed salad

Two-bean rillettes

Lentil chorba

Serves 4-6

100 g green lentils
5 tbsp olive oil
½ tsp ground cumin
½ tsp ground turmeric
½ tsp paprika
¼ tsp ground cinnamon
¼ tsp ground nutmeg
¼ tsp freshly ground black pepper
1 onion, cut into cubes
2 medium potatoes, cut into cubes
1 large carrot, cut into cubes
1 celery rib, cut into cubes
1 courgette, cut into cubes
2 tsp chopped fresh coriander and 1 tbsp chopped fresh
  mint
½ tsp red chilli paste
200 g chopped tomatoes
1½ litres vegetable stock
30 g wheat bulgur or einkorn
1 lemon, juiced
salt

Cook the lentils for 30 minutes in a large saucepan in 5 times their volume of water. Drain and set aside. Heat the olive oil over medium heat in a large saucepan and add the spices. Stir well and add the cut up vegetables. Cook for at least 5 minutes, stirring from time to time. Add the herbs and red chilli paste, and cook for a further 5 minutes. Add the chopped tomatoes and cook again for 5 minutes, stirring from time to time. The vegetables should not brown much. If they do, lower the heat. Pour in the vegetable stock and cook for 20 minutes. Adjust the seasoning if necessary. Add the bulgur and cook for another 10 minutes. Lastly, add the lentils and the lemon juice, and cook over high heat for a few minutes before serving.

Two-bean rillettes

Serves 4-6

1 small onion, finely sliced
2 garlic cloves, finely sliced
2 tbsp olive oil
2 bay leaves
225 g cooked white beans
225 g cooked red beans
1 tsp mustard
3 tsp barley miso
2 tbsp chopped chives
salt and pepper

Brown the onion and garlic in a saucepan with 1 tbsp of the olive oil (and the bay leaves) over medium heat for 5 minutes. Add the beans. Mix well and cook over low heat for 1 minute together with the remaining tbsp of olive oil. Remove the bay leaves. Put the bean mixture in the bowl of a food processor with the mustard and miso. Whiz to a coarse, slightly chunky mixture. Season to taste with salt and pepper and mix in the chives with a fork. Put into a terrine and refrigerate for 2 hours. Enjoy on slices of rustic baguette, topped with a gherkin.

For a bit more of a kick, add a few drops of liquid smoke.

QUINOA AND BUCKWHEAT, TWO UNUSUAL INGREDIENTS

Quinoa, grilled tofu, olive and sun-dried tomato salad

Serves 4

150 g white quinoa
200 g firm tofu, cubed
4 tbsp olive oil
1 tsp curry powder
1 tsp herbs de Provence
2 tsp shoyu
175 g pitted Kalamata olives
80 g sun-dried tomatoes in olive oil, finely sliced
1 lemon, quartered
salt and black pepper

Wash the quinoa and put it in a saucepan with twice its volume of water. Bring to the boil, then cook over medium heat for 10 minutes. Remove from the heat and leave to swell and absorb the water completely. Put into a fine sieve and refresh under cold water. Sauté the tofu, curry powder and herbs de Provence in a frying pan with 1 tbsp of the olive oil over high heat. When the tofu has browned nicely, remove from the heat and add the shoyu. Mix well and set aside. Mix the quinoa in a bowl with the remaining 3 tbsp of olive oil. Add the olives, sun-dried tomatoes and browned tofu. Season to taste. This salad keeps well for 24 hours in the fridge. Add a squeeze of lemon juice just before eating.

Quinoa soup

Serves 4

1 onion, finely sliced
½ red pepper, finely sliced
2 garlic cloves, finely sliced
2 tbsp olive oil
½ fresh red chilli, to taste
2 tsp ground cumin
pepper
1 medium potato, finely diced
2 tomatoes, finely diced
1½ litres water
100 g quinoa
2 tbsp chopped parsley
2 tbsp chopped fresh coriander
1 lime
salt and pepper

Brown the onion, red pepper and garlic in the olive oil in a large saucepan over high heat. Add the chilli and spices, then the potato and tomatoes. Cook for a few minutes. Add the water and season to taste. Cook for about 30 minutes over low heat. Add the quinoa and cook until it is tender and begins to uncoil. Sprinkle with the herbs and squeeze the lime juice over it when about to serve.

Inspired by the quinoa soups of the Andes, this dish makes a delicious meal rich in protein, vegetables and flavours!

inoa, grilled tofu, olive and sun-dried tomato salad

Red peppers stuffed
with buckwheat, tofu and olives

Serves 4

125 g husked buckwheat
2 tbsp olive oil
125 g firm tofu
1 shallot, finely diced
40 g pitted green olives, sliced horizontally
1 tbsp chopped parsley
1 garlic clove
1 pinch Espelette pepper
2 large red peppers
salt and pepper

Cook the buckwheat in a saucepan with twice its volume of water over low heat for about 30 minutes. It should be just tender but not too soft. Drain and refresh under cold running water. Heat the olive oil in a frying pan over high heat. Sauté the tofu with the shallot, olives, parsley and garlic. Generously season with pepper. Sauté, stirring often until the tofu and the olives are lightly browned. Taste for pepper and seasoning. Wash the peppers, cut them in half and stuff with the mixture. Place on a baking tray and bake for 20 minutes at 240°C (Gas mark 9).

peppers stuffed with buckwheat, tofu and olives

Quinoa porridge with coconut

Serves 2

75 g quinoa
60 g dessicated coconut
150 ml non-dairy milk
agave syrup

Rinse the quinoa and cook it in water until just soft. Drain, refresh, and put it back in the saucepan together with the coconut and non-dairy milk. Cook over medium heat until the quinoa swells completely, the coconut softens and the mixture has the consistency of a smooth, silky porridge. Sweeten to taste with the agave syrup.

For an even more nourishing breakfast, add dried fruit, oily seeds, cut up fresh fruit, grains or cereals, etc.

Buckwheat groats with leeks

Serves 4

1 leek, finely sliced
3 tbsp olive oil
250 g husked buckwheat
750 ml vegetable stock
200 ml soy cream
2 tbsp cashew butter
2 tbsp malted yeast
pepper

Sauté the leek with the olive oil in a saucepan over medium heat. Season with pepper. Add the buckwheat and vegetable stock. Cook for 20 minutes. Add the cream, cashew butter and malted yeast, and cook for a further 10 minutes.

Buckwheat and potato galettes

Makes 10 galettes

225 g potatoes, peeled and finely diced
100 g wholegrain buckwheat flour
300 ml soy milk
salt and pepper

Bring the potatoes to the boil then simmer until tender. Drain. Whiz the potatoes in a food processor with the flour and milk. Season to taste. Cook as you would pancakes, in a lightly oiled frying pan over medium heat, a few minutes on each side.

Serve with sautéed mushrooms, vegan taramasalata (see p. 111) or dill cream (see p. 111).

Soba with rocket pesto

Serves 4

500 g soba noodles (Japanese buckwheat noodles)
125 g rocket leaves
6 tbsp olive oil
50 g white cashew nuts
1 small garlic clove
1 tsp lemon juice
salt and pepper

Cook the soba noodles in boiling water for a few minutes. Drain. Whiz the rocket with the olive oil, cashew nuts, garlic and lemon juice. Season and serve with the soba noodles.

Suggestion: *This goes very well with tofu cooked in teriyaki sauce (see p.104) or, for an even more amazing combination of flavours, with tofu à la Provençale (see p.82).*

Try using this pesto for bruschette or to give an extra zing to pasta salads.

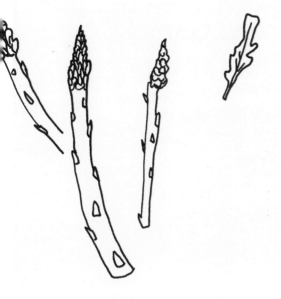

Sautéed buckwheat with rocket and red pepper

Serves 2

100 g husked buckwheat
2 tbsp olive oil
½ red pepper, finely sliced
2 garlic cloves, finely sliced
2 generous bunches rocket leaves
salt and pepper

Cook the buckwheat in twice its volume of water until tender. Heat the olive oil in a frying pan over high heat and sauté the buckwheat. Add the red pepper and garlic. Brown over high heat for about 5 minutes. Add the rocket, cook for a few minutes until it is just tender, season to taste and serve.

Vegetable and quinoa Antilles curry

Serves 3-4

4 garlic cloves, finely sliced
1 onion, finely sliced
2 medium potatoes, peeled and cut into cubes
1 sweet potato, peeled and cut into cubes
1 aubergine, cut into cubes
1 courgette, cut into cubes
4 tbsp neutral vegetable oil
5 tsp ground Antilles curry mix
1 tbsp apple cider vinegar
½ tsp red chilli paste (optional)
230 g tinned, peeled plum tomatoes, diced
600 ml vegetable stock
100 g red quinoa
100 ml soy cream
salt and pepper

Heat the oil over high heat in a large saucepan and sauté all the vegetables for 5 minutes, stirring continuously. Add the spices, the vinegar mixed with the red chilli paste, and the peeled plum tomatoes. Mix well and and cook for a few minutes. Pour in the vegetable stock and lower the heat to medium. Cover and cook for 20 minutes. Add the quinoa and about 200 ml of water. Cook, uncovered, for a further 25 minutes over medium heat. Add the cream and season to taste.

Sautéed quinoa and green asparagus salad

Serves 4-6

100 g white quinoa
100 g red quinoa
3 tbsp olive oil
2 garlic cloves, finely sliced
¼ tsp ground turmeric
1 bunch asparagus, washed, hard parts removed
40 g almonds, skin on, chopped with a knife
1 handful raisins
2 lemons, quartered

Wash the quinoa and cook in twice its volume of water in a large saucepan until tender and the grains begin to uncoil. Drain and set aside. Heat the olive oil in a large frying pan over high heat and sauté the quinoa and garlic. Add the turmeric. Cut the asparagus in small pieces and sauté with the quinoa for about 5-10 minutes, stirring often. Transfer to a bowl or plate and leave to cool. Add the almonds and raisins to the salad. Serve with lemon wedges to squeeze at the table.

Versatile tofu stuffing

Serves 2

125 g firm tofu
1 small garlic clove
1 tsp chopped chives
1 tsp olive oil
¼ tsp salt
pepper

Whiz all the ingredients in a food processor.

Use to stuff vegetables, savoury pastries, etc.

Tofu chimichurri

Serves 2

6 tbsp chopped curly parsley
3 tbsp chopped fresh coriander
1 tbsp fresh or dried oregano
1 shallot
3 garlic cloves
1 tsp fresh green chilli pepper
1 tbsp sherry vinegar
1 tbsp lemon juice
60 ml olive oil
¼ tsp salt
200 g tofu, sliced
black pepper

Whiz the herbs, the shallot, garlic and green chilli in a food processor. Put in a bowl and mix with the vinegar and lemon juice. Add the olive oil and season to taste. Marinate the tofu in the chimichurri sauce. Drizzle with a tiny bit of oil and grill on a barbecue or in a frying pan for a few minutes each side. Serve together with the rest of the sauce.

Suggestion: *This Argentinian sauce goes well with all grilled food but is also great for spicing up many other dishes.*

TOFU

Tofu nuggets

Makes about 15 nuggets

250 g firm tofu, crumbled
1 small garlic clove, crushed
3 tbsp toasted, ground flaxseeds
2 tbsp white miso
1 tbsp chopped parsley
1 pinch ground turmeric
1 pinch paprika
6 tsp arrowroot
60 ml water
breadcrumbs
vegetable oil for cooking
pepper

Put the tofu in a bowl. Add the garlic, flaxseeds, miso, parsley, turmeric and paprika and mash well with a fork to combine. Leave to rest for 15-30 minutes for the flaxseeds to release their mucilage and bind the mixture. Mix the arrowroot and the water in a ramekin. Spread the breadcrumbs on a small plate. Shape firm nuggets with your hands, roll them in the arrowroot and then in the breadcrumbs and set aside. Heat a little vegetable oil in a frying pan and brown the nuggets, pan-frying them a few minutes on each side. Drain on kitchen paper. When all the nuggets are golden brown, place them on a baking tray and bake for 20 minutes at 180°C (Gas mark 4).

Tofu nuggets

Orange and miso-glazed tofu

Serves 2-4

1 tbsp brown barley miso
3 oranges, juiced
½ tsp five-spice powder
250 g firm tofu, cut into triangles about 1 cm thick
1 tsp vegetable oil
2 tbsp agave syrup
pepper

Mix the miso and orange juice in a flat-bottomed dish and add the spices. Marinate the tofu for 1-2 hours. Oil a frying pan and cook the tofu pieces a few minutes on each side. Mix the agave syrup with the marinade and pour into the pan. Reduce the mixture over a low heat.

Tofu and vegetable past

Devilled tofu

Serves 2

3 garlic cloves, finely sliced
2 shallots, finely sliced
250 g firm tofu, cut into large cubes
2 tbsp olive oil
2 tsp dried basil
1 tbsp cognac
100 ml soy cream (or other non-dairy cream)
½ tsp chilli paste
1 tbsp tomato concentrate
1 tbsp tamari
salt and pepper

Heat the olive oil in a frying pan and sauté the garlic, shallots and tofu over medium heat. Add the dried basil and season with pepper. Cook for a few minutes to brown nicely. Add the cognac and let the alcohol evaporate. Add the cream, chilli paste, tomato concentrate and tamari. Mix well. Correct the seasoning if necessary and serve.

Inspired by a Belgian recipe for devilled scampi, this recipe differs from the French devilled sauce which contains mustard and white wine. This vegetable version, served with plain rice or sautéed noodles, is perfect for an everyday meal.

Green curry with tofu

Serves 2

2 tsp sesame oil
1 onion, cut into medium-sized pieces
1 large green pepper, cut into medium-sized pieces
250 g firm tofu, cubed
2 garlic cloves, crushed to a paste
300 ml coconut milk
2 tbsp tamari
2 tbsp Thai green curry paste
100 ml soy cream

Heat the sesame oil in a wok or frying pan over high heat. Sauté the onion and green pepper, then add the tofu and garlic paste. Brown for a few minutes, stirring continuously. Add the coconut milk, tamari and curry paste. Cook for 10 minutes and then stir in the soy cream. Serve with Thai rice.

Tofu and vegetable pastilla

Serves 4

3 tbsp olive oil
2 shallots, finely sliced
125 g firm tofu, diced
75 g grated carrots
75 g grated white cabbage
1 courgette, finely sliced
1 small fennel bulb, finely sliced
½ red pepper, finely sliced
1 tsp ras el hanout
1 tsp ground cumin
150 ml water
3 tbsp plain flour
olive oil
8 brik pastry sheets
icing sugar
ground cinnamon
salt and pepper

Heat the olive oil in a frying pan over high heat. Sauté the shallots, tofu, carrots and the cabbage together. Add the courgette, fennel, red pepper and spices. Cook for at least 5 minutes so that the vegetables and the tofu begin to brown. Season to taste. Mix the water and the flour in a small saucepan to make a sort of 'glue' for the pastry sheets. Grease a cake or springform tin. Place 1 sheet of brik pastry over a third of the bottom of the tin and leave the remainder to drape over the edge of the tin. Place 3 more sheets of pastry in the same way, so that they cover the bottom as well as drape over the sides of the tin. 'Glue' the sheets together with the flour and water mixture. Thoroughly coat the bottom and sides with the 'glue', then place 1 sheet of pastry in the centre, 'gluing' it to the other sheets. 'Glue' again and place another sheet of pastry on it in the same way. Spread the tofu and vegetable stuffing in the tin. Cover with a sheet of pastry, tuck the edges in and fold the first sheets of pastry over the pastilla, always brushing them with the 'glue' so that the pastilla remains closed. Finally, brush the top of the pastilla with the 'glue', making sure that all the edges are folded toward the centre and are 'glued' together. Cover with the last sheet of pastry and tuck the edges under pastilla. Brush with oil and bake at 180°C (Gas mark 4) for 15 minutes. Brush with oil again and bake for a further 15 minutes. Sprinkle with icing sugar and ground cinnamon. Serve hot. This recipe involves a little work, but it is worth the effort!

Quick smoked tofu

250 g firm tofu
2 tbsp liquid smoke
2 tbsp soy sauce
water

Drain the block of tofu and cut it into eight pieces. Mix the liquid smoke and the soy sauce in an airtight container. Coat each piece of tofu in this mixture and arrange them in the container. Cover with water, put the lid on, shake gently and leave in the fridge overnight. Use the next day as you would classic smoked tofu.

Homemade herbed tofu

Makes about 1 x 150 g block

1 litre soy milk
2 tsp nigari (magnesium chloride flakes)
½ tsp salt
1 tbsp lemon juice
1 tbsp chopped parsley
1 tbsp chopped chives
1 tbsp chopped basil

Bring the soy milk to the boil in a saucepan then lower to a simmer. Mix the nigari with a little water in a small bowl. Add the salt and lemon juice, then pour this mixture into the simmering soy milk. Whisk to mix and remove from the heat. Leave to stand for 15 minutes, then pour through a very fine strainer. Line a tofu press, or a container with holes in (or, as a last resort, a small, fine strainer) with cheesecloth and place over a deep dish or in a plate. In a bowl, mix the soy curds with the herbs, then pour into the cheesecloth. Close the tofu press and put a weight on top. The longer the tofu is pressed, the firmer it will be, but it needs to be pressed for at least 2 hours. It can be refrigerated as it presses. Store, covered with water, in an airtight container. Eat it soon after making it.

***Variation:** The nigari and lemon juice can be substituted by 120 ml of vinegar; this will make the tofu softer and more acidic.*

Tofu à la Provençale

Serves 2-4

250 g firm tofu, cubed
50 g pitted green olives, chopped
2 tomatoes, diced
½ red pepper, diced
2 garlic cloves, finely sliced
3 tbsp olive oil
2 tsp herbs de Provence
100 ml white wine

Heat the oil in a frying pan over high heat and sauté the vegetables and tofu for 5-8 minutes, stirring continuously. Add the herbs de Provence. Pour in the white wine and cook for 2 minutes. Season to taste and serve.

TEMPEH, FERMENTED SOY

Tempeh with satay sauce

Serves 2-4

300 g tempeh, cut into cubes
wok sauce (see p. 103)
6 tbsp peanut butter
2 tbsp soy sauce
2 tbsp freshly squeezed lime juice
1 tbsp agave syrup
1 tsp red chilli paste
1 tsp ground coriander
½ tsp fresh ginger, crushed to a paste
2 garlic cloves, crushed to a paste
100-200 ml water
1 tbsp coconut oil (optional)

Marinate the tempeh in the wok sauce for 2-4 hours. In a bowl, mix the peanut butter with the soy sauce, lime juice, agave syrup, chilli paste, ground coriander, ginger and garlic to make a paste. Add water (100 ml if using skewers; 200 ml if cooking in a frying pan) and mix well. Thread the tempeh cubes onto the skewers and cook on a barbecue or in the oven and serve with the sauce. Alternatively, grill the tempeh cubes in a pan with the tablespoon of coconut oil, then pour the sauce over the tempeh and reduce for a few minutes before serving.

Tempeh 'bacon'

Serves 4

200 g smoked tempeh, cut into long thin slices
4 tbsp tamari
2 tbsp agave syrup
1 tbsp neutral vegetable oil
1 tbsp vegetable oil for cooking
pepper

Combine the tamari, agave syrup and 1 tbsp of neutral vegetable oil in a bowl and marinate the tempeh for 30 minutes. Next, cook it in a frying pan in the cooking oil over high heat for a few minutes on each side. When cooked, add the marinade. Turn the slices often so that the tempeh absorbs the sauce. Serve hot.

Tempeh with peanut butter

Serves 4

2 onions, finely sliced
2 garlic cloves, finely sliced
2 tbsp vegetable oil
300 g tempeh, cut into large cubes
250 ml tomato passata
250 ml water
6 tbsp peanut butter
2 tbsp white miso
1 tsp tamari
½ vegetable stock cube
cayenne pepper
salt and pepper

Sauté the onions and garlic with the oil in a frying pan over high heat. Add the tempeh. Cook for 5-10 minutes over medium-high heat until everything is well browned. Add the remaining ingredients, one at a time, stirring to mix well. Season with pepper and cayenne pepper to taste. Cook for at least 10 minutes and adjust the seasoning if necessary. Serve with plain rice.

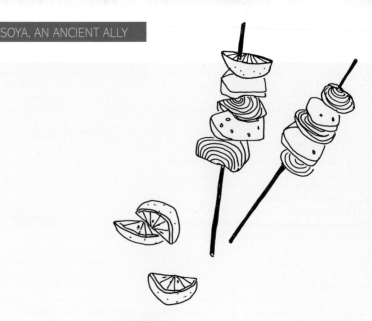

Curried tempeh croque monsieur

Makes 4

2 tbsp tahini
2 tbsp freshly squeezed lemon juice
6 tbsp water
1 tbsp chopped fresh chives
1 tsp curry powder
2 tsp agave syrup
200 g tempeh, cut into fine slices
8 slices wholegrain sandwich bread
a few fresh coriander sprigs
vegetable oil

In a bowl, combine the tahini with the lemon juice, water, chives, curry powder and agave syrup. Brown the tempeh in a frying pan with a little vegetable oil (choose a neutral-tasting oil). Spread 4 slices of bread with the curry cream and top with the tempeh slices and coriander leaves. Cover with the other 4 slices of bread and cook for 2 minutes on each side in a frying pan, or use a sandwich maker.

Sesame tempeh brochettes

Serves 6

300 g tempeh, cut into large cubes
8 tbsp shoyu or tamari
1 tbsp toasted sesame oil
3 tbsp white sesame seeds
3 tbsp black sesame seeds

Combine the soy sauce and the sesame oil and marinate the tempeh for 2 hours. Thread the tempeh onto 6 skewers and cook on a barbecue, then roll in the two kinds of sesame seeds mixed on a plate. These brochettes can also be cooked in a frying pan.

Tempeh and winter vegetable casserole

Serves 2

1 large onion, cut into large cubes
200 g tempeh, cut into large cubes
2 garlic cloves, roughly chopped
200 g red kuri squash, cut into medium-sized pieces
1 sweet potato, cut into medium-sized pieces
1 carrot, sliced
4 tbsp vegetable oil
1 tsp dried sage
1 tbsp chopped parsley
2 tbsp white miso
200 ml boiling water
200 ml soy cream
salt and pepper

Sauté the vegetables and tempeh in the oil in a high-sided frying pan over medium heat for a few minutes. Add the herbs, cover and cook gently for 10 minutes. Slake the miso with a little boiling water and pour into the pan. Cook for 5 minutes, uncovered, then add the cream and season to taste. Cook for a few minutes over medium heat to reduce the sauce, and serve at once.

Delicious with pearl barley, einkorn, buckwheat or quinoa.

rried tempeh croque monsieur and sesame tempeh brochettes

Tempeh with sautéed spinach and tahini

Serves 4

4 tbsp olive oil

2 garlic cloves, finely sliced

1 large onion, finely sliced

200 g plain or smoked tempeh, finely sliced

400 g fresh spinach, washed and roughly chopped

2 tbsp sunflower seeds

½ tbsp white sesame seeds

1 tbsp tamari

3 tbsp tahini

6 tbsp water

¼ tsp five-spice powder

½ tsp garlic powder

salt and pepper

Sauté the garlic and onion in the oil in a large frying pan over medium-high heat. Add the tempeh and brown for about 5 minutes. Add the spinach a little at a time and leave to wilt for a few minutes. Add the sunflower seeds, sesame seeds and tamari. Mix well. Mix the tahini and the water with a fork in a small bowl until creamy and well-combined. Season with the spices, salt and pepper. Add to the tempeh and spinach and cook gently for a few minutes over low heat.

Delicious served with steamed potatoes or rice.

Tempeh tagine with aubergines and olives

Serves 6-8

600 g potatoes, peeled and roughly chopped

2 large aubergines, roughly chopped

165 g pitted green olives

300 g plain tempeh, cut into cubes

6 tbsp olive oil

½ tsp ground cinnamon

½ tsp ground nutmeg

½ tsp freshly ground black pepper

2 tsp ras el hanout

65 g raisins

150 ml water

4 tbsp tamari

Put the potatoes and aubergines in a large tagine dish with the olives, tempeh, olive oil, spices and raisins. Mix the water with the tamari and pour over the vegetables and tempeh. Cover and cook over a low heat for 1½ hours.

Quick BBQ tempeh

Serves 2-4

200 g tempeh, cut into thick slices
1 onion, cut into medium slices
2 garlic cloves, finely sliced
2 tbsp neutral vegetable oil
pepper
2 tsp ground coriander
1 tsp dried oregano
3 tbsp tamari
2 tsp liquid smoke
125 ml ketchup

Brown the tempeh and the onion in the oil in a frying pan over medium-high heat for 5 minutes. Add pepper, the coriander, oregano and garlic. Mix well and cook for a further 2-3 minutes. Lower the heat to medium. Add the tamari. Combine the liquid smoke and the ketchup in a bowl and add to the pan. Mix well and cook for a few minutes.

Great for flavoursome sandwiches, with chips and even for an apéro or aperitif snack (in which case the tempeh should be cut into cubes). If you leave out the ketchup and the liquid smoke, you have a delicious sautéed tempeh dish that goes well with vegetables.

Quiche Lorraine with tempeh 'lardons'

Serves 4-6

200 g smoked tempeh, cut into matchsticks
2 tbsp olive oil
2 tbsp tamari, plus 4 tsp extra
250 g firm tofu
125 g tamari-marinated lacto-fermented tofu
300 ml soy cream
2 tbsp arrowroot
2 tbsp tahini
2 tsp Dijon mustard
2 tbsp malted yeast
1 pinch ground turmeric
1 quantity shortcrust pastry dough (or recipe p. 244)
pepper

Sauté the tempeh in the olive oil for a few minutes. Add the 2 tbsp of tamari, cook for 1 minute and set aside. Whiz the tofu, soy cream, arrowroot, tahini, mustard, the 4 tsp of tamari, the malted yeast, turmeric and pepper to taste in a food processor. Line a tart tin with the pastry and bake blind for 5 minutes. Put the tempeh into the pastry crust and pour the mixture over it. Bake for 25 minutes at 180°C (Gas mark 4).

Lemon and herb-marinated tempeh brochettes

Makes 4 brochettes

2 lemons, zested and juiced
¼ tsp freshly ground black pepper
¼ tsp garlic powder
1 tsp ground coriander
¼ tsp ground turmeric
2 tbsp toasted sesame oil
2 tsp shoyu
3 tbsp chopped fresh coriander
1 onion, peeled and quartered
200 g tempeh, cut into large cubes

Put the lemon zest and juice into an airtight container. Add the spices, sesame oil, shoyu and fresh coriander. Separate the onion layers and put them into the marinade. Add the tempeh. Put the lid on the container and shake. Leave to marinate at room temperature for 4 hours, regularly giving the container a good shake. Thread, alternating onion and tempeh, onto skewers and grill for 2-3 minutes on each side.

Soy 'spare ribs', soy stir-fry and enchil

TEXTURED SOY PROTEIN

Caramelised soy 'spare ribs'

Serves 3-4

50 g textured soy protein, in 'matchsticks'
3 tbsp tamari
½ vegetable stock cube
5 tbsp agave syrup
3 tbsp tamari
vegetable oil for cooking

Combine the soy protein in a bowl with the tamari and the ½ vegetable stock cube. Cover with boiling water and leave to hydrate for 30 minutes. Mix the agave syrup and tamari in a bowl. Thread the soy protein pieces onto skewers, making sure they are close together. Cut off the ends of the skewers that stick out. Oil a frying pan and cook for a few minutes on each side. Pour the agave/tamari mixture over the brochettes and cook for 1 minute on each side. Serve immediately.

Sweet and sour soy stir-fry

Serves 4

50 g textured soy protein, 'morsel' size
3 tbsp tamari
½ vegetable stock cube
1 onion, cut into medium-sized pieces
1 red pepper, cut into medium-sized pieces
1 green pepper, cut into medium-sized pieces
200 g pineapple, cut into medium-sized pieces
2 tomatoes, cut into medium-sized pieces
2 tbsp olive oil
2 garlic cloves, finely sliced
3 tbsp tamari
2 tbsp apple cider vinegar
3 tbsp sugar
pepper

Combine the soy protein in a bowl with the tamari and the ½ vegetable stock cube. Cover with boiling water and leave to hydrate for at least 30 minutes. Heat the olive oil in a large frying pan and sauté the onion, peppers, soy protein and garlic. Cook for 5 minutes. Add the pineapple, tamari, vinegar, sugar and tomatoes. Generously season with pepper. Mix well and cook for 10 minutes over low heat. Serve with rice.

Bell pepper enchiladas

Serves 4

40 g textured soy protein, in 'matchsticks'
2 tbsp tamari, plus 2 tbsp extra
½ tsp garlic powder
1 tsp ground cumin, plus 2 tsp extra
1 onion, finely sliced
2 garlic cloves, finely sliced
1 red pepper, finely sliced
2 tbsp olive oil
200 g peeled, chopped tomatoes
1 tsp oregano
½ tsp paprika
3 tsp chipotle chilli sauce
4 wheat or corn tortillas
100 ml cream
salt and pepper

Combine the soy protein with 2 tbsp of the tamari, the garlic powder, the 1 tsp of cumin and pepper to taste. Cover with boiling water and leave to hydrate for 30 minutes. Heat the olive oil in a large frying pan and sauté the vegetables and the soy protein for 5 minutes. Add the tomatoes and the remaining spices, the other 2 tbsp of tamari and the chipotle chilli sauce. Cook for a few minutes and season to taste. Fill 4 tortillas (keeping aside 3 tbsp of the filling), fold them and place them side by side on a serving dish. Pour the cream along the centre of the tortillas and top with the remaining filling. Cook for 10 minutes at 180°C (Gas mark 4).

Middle Eastern briks

Makes about 20 briks

50 g textured soy protein
½ tsp garlic powder
1 tsp ground cumin, plus 2 tsp extra
1 tbsp brown barley miso
2 tbsp olive oil
2 large onions, finely sliced
¼ tsp ground cinnamon
2 tsp ground coriander
¼ tsp ground nutmeg
cayenne pepper
1 tbsp tamari
2 tbsp plain flour
6 tbsp water
8 brik pastry sheets
vegetable oil for cooking

Put the soy protein, garlic powder, the 1 tsp of cumin and the miso in a bowl. Cover with boiling water and leave to hydrate for 15-30 minutes. Heat the olive oil in a frying pan and sauté the onions for a few minutes. Add the drained and chopped soy protein (keep the soaking liquid) and the remaining spices, and sauté for a few minutes. Add the tamari and lastly the soaking liquid. Allow it to absorb the liquid. Remove from the heat and leave to cool. In a small saucepan, combine the flour and the water over high heat, stirring continuously. Remove from the heat when this 'glue' has the consistency of porridge. Cut the brik pastry sheets in half. Place the curved side away from you, then fold three quarters of it towards you. Place a tablespoon of the stuffing onto it and fold into a triangle. Seal with the flour and water 'glue'. Heat enough oil to cover the bottom of a large frying pan and fry the briks, turning them constantly until they are golden brown and crispy. If possible, cook them just before serving. If this is not possible, line an oven tray with parchment paper and, after cooking the briks, place them on the tray. Just before serving, reheat them in a very hot oven.

Soy Bolognese sauce

Serves 2-3

30 g textured soy protein (small pieces)
1 tbsp brown barley miso
1 tsp dried thyme
1 onion, finely sliced
2 garlic cloves, finely sliced
1 medium carrot, washed and finely diced
2 tbsp olive oil
400 g peeled, chopped tomatoes
150 ml tomato passata
1 tbsp tamari or shoyu
2 tbsp white miso
1 tbsp chopped basil
pepper

Put the soy protein in a bowl and cover with boiling water. Add the miso and thyme and leave for 15 minutes to swell. Brown the onion, garlic and carrots in a frying pan with the olive oil over high heat. Add the soy protein and soaking liquid. Leave to reduce for a few minutes. Add the tomatoes, tomato passata, tamari and basil. Add pepper to taste and mix well. Cook for 15 minutes over low heat.

Use as a sauce for spaghetti, for lasagne, to stuff cannelloni, etc.

ddle Eastern briks

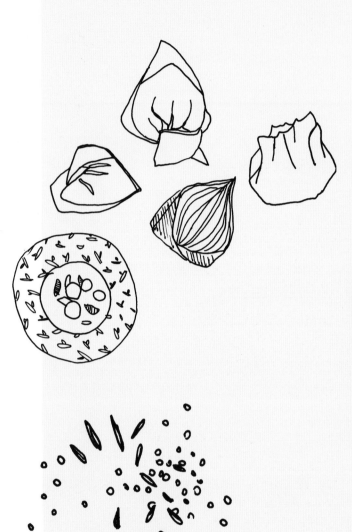

Wontons

Serves 4

150 ml boiling water
2 tbsp tamari
35 g textured soy protein
1 tbsp sunflower oil (or neutral vegetable oil)
½ leek, finely sliced
1 small onion, finely sliced
2 garlic cloves, finely sliced
½ tsp chopped fresh ginger
½ tsp five-spice powder
cayenne pepper
1 tsp tamari
20 wonton wrappers (available from Asian supermarkets)
miso and coconut soup for 4 people (see p. 177)
  or any stock you choose
pepper

Mix the boiling water and the tamari in a bowl. Add the soy protein and leave to hydrate for at least 30 minutes. Heat the oil in a frying pan and sauté the leek with the onion, garlic and ginger for a few minutes over high heat. Add the soy protein, five-spice powder, a tiny pinch of cayenne pepper, pepper to taste and the tamari. Mix well and cook for a few minutes, stirring often. Set aside. Place a teaspoonful of the stuffing in the middle of a wonton wrapper. Run a wet finger over the inner edge of the wrapper and fold over, pressing to seal. When all the wontons have been made, cook in the miso and coconut soup, ladle into bowls and serve immediately.

Soy Parmentier

Serves 4-6

500 ml boiling water
1 tbsp barley miso
1 tbsp vegetable stock paste
1 tbsp tahini
2 tbsp shoyu
2 tbsp dried onion
80 g textured soy protein (small pieces)
2 tbsp olive oil, plus 3 tbsp extra
1 large onion, finely sliced
2 garlic cloves, finely sliced
3 tbsp chopped parsley
potato purée (see p. 275)
5 tbsp malted yeast
7 tbsp soy cream

In a bowl, whisk the miso, stock paste, tahini, shoyu and dried onion into the boiling water. Add the soy protein and leave to hydrate for 30 minutes. Heat the 2 tbsp of olive oil in a frying pan and sauté the onion and garlic over high heat. Drain the soy protein, keeping the soaking liquid. Add the soy and the parsley to the pan and sauté for 5 minutes. Add 100 ml of the soaking liquid and cook for a few minutes. Put the soy protein in an oven-proof dish and cover with the potato purée. Mix the malted yeast in a bowl with the other 3 tbsp of olive oil and the soy cream. Spread this mixture over the potato purée. Bake for 25-30 minutes at 180°C (Gas mark 4).

Soy medallions in a white wine and shallot sauce

Serves 4

50 g textured soy protein, in 'medallions'
350 ml vegetable stock
2 tbsp tamari
2 tbsp olive oil, plus 1 tbsp extra
3 shallots, finely sliced
1 garlic clove, finely sliced
200 ml white wine
200 ml soy cream
100 ml vegetable stock
2 tbsp cornflour

Hydrate the soy medallions in the stock mixed with the tamari for 30 minutes. Remove the medallions from the stock. Heat the 2 tbsp of olive oil in a frying pan and brown them for a few minutes each side over high heat. Heat the 1 tbsp of olive oil in another frying pan and sauté the shallots and garlic for a few minutes. Add the white wine and allow it to reduce for 2-3 minutes. Add the cream and vegetable stock. Slake the cornflour and add to the pan. Cook for a few minutes over medium heat to reduce the sauce. Pour the sauce over the medallions and serve.

This dish goes perfectly with potatoes or rice, and served with green beans or sautéed vegetables.

Fig and lemon to

Vegetable moussaka

Serves 4

3 large aubergines, washed and cut into slices lengthways
olive oil
1 large onion, finely sliced
2 garlic cloves, finely sliced
60 g textured soy protein, small pieces
2 tbsp barley miso
1 tsp garlic powder
400 g chopped tomatoes
300 ml tomato passata
1 tsp dried basil
2 tbsp tamari
béchamel (see p. 163)
salt and pepper

Sauté the aubergine slices in a little olive oil over high heat for a few minutes each side. They should be cooked through and well browned. Set aside. Combine the soy protein in a bowl with the miso and garlic powder and cover with water. Leave to hydrate for 15 minutes. Heat 2 tbsp of olive oil in a frying pan and sauté the onion and garlic. Add the hydrated soy protein and cook for a few minutes. Add the tomatoes, tomato passata, basil and tamari. Mix well and cook for 5 minutes over high heat. In an oven-proof dish, alternate layers of sauce and slices of aubergine. Finish with a layer of béchamel and bake in the oven for 20 minutes at 180°C (Gas mark 4).

Fig and lemon tagine

Serves 8

50 g textured soy protein,
   (large pieces, medallions or morsels)
2 tbsp barley miso
300 g onions, peeled and quartered
600 g potatoes, peeled and cut into large pieces
300 g peeled carrots, cut into thick slices
4 tbsp olive oil
1 tsp ground turmeric
2 tsp ground coriander
1 tsp ground cinnamon
½ tsp ground nutmeg
150 g dried figs, cut in half
2 lemons, cut into pieces
150 ml water
2 tbsp tamari

Mix the miso with sufficient boiling water to cover the soy protein in a large bowl. Hydrate for 30 minutes. Heat the olive oil in a tagine dish on the stove and sauté the vegetables for a few minutes over medium heat, then turn the heat to low. Add the spices and soy protein. Add the figs and lemons to the dish. Mix the water with the tamari and pour over the vegetables. Cover. Cook for 1½ hours, without removing the lid.

Country-style seitan

Serves 4

Dry ingredients
150 g gluten
75 g chickpea flour
2 tsp dried onion
¼ tsp paprika
¼ tsp Cayenne pepper

Liquid ingredients
250 ml boiling water
2 tbsp tamari
1 tbsp vegetable stock paste
1 tbsp barley miso
1 tsp toasted sesame oil
½ tsp liquid smoke

Stock
1½ litres boiling water
1 tbsp vegetable stock paste
1 tbsp barley miso
1 tsp balsamic vinegar
1 tbsp tamari
1 tsp garlic powder
½ tsp red chilli paste
a few bay leaves

Combine all the dry ingredients in a mixing bowl. Combine all the liquid ingredients in a bowl. Pour onto the dry ingredients and immediately mix with your hands, then knead for a few minutes. Add a little gluten if the mixture is too sticky. Put all the ingredients for the stock into a large saucepan. Cut the seitan into pieces and put it into the stock. Boil for a few minutes, then lower the heat to medium. Cook for 30 minutes.

The seitan will keep in the fridge for 48 hours if kept in its cooking stock in an airtight container. It will be tastier the day after making. It can be baked, sautéed, served with a sauce, or used as a stuffing. It also freezes well.

SEITAN

Classic seitan

Serves 4

Dry ingredients
150 g gluten
30 g ground almonds
1 tbsp malted yeast
½ tsp garlic powder
¼ tsp paprika
¼ tsp salt

Liquid ingredients
160 ml hot water
2 tbsp shoyu
1 tbsp white miso
1 tsp vegetable stock paste (or ½ cube)

Stock
1½ litres boiling water
1 tbsp vegetable stock paste (or 1 ½ cubes)
1 tbsp barley miso
1 bunch of thyme
2 bay leaves

Combine all the dry ingredients in a bowl. Combine all the liquid ingredients in a glass. Pour the liquid ingredients in to the bowl and mix with a spoon, then knead with your hands for a few minutes. On a chopping board, cut the seitan into pieces or slices. Bring the stock ingredients to the boil in a large saucepan. Add the pieces of seitan and cook over medium heat for 20-30 minutes, depending on the size of the pieces. Put the seitan and the stock in an airtight container in the fridge for 24 hours if possible. The seitan is now ready to be cut up or cooked.

Perfect for sautéing, served with a sauce, as a stuffing, marinated, etc.

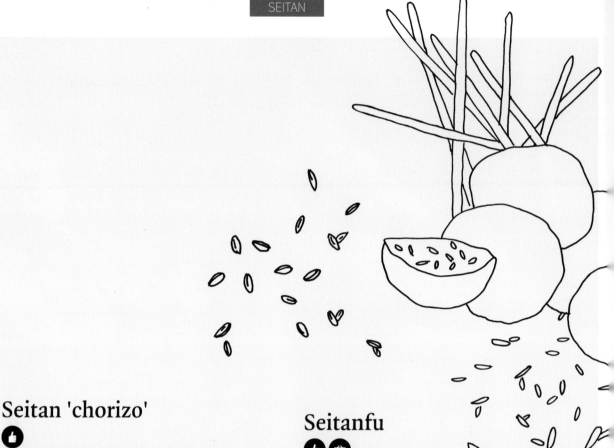

Seitan 'chorizo'

150 g gluten
2 tbsp olive oil, plus 2 tsp extra
2 tbsp tamari
1 tbsp barley miso
1 tbsp shiro miso
4 tsp chipotle chilli sauce
3 tsp garlic powder
2 tsp paprika
½ tsp liquid smoke
100 ml hot water
1 tsp paprika

Put the gluten in a bowl. Put all the other ingredients (except the 1 tsp of paprika) into a measuring jug and slake with a little of the hot water. Then add the rest of the hot water. Mix well. Pour onto the gluten, mix in and then quickly knead with your hands. Divide the dough and shape into two 'chorizos'. Roll each one in a sheet of parchment paper. Tie with kitchen string, but not too tightly as the seitan will swell a little as it cooks. Make sure the ends are well-closed to avoid the cooking liquid from entering. Cook for 30 minutes in a large pan of boiling water. Remove the parchment paper and sauté both 'chorizos' for 2 minutes in a frying pan with the 2 tsp of olive oil and the 1 tsp paprika. Wrap and refrigerate for 24 hours before eating.

Cut into fine slices just before serving. Keeps for 4 days in the fridge.

Seitanfu

Makes about 1.2 kg

Dry ingredients
350 g gluten
1 tbsp malted yeast
1 tsp ground coriander
1 tsp garlic powder

Liquid ingredients
240 g silken tofu
200 ml warm water
5 tbsp tamari
1 tbsp white miso
2 tsp toasted sesame oil

Stock
3 litres water
2 tbsp vegetable stock paste
2 tbsp barley miso
2 tbsp tamari
black pepper

Combine all the dry ingredients in a mixing bowl. Combine all the liquid ingredients then pour them onto the dry ingredients. Mix in and knead with your hands to make a large ball of dough. Cut into slices and cook in the stock for 30 minutes over high heat. Drain and put into a container. Cover with stock, leave to cool, then refrigerate for 24 hours before cooking it.

an 'chorizo'

Tandoori seitan and red ser

Tandoori seitan

Serves 4-6

500 g seitanfu (see p. 98)

2 x 100 g pots soy yoghurt, plus ½ yoghurt extra

1-2 tbsp tandoori paste

juice of ½ lemon, plus juice of 1 lemon

1 onion, sliced

1 tbsp sugar

1 pinch ground turmeric

1 pinch ground coriander

300 g Basmati rice

cumin seeds

Cut the seitan into large bite-sized pieces. Mix the 2 yoghurts with the tandoori paste and the juice of the ½ lemon. Add the seitan and leave to marinate for 2 hours. Put into an oven-proof dish and bake for 10 minutes at 240°C (Gas mark 9). Combine the onion with the juice of the whole lemon. Add the sugar, spices and the other ½ yoghurt. Cook the basmati rice. Serve the tandoori seitan with the rice, and the onion and yoghurt sprinkled with cumin seeds.

Smoked seitan

Serves 6

200 g gluten

½ tsp garlic powder

½ tsp ground cumin

1 vegetable stock cube, crumbled

250 ml boiling water

2 tsp liquid smoke

Stock

2 litres boiling water

3 tbsp tamari

2 tsp liquid smoke

1 vegetable stock cube

Combine the garlic powder, cumin and stock cube in a bowl. Mix in the liquid ingredients and lastly add the gluten. Mix with a spoon and then knead for a few minutes. Bring the stock ingredients to the boil. Cut the seitan into slices or pieces and cook in the stock for 30 minutes. Leave to cool. Store in an airtight container in the fridge. Leave in the fridge for 24 hours before cooking it.

Red seitan

Makes about 1.5 kg

400 g gluten

1 tbsp sweet paprika

1 tsp garlic powder

150 g cooked red beans

250 ml warm water

1 tbsp brown barley miso

5 tbsp tamari

5 tbsp tomato passata

Stock

3 litres water

2 tbsp vegetable stock paste

2 tbsp barley miso

2 tbsp tamari

black pepper

Combine the dry ingredients in a mixing bowl. Whiz the red beans with the water, miso, tamari and tomato passata in a food processor. Pour into the bowl, mix well and then knead with your hands to make a large ball of dough. Cut into slices and cook in the stock for 30 minutes.

Tip: Replace the minced meat in any recipe with the same amount of red seitan. Simply whiz in a food processor fitted with an S-shaped blade for a few seconds and it's ready!

Seitan rillettes

Serves 4

115 g 'grilled gourmet seitan'
1 small onion, finely sliced
1 garlic clove, finely sliced
1 tbsp olive oil
100 g smoked tofu, crumbled
4 tbsp white wine
150 ml water
1 tsp agar-agar
salt and pepper

Chop the seitan in a food processor. Lightly brown the onion and garlic in a little saucepan with the olive oil. Then add the seitan and tofu. Cook for a few minutes. Add the white wine and cook a few minutes longer. Season with salt and pepper. Put into a small dish and press down well. In the same saucepan, mix the water with the agar-agar and bring to the boil. Cook for 2 minutes, stirring, then pour onto the seitan/tofu mixture. Mix together. Leave to cool and refrigerate overnight.

- -

Seitan stuffing

Serves 4

300 g homemade seitan (see p. 96)
1-2 garlic cloves
2 tbsp chopped flat-leaf parsley
1 tbsp chopped fresh chives
salt and pepper

Put all of the ingredients into the bowl of a food processor fitted with an S-shaped blade. Whiz until the consistency is right for a stuffing.

Use to stuff vegetables, as a quick sauce, for gratins, etc.

Seitan nuggets

Makes about 20 nuggets

6 tbsp water
2 tbsp ground toasted flaxseeds
300 g seitanfu (see p. 98)
breadcrumbs
vegetable oil for cooking

Combine the water and flaxseeds in a bowl and leave to soak for 15 minutes. Cut the seitan into medium-sized pieces, about ½ cm thick. Coat them in the flaxseed mixture and then toss in the breadcrumbs. Heat a little oil in a frying pan and brown the nuggets on both sides over high heat.

- -

Seitan à la Basquaise

Serves 4

400 g homemade seitan (see p. 96), cut into large pieces
3 tbsp olive oil
1 red pepper, finely sliced
1 green pepper, finely sliced
2 onions, finely sliced
2 garlic cloves, finely sliced
2 sprigs fresh thyme
2 bay leaves
400 g peeled, chopped tomatoes
350 ml vegetable stock
salt and pepper

Heat 2 tbsp of the olive oil in a saucepan and brown the seitan over high heat. Add the vegetables to the pan and lower the heat to medium. Cook for 5 minutes, stirring from time to time. Add the thyme, the bay leaves and the chopped tomatoes. Season to taste and pour in the vegetable stock. Cover and cook for 5 minutes over medium heat, then for 15 minutes, uncovered, over low heat. Remove the bay leaves and the sprig of thyme, and adjust the seasoning if necessary.

Serve with plain, long-grain rice or homemade potato purée (see p. 275).

Miso gravy

Serves 4

1 shallot, finely sliced
2 tbsp olive oil
3 tbsp white miso
1 tbsp brown barley miso
400 ml boiling water
2 tbsp cornflour
pepper

Heat the oil and the two misos in a medium-sized saucepan over high heat. When the mixture begins to boil, add the shallots and turn the heat down to medium. Cook for a few minutes, stirring continuously so it does not catch on the bottom of the pan. Whisk in half of the water, add the cornflour and mix it in well. Add the rest of the water and whisk continuously for a few minutes until the sauce thickens. Season with pepper and serve.

Suggestion: *This sauce should be prepared just before serving. It is delicious with seitan, tofu, vegan roasts and potato dishes. Astonish your grandmother with this gravy recipe and show her that it is possible to make a good brown sauce without any meat juices!*

Ginger, lemon and garlic wok sauce

Makes 1 x 125 ml bottle

125 ml tamari
2 tsp finely chopped fresh ginger
2 tsp freshly squeezed lemon juice
1 tsp garlic, crushed to a paste

Combine all the ingredients in a jar. Refrigerate and leave to marinate for 3-5 days. Strain and pour into a small bottle. Keeps for a fortnight in the fridge.

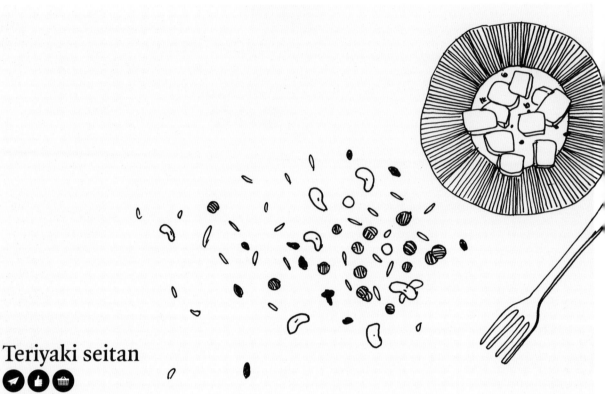

Teriyaki seitan

Serves 2-3

250 g seitanfu (see p. 98)
   or classic seitan (see p.96), cut into thick slices
2 tsp sesame oil
spring onions, finely sliced
<u>Teriyaki sauce</u>
4 tbsp tamari
4 tbsp mirin
4 tbsp water
2 tbsp cane sugar
1 tbsp cornflour

Combine all of the sauce ingredients in a small saucepan and cook over medium heat for a few minutes to dissolve the sugar. Then turn up the heat to high and whisk to thicken the sauce. Be careful as this happens very quickly. When the sauce has begun to brown it will thicken at once. Remove from the heat and pour into a small container. Marinate the seitan in the sauce for 1 hour. Heat the sesame oil in a frying pan and fry the seitan before adding the sauce. Remove from the heat and cover the seitan with the sauce. Serve, topped with some spring onions. Delicious served with rice and vegetables.

Tip: *Teriyaki sauce can be used with tofu, tempeh, soy protein and even vegetables. Teriyaki broccoli is fabulous! If serving as a snack or as part of a buffet, cut the seitan (or tofu) into cubes and roll in sesame seeds after cooking. Serve on a platter, stuck with toothpicks.*

Glazed seitan

Serves 3 -4

300 g red seitan (see p. 101), cut into thick slices
50 ml tamari
50 ml maple syrup
1½ tbsp vegan Worcestershire *sauce*
⅛ tsp ground vanilla powder
1 pinch Espelette pepper
1 tbsp vegetable oil
black pepper

Combine all the ingredients except for the oil and marinate the seitan for 1 hour. Heat the oil in a frying pan and brown the seitan over high heat for a few minutes. Pour in half of the marinade and reduce over medium heat, turning the slices of seitan every now and again. Arrange the slices on a serving dish. Pour the rest of the marinade into the pan and reduce. Pour over the seitan and serve.

ed seitan

Seitan brochettes

Makes 8 brochettes

75 ml olive oil

2 tbsp vegan Worcestershire sauce

1 tsp garlic powder

2 tsp herbs de Provence

350 g seitanfu (see p. 98) or classic seitan (see p. 96),
    cut into large cubes

1 red pepper, cut into medium-sized pieces

1 large onion, cut into medium-sized pieces

salt and pepper

Combine the olive oil and Worcestershire sauce, garlic and herbs de Provence in a bowl. Season with salt and pepper. Cover the seitan with the marinade and leave to marinate for 2-6 hours. Prepare the brochettes, alternating the seitan and the vegetables as you thread them onto the skewers. Grill on a barbecue for a few minutes each side, brushing with the marinade for an even tastier result.

Seitan escalopes in a cream sauce

Serves 4

2 tsp olive oil

4 classic seitan escalopes (see p. 96)

1 garlic clove, finely sliced

2 shallots, finely sliced

1 x 235 g pot lacto-fermented soy cream

100 ml water

2 tsp shiro miso

1 tbsp chopped fresh chives

a few fresh thyme sprigs

salt and pepper

Heat the olive oil in a medium-sized frying pan over high heat. Brown the seitan escalopes with the garlic and shallots. Add the cream and the water and mix well. Slake the miso in the cream and add the herbs. Season with salt and pepper and turn the heat to very low. Simmer for a few minutes and serve.

Delicious with green beans and potatoes.

Crumbed seitan wraps

Serves 4

150 g seitan, cut into slices (see p. 96)

2 tbsp cornflour

4 tbsp water

breadcrumbs

neutral vegetable oil

4 wheat tortillas

4 lettuce leaves

1 bowl tartare sauce (see p. 163)

½ cucumber, sliced

1 large tomato, cut into thin wedges

Mix the cornflour and the water. Dip the seitan slices in the batter and then coat with the breadcrumbs. Brown the seitan in a frying pan with a little olive oil. Heat the tortillas in the oven for 1-2 minutes. Place a lettuce leaf in the centre of each tortilla and spread with some of the tartare sauce. Add a few seitan slices, a few cucumber slices and two wedges of tomato. Fold in the base of the tortillas, and then fold in from the sides.

Neapolitan escalopes in a cream sauce

Herbed puff pastry parcel with seaw

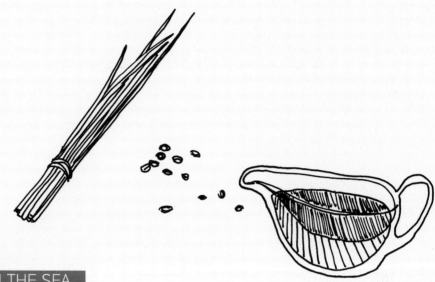

Herbed puff pastry parcel with seaweed

Serves 8

2 tbsp olive oil
1 onion, finely sliced
2 garlic cloves, finely sliced
1 celery rib, finely sliced
1 bunch of parsley, chopped
250 g firm tofu, crumbled
125 g smoked tofu, crumbled
100 ml soy cream
1 tbsp white miso
¼ sheet of yaki nori, cut into very fine slivers
¼ tsp ground nutmeg
2 tbsp chopped fresh chives
50 ml water
1 sheet puff pastry
salt and pepper

Heat a little olive oil in a large pan. Sauté the onion and garlic. Add the celery and parsley. Add the tofus and then the soy cream and miso. Add the yaki nori, nutmeg, chives and water. Mix and leave to cook until the stuffing is quite dense. Season to taste. Roll out the pastry and spoon the stuffing down the centre, along the length of the dough. Fold the sides to the centre and seal the ends with the tines of a fork or, for a very beautiful presentation, cut the sides into strips about 1 cm wide and fold over towards the centre, alternating the strips to give an almost plaited look. Bake for 30 minutes at 180°C (Gas mark 4).

Seaweed and miso stock

200 ml water
2 tbsp white miso
5 g dried hijiki seaweed

Bring the water to the boil in a small saucepan. Dissolve the miso in it and add the seaweed. Cook over high heat for a few minutes so that it acquires a good flavour, in particular if it is going to be used as a marinade for tofu. Strain the stock. Reduce it if it is going to be used to flavour a stuffing or a sauce. Use as it is to make breaded seaweed tofu (see the following recipe).

- -

Breaded seaweed tofu

Serves 2

125 g firm tofu, cut into cubes
seaweed and miso stock (see previous recipe)
breadcrumbs
vegetable oil for cooking

Cook the tofu in the seaweed and miso stock in a small saucepan over medium heat for 5 minutes. Remove from the heat and leave to cool completely. Dredge the pieces of tofu in the breadcrumbs, then coat them in the stock again and dredge again in the breadcrumbs. Heat a little oil in a frying pan and brown the tofu in the hot oil.

Serve with the tartare sauce (see p. 163).

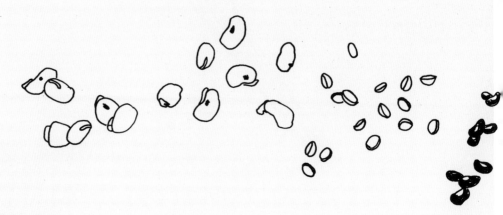

Vegetable bisque

Serves 4-6

1 litre water
4 tbsp white miso
10 g dried hijiki
1 piece kombu seaweed
1 onion, finely sliced
1 leek, finely sliced
2 celery ribs, finely sliced
4 tbsp neutral vegetable oil
2 bay leaves
200 ml white wine, plus extra 50 ml
3 garlic cloves, finely sliced
500 g tomato pulp
200 ml soy cream
½ tsp Espelette pepper
1 tsp salt
2 tbsp light brown sugar
1 tbsp cashew butter
pepper

Prepare the stock: Bring the water to the boil and dissolve the miso in it. Add the seaweeds and boil for 5 minutes. Strain. Heat the oil in a large saucepan over high heat. Put in the vegetables and the bay leaves and sauté for 5 minutes, stirring to mix well. Add the 200 ml of white wine and the garlic, and cook for 2 minutes. Add the tomato pulp and cook for 5 minutes. Add the seaweed stock and cook over high heat for 15 minutes. Remove the bay leaves. Pour in the cream and the rest of the wine. Add the salt, Espelette pepper, sugar, cashew butter and some pepper. Mix well and turn the heat to low.

Serve with homemade garlic and parsley croutons.

Sea-flavoured crudité sandwich

Makes 8 sandwiches

250 g cooked chickpeas
6 tbsp vegenaise (see p. 163)
1 small celery rib, finely sliced
1 tsp chopped spring onion
2 tsp chopped dill
4 tbsp reduced seaweed and miso stock (see p. 109)
4 lettuce leaves
16 slices sandwich bread
2 large tomatoes, sliced
½ cucumber, very finely sliced

Whiz the chickpeas in a food processor just long enough to break them up, but do not purée them. In a large bowl, mix the vegenaise with the spices and the reduced stock, then add the chickpeas. Mix well. For each sandwich, place a lettuce leaf on 1 slice of bread and spread a layer of mashed chickpeas on top. Top with 1 or 2 slices of tomato and a few slices of cucumber. Top with another slice of bread and cut diagonally to make 2 triangles.

Tip: The filling for this sandwich, vaguely reminiscent of a tuna-mayonnaise mixture, can also be used to stuff halved avocados, California maki rolls, bagels and raw tomatoes.

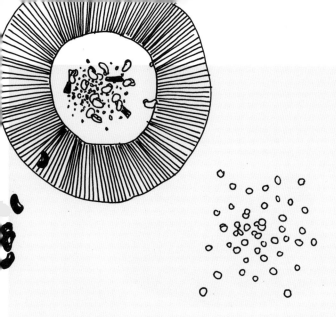

Dill cream

Makes 1 bowl

1 bowl soy crème fraîche (see p. 143)
2 tbsp freshly squeezed lemon juice
2 tsp chopped dill
salt and pepper

Mix all of the ingredients together with a fork and store in the fridge before using.

Vegan taramasalata

Makes 1 small bowl

125 g firm tofu, crumbled
¼ sheet of yaki nori, cut into pieces
2 tbsp lacto-fermented soy cream
1½ tbsp tomato passata
2 tsp freshly squeezed lemon juice
1 tsp neutral vegetable oil
½ tsp salt
15 drops liquid smoke

Whiz the tofu in a food processor. Cut the yaki nori into very fine slivers with a mini-chopper. Add it to the tofu together with the other ingredients and process. Put into a bowl, cover and refrigerate for 2 hours. Serve with toasted bread or blinis.

Galettes Bretonnes

Serves 4

50 g samphire
1 shallot, finely sliced
100 g smoked tofu, cut into matchsticks
1 tbsp white wine
8 buckwheat galettes (see p.151)
1 x 235 g pot thick lacto-fermented soy cream
vegetable oil of your choice
pepper

Soak the samphire for 10 minutes. Refresh under cold water to get rid of the salt. Heat 1 tbsp of oil in a small frying pan and sauté the shallot together with the samphire and the tofu. Season with pepper and brown nicely. Deglaze the pan with the white wine. Set aside. In a large, oiled frying pan, heat a buckwheat galette for 30 seconds each side. Place a tablespoon of thick cream in the centre and add a little of the tofu and samphire stuffing. Fold the galette over and heat it for 2 minutes before serving.

Suggestion: *For anyone not fond of seaweed and its iodic smell, it can be substituted by 1 small, finely sliced leek.*

Sea-flavoured rillettes, herbed seaweed rolls and samphire s...

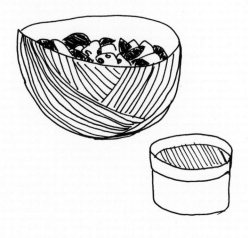

Herbed seaweed rolls

Makes 2 rolls

125 g firm tofu

3 tbsp soy cream

2 tbsp soy yoghurt

2 tbsp chopped flat-leaf parsley

1 tbsp chopped dill

1 tbsp chopped chives

2 sheets yaki nori

1 tsp finely sliced shallot

1 tbsp olive oil

2 tbsp ground flaxseeds

salt and pepper

Blend the tofu together with the soy cream and yoghurt. Mix with the herbs, shallot, olive oil and flaxseeds. Season to taste. Spread half of the mixture on a sheet of yaki nori and roll it up. Prepare the other roll in the same way. Serve immediately with a salad and bread.

For larger rolls, use ½ a sheet of nori per person.

Samphire salad

Serves 2

150 g samphire from a jar, rinsed and drained

125 g cherry tomatoes, quartered

½ shallot, finely sliced

½ pomegranate, seeds removed

2 tbsp chopped flat-leaf parsley

olive oil

sunflower seeds

gomasio

Combine the samphire, cherry tomatoes, shallot, pomegranate seeds and parsley in a bowl. Drizzle with a little olive oil and sprinkle with sunflower seeds and gomasio.

Sea-flavoured rillettes

Serves 4

200 g hearts of palm in a jar, drained and finely chopped

1 tbsp olive oil

a few drops liquid smoke

125 g white beans

2 tbsp mustard

5 tbsp neutral vegetable oil

3 tsp soy cream

½ sheet of yaki nori

2 tsp tomato concentrate

2 tbsp chopped flat-leaf parsley

1 tbsp chopped dill

1 tsp ground flaxseeds

salt and pepper

Sauté the hearts of palm in a frying pan in the olive oil over medium heat for 5 minutes. Season with salt and pepper and add a few drops of liquid smoke. Set aside. Whiz the beans with the mustard and neutral vegetable oil in a food processor. Add the cream, yaki nori, tomato concentrate and herbs and whiz again. Mix the cream mixture with the hearts of palm and add the ground flaxseeds. Taste for salt and pepper. If the smoky taste if too mild, add a few more drops of liquid smoke. Put into a serving dish and refrigerate for 1 hour before serving.

For a more pronounced sea flavour, use a whole sheet of yaki nori.

Sea-flavoured risotto

Serves 4

1 litre hot vegetable stock
½ piece kombu
3 tbsp olive oil
400 g risotto rice
2 celery ribs, diced
2 garlic cloves, finely sliced
200 ml white wine
2 tbsp chopped parsley
100 ml soy cream
2 tbsp cashew butter
salt and pepper

Prepare the vegetable stock then pour it into a jug and add the kombu. Heat the olive oil in a large saucepan over medium heat and sauté the rice together with the celery and garlic. When the rice is translucent, pour in the white wine and allow it to be absorbed. Cover with a ladleful of stock, add the parsley and stir until the rice has absorbed the liquid. Repeat the process until all the stock has been used up. Add the cream and cashew butter. Adjust the seasoning if necessary, stir and serve at once.

Ocean salad

Serves 2

100 g little gem lettuces
100 g cherry tomatoes, cut in quarters
½ cucumber, cut into half-moon slices
dill cream (see p.111)
breaded seaweed tofu for 2 (see p. 109)
100 g garlic croutons

Arrange the lettuce, tomatoes and cucumber on 2 plates. Pour 2-3 tbsp of dill cream over the salad. Add the breaded seaweed tofu and sprinkle with garlic croutons.

Hollandaise sauce

Serves 4

50 g cornflour
100 ml water
100 ml freshly squeezed lemon juice
1 pinch ground turmeric
50 g margarine, cut into pieces
200 ml soy milk
salt

In a saucepan, whisk the cornflour with the water, lemon juice and turmeric. Turn the heat to high and add the margarine. Whisk together. When the mixture is thick, remove from the heat and continue to whisk. Add the soy milk a little at a time. Season with salt. Serve immediately.

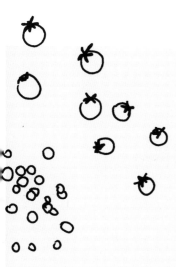

Buckwheat flour pizza

Serves 4

90 g wholegrain buckwheat flour
210 g plain flour
10 g sachet dried baker's yeast
1 tbsp light brown sugar
1 tsp salt
150 ml warm water
1 tbsp olive oil, plus extra to drizzle
1 onion, finely sliced
65 g smoked tofu, cut into matchsticks
6 tbsp soya cream
½ sheet of yaki nori
salt and pepper

Mix the flours in a bowl. Mix the yeast with the sugar, salt and the warm water in a measuring jug. Leave to rest for 5 minutes. Pour the yeast mixture into the flours and mix in with a spoon. Then knead just until the dough comes together. Add the olive oil and knead a few minutes longer. Leave to rise in a bowl covered with a tea towel at 25°C minimum, for 1 hour. Roll out the dough on parchment paper, and put it on a baking tray. Spread the cream on the dough. Season with salt and pepper. Top with the onion and tofu, drizzle with olive oil and bake for 20 minutes at 180°C (Gas mark 4). Use scissors to cut the yaki nori into very fine slivers. Cut the pizza into portions and sprinkle with the yaki nori.

Yaki nori and sesame chips

Serves 4

3 sheets of yaki nori
1½ tsp sesame oil
salt

Cut each sheet of yaki nori into 8 rectangles. Rub both sides of the yaki nori pieces with sesame oil. Sprinkle with a little salt. Heat a small frying pan over medium-high heat and cook the yaki nori pieces for a few seconds on each side. They will shrink very quickly. Do not heat them too long or allow them to brown. If they do begin to brown, turn down the heat. Prepare just before serving to ensure they are crispy.

Sea-flavoured linguine

Serves 4

300 g linguine
1 onion, finely sliced
4 celery ribs, finely sliced
2 garlic cloves, finely sliced
2 tbsp olive oil
125 g soft, smoked tofu, cut into cubes
2 tbsp chopped parsley
100 ml white wine
200 ml soy cream (or other non-dairy cream)
salt and pepper

Cook the linguine in abundant boiling water with a pinch of salt and a drizzle of olive oil. Brown the onion, celery and garlic in a frying pan with the olive oil. Add the smoked tofu and parsley. Season and leave to brown for a few minutes. Add the white wine and remove from the heat. Season the soy cream with salt and pepper and mix well. Drain the linguine, put in a serving dish and pour the cream and the contents of the pan over the pasta. Mix well and serve at once.

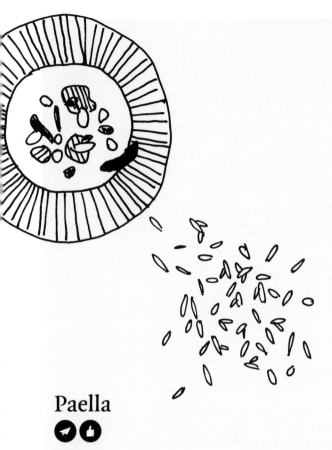

Paella

Serves 4

3 tbsp olive oil

1 pinch saffron strands or ¼ tsp turmeric plus ¼ tsp
   paprika

1 large onion, finely sliced

3 garlic cloves, finely sliced

1 red pepper, sliced

100 g smoked tofu, cut into cubes

2 large ripe tomatoes, peeled and finely chopped

100 ml white wine

400 g short-grain rice

1 litre vegetable stock

Espelette pepper

50 g fresh or frozen petits pois

4 artichoke hearts, sliced

1 lemon, quartered

salt and pepper

Heat the olive oil in a large frying pan. Add the saffron or the turmeric/paprika mix and sauté the onion, garlic, pepper and tofu. After a few minutes, add the tomatoes and white wine. Add the rice and mix well. Lower the heat, cook for a few minutes and then pour in the vegetable stock. Adjust the seasoning, pepper to taste, and add the petit pois and artichoke hearts. Mix and cook for 20 minutes. Serve with lemon wedges to squeeze at the table.

Tofu escabeche

Serves 2-4

3 tbsp olive oil

1 red onion, finely sliced

5 large garlic cloves, finely sliced

200 g tofu, cut into cubes

1 large tomato, diced

50 ml white balsamic vinegar

1 sprig parsley

chilli sauce

salt and pepper

Heat the olive oil in a saucepan over high heat. Sweat the onion for a few minutes before adding the garlic and tofu. Leave to cook for 5 minutes, stirring often. Add the tomato and vinegar. Season with salt and pepper and add chilli sauce to taste. Cook for a few minutes longer. Add the parsley. Transfer to a bowl or airtight container. Can be eaten hot or cold. Keeps for two days in the fridge.

A perfect dish for a summer snack together with some olives, or as a filling for a sandwich.

Potatoes
à la marinière

Serves 4-8

800 g firm-fleshed potatoes, peeled, washed and cut into
   cubes

60 ml vegetable oil

3 onions, finely sliced

1 celery rib, finely sliced

200 ml white wine

2 sprigs curly parsley, chopped

salt and pepper

Heat the oil in a frying pan or saucepan over medium heat. Sauté the potatoes for 10 minutes. Add the onions and celery. Cook for a further 10 minutes. Season with salt and pepper and add the white wine. Cook for another 10 minutes over low heat until the potatoes are just soft. Serve sprinkled with the curly parsley.

escabeche

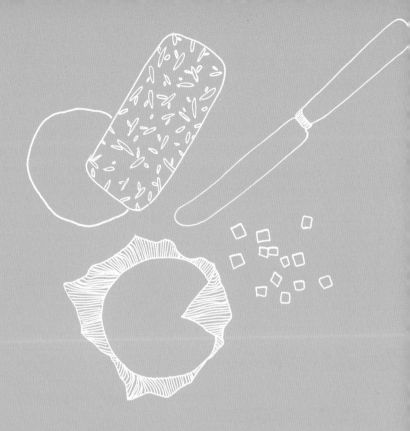

SUBSTITUTING DAIRY PRODUCTS AND EGGS

-- NON-DAIRY MILK --

-- NON-DAIRY CHEESE --

-- NON-DAIRY CREAMS AND FATS --

-- DOING AWAY WITH EGGS --

Almond milk

Makes 1 litre

100 g almonds
1 litre water
1-2 tbsp agave syrup (optional)

Soak the almonds in a large container of water overnight or for at least 3 hours (in which case, use warm water). Discard the soaking water (or keep it for watering the plants!). Whiz the almonds in a blender with the litre of water. For a sweeter milk, add the agave syrup before blending. Filter through a fine sieve lined with cheesecloth (or use a nut milk bag or a stocking). Squeeze the cheese-cloth tightly. Keep the almond solids for making biscuits, terrines or vegetable galettes. Keep refrigerated in an airtight bottle and drink within 3 days.

A closer look: Okara, what is it?

It is the Japanese word for the soy pulp that remains after soy milk has been made. By extension, this word is used to refer to the pulp or flesh that remains after other non-dairy milks have been made. Okara can come from almonds, cashew nuts, etc. and is a traditional ingredient in Japanese and Korean cooking. In the West, its popularity has come about thanks to vegetarian and vegan-style cooking. Okara is full of nutrients and it is a pity that it is not used more!

Soy and vanilla yoghurt

Makes about 8 yoghurts

1 litre soy milk
1 x 100 g pot soy yoghurt
2-3 tbsp agave syrup
1-2 tsp vanilla extract

Whiz all the ingredients in a blender, then divide among the glass yoghurt pots and leave in a yoghurt maker for about 12 hours. Leave to cool, put the lids on and refrigerate. Eat within a week.

ond milk

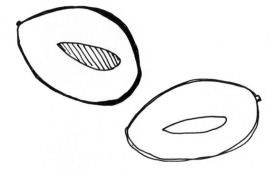

Pastry cream

Serves 4

10 tbsp light brown sugar
1 tbsp cornflour
4 tbsp flour
3 tbsp cashew butter
3 tbsp water
500 ml soy milk, heated
margarine

Mix the sugar with the cornflour and flour in a saucepan. Add the cashew butter and water and mix well until smooth. Gradually whisk in the hot milk. Bring to a simmer over medium heat and whisk for a few minutes until the cream is thick and smooth. Pour into a large bowl and rub a little margarine over the top of the pastry cream to avoid a skin forming.

Banana and date milk-shake

Makes 1 large glass

150 ml non-dairy milk
1 banana
4 dates, pitted
1 handful ice cubes
1 pinch ground vanilla
1 pinch ground cinnamon

Whiz all the ingredients in a blender for a few minutes. Serve immediately.

Tigernut horchata

Makes 1 litre

200 g dried tigernuts
1 litre water
100 g light brown sugar (or more to taste)
⅛ tsp ground cinnamon
⅛ tsp ground vanilla
shaved ice (optional)

Soak the tigernuts in warm water for 48 hours, changing the water regularly. Rub them together in the warm water to get rid of any earth. Rinse the tigernuts and repeat the process until the water stays clean. Put 500 ml of the water and 1 handful of the tigernuts in the blender. Add another handful of tigernuts and whiz. Add the rest of the water, the sugar, cinnamon and vanilla together with the last handful of tigernuts. Set aside in the fridge for 1 hour. Blend again for a few seconds and filter through a sieve lined with cheese-cloth. Squeeze well to obtain all the liquid. Serve cold or over shaved ice.

FYI: This traditional drink from Valencia is usually very sweet so adjust the amount of sugar to taste. Manufactured horchata sometimes contains dairy milk, but this recipe is 100% non-dairy. In Mexico, they make horchata in the same way but with rice. It is also served cold and is perfumed with cinnamon.

Rice and chestnut milk

Makes 1 litre

70 g rice
100 g pre-cooked chestnuts, peeled
1 litre water, plus 250 ml extra
1 tbsp agave syrup

Place the rice, chestnuts and the litre of water in a saucepan. Cook over high heat for 15 minutes. Remove from the heat and leave to cool for 15 minutes. Mix with an immersion blender or whiz in a blender. Filter through a fine sieve lined with cheesecloth. Add the 250 ml of water and the agave syrup. Store in a glass bottle in the fridge.

Mango lassi

Serves 4

350 ml soy milk
2 x 100 g pots soy yoghurts
1 very ripe mango, peeled and the flesh cut into pieces
2 tbsp light brown sugar
1 tsp freshly squeezed lemon juice

Put the soy milk and yoghurts in the jar of a blender. Add the mango, sugar and lemon juice and whiz until like a very smooth milk-shake. Drink it immediately.

Bergamot puddings

Makes 6 puddings

350 ml non-dairy milk
150 ml soy cream
¾ tsp agar-agar powder
100 g sugar
1 bergamot

Combine the milk with the cream, agar-agar and sugar in a saucepan. Zest the bergamot and juice it. Add the zest and juice to the saucepan and bring to the boil, stirring continuously. Whisk for 2 minutes and divide among 6 ramekins. Leave to cool and refrigerate for 2 hours.

Custard

Serves 4

500 ml soy milk
4 tbsp light brown sugar
3 tbsp cornflour
1 tbsp cashew butter
⅛ tsp ground vanilla
a tiny pinch ground turmeric (for colour, optional)

Whisk all the ingredients together in a medium-sized saucepan. Simmer over medium heat, whisking continuously, until it thickens and becomes smooth and creamy but not too thick (be careful, if it cooks too long it will become a creamy dessert!).

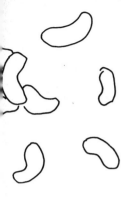

Almond milk spread

Makes 1 pot

1 litre almond milk
250 g light brown sugar
¼ tsp ground vanilla powder

Combine all the ingredients in a large saucepan. Bring to the boil then turn down the heat to low and cook, stirring often, for 2 hours until the consistency of the mixture is like cream. Pour into a jar and leave to thicken for 24 hours.

- -

Cashew-hazelnut milk

Makes 1 litre

60 g cashew nuts
40 g hazelnuts
1 litre water

Soak the cashew nuts and the hazelnuts in a large bowl of water overnight. Discard the soaking water. Whiz the nuts with the litre of water in a blender. Filter through a fine sieve lined with cheesecloth (or use a nut milk bag or a stocking). Squeeze well to obtain all the liquid. Store the milk in the fridge in an airtight bottle. Drink within 3 days.

Soft cashew and hazelnut okara biscuits

Makes about 12 biscuits

150 g cashew-hazelnut okara (see previous recipe and p. 120)
1 tbsp ground flaxseeds
75 g light brown sugar
3 tbsp neutral vegetable oil
2 tbsp cashew butter
1 tbsp hazelnut butter
125 ml soy milk
225 g type T45 flour
½ tsp baking powder
½ tsp bicarbonate of soda
¼ tsp ground vanilla
¼ tsp salt
25 g toasted cashew nuts, chopped

Mix the okara with the flaxseeds, sugar, oil, the two butters and the soy milk. In another bowl, mix the flour with the remaining dry ingredients (except for the cashew nuts) and then combine with the liquid mixture. With moistened hands, make a little ball of dough and place it on a baking tray lined with parchment paper. Flatten it and top with some cashew nuts. Repeat the process with the rest of the dough. Bake for 15 minutes at 180°C (Gas mark 4).

...hew and hazelnut milk, soft okara biscuits and almond milk spread

Apple and cinnamon rice pudding with maple syrup

Almond okara and green olive terrine

Serves 2

175 g almond okara (see p. 120)
versatile tofu stuffing (see p. 76)
50 g pitted green olives
1 tbsp malted yeast flakes
1 tbsp ground flaxseeds
2 tsp olive oil
2 tsp freshly squeezed lemon juice
1 tsp tamari
1 pinch Espelette pepper
salt and pepper

Whiz all the ingredients in a food processor. Put into a terrine, press down well and refrigerate for 2 hours.

Use as a spread on bread or as a sandwich filling.

- -

Matcha latte

Serves 1

300 ml almond milk
1 tsp matcha green tea powder
2-3 tsp agave syrup

Heat the almond milk gently without boiling it. Whisk in the matcha. Add the agave syrup and heat for 1-2 minutes. Strain through a small, fine strainer before serving.

Apple and cinnamon rice pudding with maple syrup

Serves 4

700 ml soy milk
120 g short-grain white rice
¼ tsp ground vanilla
1 large apple
1 tsp neutral vegetable oil or margarine
¼ tsp ground cinnamon
6 tbsp maple syrup
50 g light brown sugar

Bring the milk to the boil in a large saucepan. Sprinkle in the rice and mix. Add the vanilla and turn down the heat to low. Cook for 30-40 minutes until the rice is tender. Stir often to avoid the rice catching on the bottom of the saucepan. Cut the apple into small dice. Sauté in a little frying pan with the oil or margarine. Add the apple, maple syrup and sugar to the rice and mix well. Cook for about 10 minutes until the rice is very creamy. Divide among 4 ramekins. Leave to cool before serving.

FRESH AND CREAMY CHEESES

Soy mozzarella

Makes 1 large ball

200 g silken tofu
125 g soy yoghurt
100 ml soy milk
1½ tbsp freshly squeezed lemon juice
1 tbsp olive oil
1 tbsp arrowroot
½ tsp agar-agar powder
½ tsp salt

Whiz all the ingredients with an immersion blender until smooth. Pour into a small saucepan and bring to the boil. Cook for a few minutes to thicken, whisking constantly, until it is like a thick béchamel. Line a bowl with a large piece of cling film and pour in the thick cream. Pull the remaining film up and tie to close. Leave to cool and then freeze for 30 minutes. Store in the fridge. Remove the cling film before serving.

Use as you would mozzarella, and it melts like the real thing.

Soy ricotta

Makes 1 bowl

150 g firm tofu, crumbled
1 tbsp tahini
6 tbsp soy cream
½ tsp onion powder
¼ tsp garlic powder
¼ tsp salt
1 tsp freshly squeezed lemon juice
pepper

Put the tofu in a bowl and mix with the tahini, soy cream and the onion and garlic powders. Season to taste and add the lemon juice. Refrigerate.

Use as it is, like a fresh cheese, or with a sauce, as a stuffing, in tarts, with pasta, etc.

Cottage cheese

Makes 1 bowl

400 g silken tofu
1 x 100 g pot soy yoghurt
1 tsp salt
2 tbsp freshly squeezed lemon juice

Mash the silken tofu and the soy yoghurt together with a fork. Add the salt and lemon juice. Mix well. Line a fine sieve with cheesecloth and pour in the mixture. Cover with a tea towel and leave to drip for 1 hour. Hold up the ends of the cheesecloth with one hand, and gently twist and press to drain the excess water. Put into a bowl and serve seasoned with fresh herbs and olive oil.

Cream cheese

Makes 1 bowl

200 g silken tofu
150 ml soy cream
1 tbsp arrowroot
1 tsp agave syrup
½ tsp salt
½ tsp agar-agar powder

Whiz all the ingredients together in a blender and then bring the mixture to the boil, stirring continuously with a wooden spoon for 2-3 minutes. Pour into an airtight container. Leave to cool to room temperature and then refrigerate. Leave to rest in the fridge for 2 hours before eating it.

Spread it on bread or toast, serve with herbs or fresh vegetables, use as a sandwich filling, etc.

Cashew nut mascarpone

Makes 300 g

150 g raw cashew nuts
3 tbsp soy yoghurt
100 ml soy cream
4 tsp freshly squeezed lemon juice
1 pinch salt

Soak the cashew nuts In a large bowl for 2-3 hours. Drain and whiz them with the yoghurt and soy cream in a food processor. Add the lemon juice a little at a time, pulsing between each spoonful. Lastly, add salt and whiz well. Refrigerate for 1-2 hours before using. Store in an airtight container. Keeps for 48 hours in the fridge.

FERMENTED CHEESES

Herb log

Serves 4

150 g raw cashew nuts
50 ml grain milk
¾ tsp salt
1 tsp malted yeast
3 tbsp chopped fresh chives
3 tbsp chopped fresh coriander
½ tbsp chopped thyme leaves

Soak the cashew nuts in water for 6-8 hours, then drain. Whiz at length in a food processor with the grain milk until thick and creamy. Place in an airtight container, close it and leave to ferment at room temperature for 12-48 hours (on average, it takes 24 hours). Add the salt and the yeast and mix well. Refrigerate for 8-12 hours. The cheese will harden. Sprinkle the chopped herbs on a piece of cling film and put the cheese on it, in an elongated mound. Roll the cheese in the cling film to shape into a log. Close tightly, twisting the ends well, and refrigerate for 12 hours before eating. Keeps for 1 week in the fridge.

Fermented tofu and miso feta

Serves 2

125 g firm tofu
1 pack shiro miso

Cut the block of tofu into 3 slices horizontally (to obtain thin slices). Cover them with miso and place one on top of the other in an airtight container. Close and leave to ferment for 24-48 hours at room temperature (if it is very cold, it can be left up to 72 hours). Rinse the tofu slices with water to remove the miso and keep for a few days in the refrigerator in an airtight container.

Use it as it is, diced in a salad, with pasta, with bread and olive oil, in short as you would use feta.

Soft cashew nut cheese

Serves 2-4

175 g raw cashew nuts
80 ml grain milk
1 tsp salt
1 tsp white miso
2 tbsp malted yeast
1 tsp tahini

Soak the cashew nuts in water for 6-8 hours, then drain. Whiz at length in a food processor with the grain milk until thick and creamy. Place in an airtight container, close it and leave to ferment at room temperature for 12-48 hours (on average, it takes 24 hours). Add the other ingredients, mix well and refrigerate for 8 hours. The cheese can be stored in the airtight container or shaped with a ring mould before serving. Keeps for 1 week in the fridge in an airtight container or wrapped in cling film.

Variations: *After unmoulding, sprinkle with herbs de Provence, or chop some dried fruit and nuts and mix with the cheese before shaping it.*

Almond, shallot and chive crottin

Serves 2

130 g almonds, skinned
75 ml grain milk
½ tsp salt
1 tsp malted yeast
1 tsp chopped shallot
1 tbsp chopped chives

Soak the almonds in water for 8 hours. Drain and whiz the almonds in a food processor with the grain milk at length until like cream cheese in texture. Place in an airtight container, close it and leave to ferment at room temperature for 12-48 hours (on average 24 hours). Add the salt, the yeast, the shallot and chives and mix well. Line a flat-bottomed ramekin with a sheet of cling film and place the almond cheese into it, pressing down well. Cover completely. Refrigerate for 12 hours before unmoulding. Keeps for 1 week in the fridge, covered in cling film.

Crottin, log, soft cheese and feta

Garlic and herb cheese spr

Rejuvelac (grain milk)

Makes 500 ml

2 tbsp wheat grains for germinating (or any other grain you choose)

500 ml water

Soak the grains for 8-12 hours and then put them in a germination box, jar or bowl. Leave to germinate for 2-3 days, rinsing them three times a day. Put the germinated grains in an airtight jar and cover with water. Close the container and leave to ferment at room temperature for 24-72 hours. The liquid, which will become white and opaque, will have a pronounced fermented smell.

This simplified way of making grain milk will enable you to create a number of fermented, non-dairy cheeses. If you wish to drink the grain milk, you'll have to make a lot more!

MELTY AND SPREADABLE CHEESES

Versatile cream cheese

Serves 2-4

250 ml soy cream

3 tbsp malted yeast

1 tbsp cashew butter

1 tbsp white miso

2 tsp chopped fresh chives

½ tsp mustard powder

½ tsp salt

¼ tsp garlic powder

⅛ tsp ground turmeric

Whiz all the ingredients with an immersion blender. Put into a small saucepan and cook for a few minutes over high heat. Use it immediately.

Use for cheese sauces, with pasta, for gratins, like melted cheese, as a dip or to stuff ravioli or puff pastry parcels.

Garlic and herb cheese spread

Makes 1 bowl

50 g white cashew nuts

175 g tamari-marinated lacto-fermented tofu

100 ml water

1 garlic clove

1 tsp chopped basil

1 tsp chopped parsley

1 tsp chopped fresh coriander

¼ tsp salt

Soak the cashew nuts in water for 1 hour. Whiz all the ingredients in a food processor until thick and creamy. Store in the fridge in an airtight container. Use within 4 days.

Petit Breton with nuts

Serves 2-4

60 g raw cashew nuts

5 fresh walnuts

125 g firm tofu

60 ml organic cider (unfiltered)

1 tsp salt

1 tsp freshly squeezed fresh lemon juice

½ tsp grated onion

Soak the cashew nuts in water for 30 minutes. Shell the walnuts. Whiz all the ingredients in a food processor to obtain a smooth, fresh cheese. Put in an airtight container or shape with a metal ring mould and remove it just before serving. Eat within 24 hours.

Suggestion: This cheese may be light, but it is very flavoursome. For a milder-tasting cheese, leave out the onion. The fresh walnuts are essential for the taste and the texture. It is therefore a seasonal cheese to be enjoyed in the autumn!

Gratable chee

Melty cheese

Serves 4-6

150 g raw cashew nuts
3 tbsp malted yeast
1 tsp sea salt
3 tbsp olive oil
200 ml water
6 tsp agar-agar powder

Whiz the cashew nuts, the yeast, the salt and the olive oil in a food processor at length until very smooth. Whisk the water and the agar-agar together in a small saucepan. Bring to the boil and stir for 1 minute. Pour the agar-agar mixture into the food processor and whiz again. Line a small rectangular container with cling film. Put in the mixture and press down well. Smooth the surface with a spatula. Freeze for 40 minutes before unmoulding. Store it covered with cling film and slice before using.

Great for grilled sandwiches, burgers and even pizzas. This non-dairy melty cheese won't go gooey after cooking and doesn't go stringy.

Cheese with pepper and tarragon

Serves 2-4

200 g lacto-fermented tofu
100 g raw cashew nuts
2 tbsp olive oil
1 tbsp malted yeast
½ tsp salt
½ tsp coarsely ground black pepper
1 tbsp chopped tarragon

Whiz the tofu with the cashew nuts, the olive oil, the yeast and the salt in a food processor until smooth and creamy. Mix in the pepper and the tarragon with a fork. Line a large ramekin with cling film. Put in the cheese and press down well. Refrigerate for 1 hour and unmould onto a plate just before serving. Eat within 48 hours.

Gratable cheese

Serves 4-6

260 g lupin beans in brine, drained
3 tsp malted yeast
50 g unscented coconut oil
½ tsp salt
2 tbsp water

Put the lupin beans and the malted yeast, the coconut oil and the salt in the bowl of a food processor. Whiz at length to obtain a smooth paste. Add the water and whiz again. The paste should hold its shape. Line a ramekin or rectangular container with cling film. Put in the cheese and press down well. Freeze for 45 minutes, then store in the fridge, covered in the cling film. Grate on a hand-held grater with large holes. Do not use a food processor or a fine grater. Use for gratins, pasta, nachos, as a pizza topping, etc.

Variation: Instead of grating it, use as you would cheddar, diced or sliced to top a burger.

FYI: Lupin beans in brine, called tramousses in the South of France and tremoços in Portugal, are a common aperitif snack. They are usually bought in jars or by the weight where olives are sold. These pulses are rich in protein and the salty taste from the brine gives them an interesting cheese-like flavour.

FULL-BODIED AND SCENTED CHEESES

Full-bodied tempeh cheese

Serves 2-4

50 g raw cashew nuts
100 g plain tempeh
50 ml water
2 tbsp white miso
1 tbsp malted yeast
1 tbsp cashew butter
2 tsp freshly squeezed lemon juice
1 tsp garlic powder

Soak the cashew nuts in water for 30 minutes. Drain. Put them in the bowl of a food processor with all the other ingredients. Whiz at length to obtain a smooth paste. Place an 8 cm ring mould on a plate covered with parchment paper and pour in the mixture. Bake for 25 minutes at 180°C (Gas mark 4). Leave to cool and then unmould by gently running the tip of a knife around the inside of the ring mould.

- -

Non-dairy Parmesan

Makes 1 small jar

115 g raw cashew nuts
1 tbsp malted yeast
1 tsp white sesame seeds
½ tsp salt

Whiz in a food processor until like a fine powder. Store in an airtight jar in the fridge.

Sliceable cheese with cumin

Serves 6

200 g lacto-fermented tofu, crumbled
2 tbsp lacto-fermented soy cream
2 tbsp cashew butter
3 tbsp tahini
3 tbsp malted yeast
½ tsp salt
4 tbsp unscented coconut oil, melted
4 tsp agar-agar powder
150 ml water
2 tsp cumin seeds

Whiz the tofu, the soy cream, the cashew butter, the tahini, the yeast, salt and the oil in a food processor. Mix the water with the agar-agar in a small saucepan and bring to the boil. Stir for 1 minute, then pour the agar-agar mixture into the food processor. Whiz until soft and smooth in texture. Mix in the cumin seeds with a spoon. Line a rectangular container with cling film. Pour in the mixture, press down well and smooth the surface with a spatula. Freeze for 30 minutes, then unmould and store in the fridge, covered in the cling film. Slice just before serving.

- -

Spiced pavé

Serves 2-4

125 g raw cashew nuts
1 tsp salt
4 tbsp malted yeast
3 tsp dried onion
½ tsp Espelette pepper
½ tsp paprika
1 tsp garlic powder
½ tsp ground five-pepper mix
30 g coconut oil
50 ml water

Whiz the cashew nuts and spices in a food processor. Add the oil and water and whiz again to a thick cream. Line a ramekin or rectangular container with cling film. Put in the cheese and press down well. Freeze for 15 minutes, then unmould onto a serving plate.

Suggestion: *For an even more perfumed touch, add 1 tsp of dried dill.*

odied tempeh cheese, cheese with cumin and slices of melty cheese

COOKING WITH NON-DAIRY CHEESE

Herb-marinated feta

Serves 4

200 g lacto-fermented tofu
  or homemade feta (see p.130), diced
200 ml olive oil
2 tsp dried onion
1 tsp herbs de Provence
1 tsp coriander seeds
1 tsp dried basil
½ tsp garlic powder
¼ tsp salt
1 sprig fresh thyme
pepper

Mix the tofu, the oil, the spices and the herbs in a mixing bowl. Put everything in a large jar.

Tip: *Some pickled gherkin brands have a handy little basket in the bottom of the jar. Reuse one of these to lift out the non-dairy feta cubes. Reuse the oil for another jar of marinated non-dairy feta or to marinate anything you choose (sun-dried tomatoes, grilled peppers, garlic, etc.).*

Cream cheese with grilled peppers

Makes 1 bowl

1 small red pepper
200 g silken tofu
125 g soy yoghurt
½ tsp salt
1 tsp agar-agar powder
¼ tsp garlic powder
2 tsp unscented coconut oil

Preheat the oven to 240°C (Gas mark 9), roast the pepper (or alternatively grill) until the skin begins to char. Peel off the skin and cut into pieces. Whiz in a food processor with the tofu, yoghurt, salt, agar-agar and garlic until smooth and creamy. Melt the coconut oil in a small saucepan and then pour in the red pepper cream and stir well. Bring to a simmer and cook for 1 minute, stirring continuously. Pour into a container. When it has cooled to room temperature, refrigerate for 2 hours. Keeps for 48 hours in an airtight container in the fridge.

Potato
tartiflette gratin

Serves 4

4 large potatoes (700 g), peeled
2 tsp olive oil
1 onion, finely sliced
125 g smoked tofu, finely sliced
1 bowl two-cheese sauce (see previous recipe)
150 g melty cheese (see p. 135), cut into thick slices
100 ml soy cream
salt and pepper

Put the potatoes in a saucepan of boiling water. Cook for 10 minutes when it comes back to the boil. Sauté the onion and tofu in a frying pan for a few minutes in the olive oil. When the potatoes are done, slice them horizontally. Oil a gratin dish and arrange a layer of potato slices in it. Spread half of the two-cheese sauce on top and then cover with half of the onion and tofu mixture. Next, add a second layer of potato slices followed by the rest of the sauce then the rest of the onion and tofu mixture. Finish off with a layer of potato slices. Top with the slices of melty cheese and a generous amount of soy cream. Sprinkle with salt and pepper and bake for 20-25 minutes at 180°C (Gas mark 4).

Two-cheese
sauce

Makes 1 bowl

200 ml soy milk
100 g gratable cheese (see p. 135), crumbled
125 g melty cheese (see p. 135), crumbled
salt and pepper

Heat the soy milk in a small saucepan over medium heat. Add the crumbled cheeses. Increase the heat to high and whisk well to melt the cheeses. Season with salt and pepper to taste.

Use: *For pasta dishes, vegetable gratins, burritos, to substitute melted cheese.*

Cheese croquettes

Makes about 12 croquettes

2 tbsp cornflour
4 tbsp water
breadcrumbs
1 block gratable cheese (see p. 135)
sunflower oil

Combine the cornflour and water in a mixing bowl. Place a generous layer of breadcrumbs on a plate. Take a small amount of the cheese and roll it between your hands to shape into a ball. Roll each one in the cornflour and water mixture and then in the breadcrumbs. Repeat the process 1 or 2 times if necessary. Repeat for all of the croquettes. Heat about 4 cm of oil In a saucepan. When the oil is hot (but not smoking), put in 2 croquettes. Turn them continuously for about 1 minute and remove when they are golden brown. Fry all the croquettes in the same way and place on kitchen paper to absorb any excess oil. Serve immediately.

se croquettes

WHICH FATS TO CHOOSE?

Oils

In truth, no oil is better than another as each has its particular nutritional profile; if you want to ensure a balanced fatty acid intake, being as diverse as possible is the best way to go. However, in terms of health and environmental impact, all oils are not the same. It is always better to choose virgin oils obtained by cold pressing from organic producers as these are free of toxic substances and have not undergone any modification.

To vary the oils used every day as well as those for cooking, buy:

- Cold-pressed virgin olive oil; it is very versatile and can be used for almost anything, even for cakes.

- An oil rich in omega-3 (rapeseed, flaxseed, hemp or a mixture of organic oils rich in omega-3) to liven up salads, soups and purées.

- A neutral oil for cooking and baking (grape seed, rapeseed, sunflower or a mixture of oils suitable for cooking, if possible, unscented).

- If your budget allows, it is worth buying some interesting aromatic gourmet oils: sesame, hazelnut, coconut, etc. They are slightly pricier, but a little goes a long way and they can be purchased in small quantities.

Margarine and palm oil

Organic, 100% non-dairy, plant-based margarine is a far cry from traditional margarines that are loaded with hydrogenated oil, dreadful 'trans' fats and suspicious additives. But they contain an ingredient that more and more consumers are rejecting for health, environmental and ethical reasons; palm oil. So, is organic palm oil being lumped in the same basket as its conventionally cultivated relation? The debate on this issue among those who believe in a responsible way of eating is ongoing. Here are some things to think about.

In health terms, non-hydrogenated, organic palm oil does not pose a risk to one's health as it is only consumed occasionally (for puff pastry, a recipe where margarine's texture is necessary, spread on toast once in a while, etc), especially if a variety of good-quality oils are used on a daily basis. However, eating processed organic foods on a regular basis that contain it should be avoided. It is when it is hidden in many products and we eat it without realising, that it can become dangerous to our health.

With regard to ecology and ethics, the production of organic palm oil theoretically meets strict criteria. Production is very limited compared to that of the non-organic sector (about 0.2% of the market). Most organic palm oil comes from Colombia, from plantations that are, in principle, not involved in deforestation, the destruction of biodiversity or the natural habitats of animals, and they reject inhuman working conditions – virtually the opposite of conditions for the production of conventional palm oil.

My advice: Limit minimum consumption at home and opt for organic palm oil when buying products that contain it. Replace it whenever possible with coconut oil, the only other oil that is solid below 25°C, and try to make homemade margarine without palm oil!

Coconut Chantilly cream

Serves 4

1 x 400 g tin coconut milk
50 g icing sugar

Refrigerate the coconut milk for 12 hours. Open the tin and remove the white layer that has separated from the water and put it in a bowl with the sugar. Mix with a spoon and then whisk for a few minutes. For a pretty presentation, use a piping bag with a star nozzle. Refrigerate before serving.

Soy crème fraîche

Makes 1 bowl

8 tbsp soy cream
6 tbsp soy yoghurt
¼ tsp salt

Use a spoon to mix the ingredients in a bowl.

Use cold, in sauces.

- -

Thick cashew nut cream

Makes 1 small bowl

130 g white cashew nuts
100 ml water
salt

Soak the cashew nuts in water for 1 hour. Whiz in a food processor with the water and a pinch of salt.

Thick cashew nut cream, soy crème fraîche and coconut Chantilly cream

Vegan buttermilk

Makes 1 bowl

250 ml soy milk

1 tsp apple cider vinegar

Mix the ingredients together and leave to curdle for 5 minutes, then refrigerate.

Buttermilk is a commonly used ingredient in baking in the United States. This is a very easy non-dairy version to substitute it. Non-dairy milk can be substituted with the same amount of vegan buttermilk in homemade cakes. The acidity of the vinegar reacts with the baking powder, resulting in soft and beautifully risen cakes.

Sesame cream

Makes 1 small bowl

4 tbsp tahini

3 tbsp freshly squeezed lemon juice

2 tbsp water

1 tbsp olive oil

salt and pepper

Mix the tahini and lemon juice with a fork. Add the water to make a cream-like texture. Next, add the oil, a little at a time until smooth and creamy. Season to taste.

Use as a dip for crudités, as a salad dressing, with falafels, as a sandwich spread, on vegetables, in short… everywhere!

Homemade margarine

Makes the equivalent of 1 small tub

120 g unscented coconut oil

4 tbsp oat milk

3 tbsp olive oil

3 tsp soy lecithin

Melt the coconut oil in a bain-marie. Blend for a few minutes with the other ingredients. Put into a bowl, cover and refrigerate for at least 2 hours before using it.

Can be used for cooking or as a spread.

Soy Chantilly cream

Serves 4-6

1 x 235 g pot thick lacto-fermented soy cream, very cold

200 ml soy cream, very cold

2 tbsp unscented coconut oil, melted

1 sachet whipped cream stabiliser

100 g icing sugar

⅛ tsp vanilla extract

Leave a bowl to chill well in the freezer. When it is very cold, whisk the two creams together. Whisk in the coconut oil. Add the sachet of whipped cream stabiliser, icing sugar and vanilla, and whip until thick and airy. Put in a piping bag fitted with a large star nozzle and refrigerate for 1 hour before using.

For a lighter and airier cream, put in a syphon and insert a gas cartridge. Refrigerate.

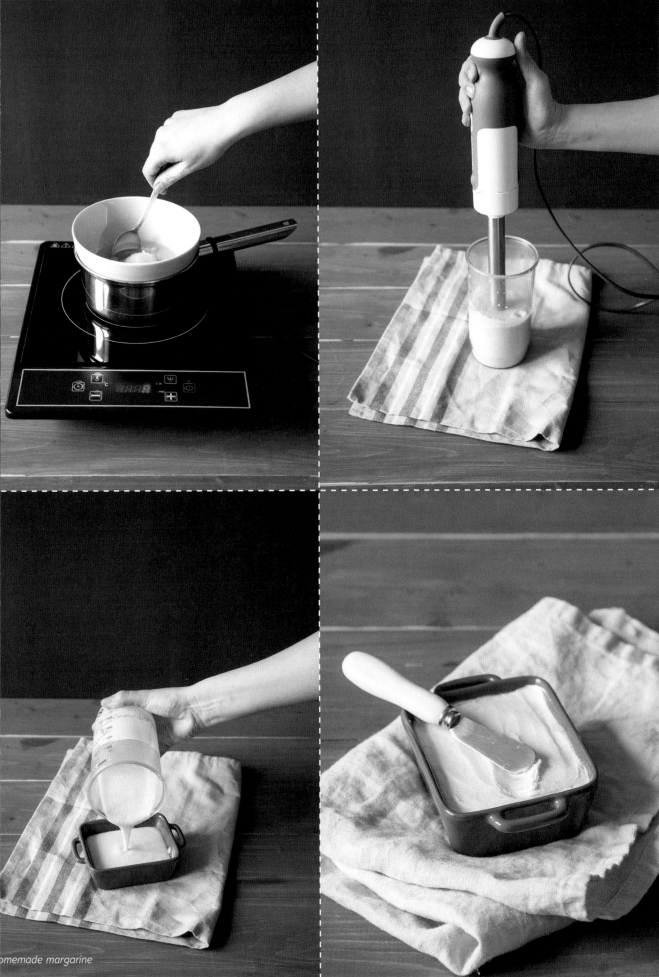

Almond crème fraîche

Makes 1 bowl

200 ml almond milk
2 sachets whipped cream stabiliser
2 tsp freshly squeezed lemon juice

Whisk the almond milk with the whipped cream stabiliser in a large bowl. Add the lemon juice. Store in the fridge in an airtight container. Eat within 48 hours.

Light soy margarine spread

Makes the equivalent of 1 tub

240 g silken tofu
1 sachet whipped cream stabiliser
2 tsp freshly squeezed lemon juice
¼ tsp salt
1 tbsp olive oil
50 g unscented coconut oil, melted
1 pinch ground turmeric

Whiz the tofu with the whipped cream stabiliser, lemon juice, salt, and olive oil in a blender. Add the coconut oil and turmeric, and blend again. Place in a mini-casserole type container with a lid. Refrigerate for 12 hours before using.

Coconut butter

Makes 1 pot

400 g dessicated coconut
2 tbsp coconut oil

Whiz the ingredients in a food processor until it becomes a smooth cream (use the pulse button if necessary). Store in a glass jar with a lid and allow the coconut butter to solidify. (If the weather is very warm, leave in the fridge just long enough for it to solidify.) Store in a dry place or cupboard but not in the fridge as it will solidify too much.

Use as you would dairy butter, for cooking vegetables and tofu, as a spread, or for baking.

Almond crème fraîche

coconut butter

WHAT ABOUT EGGS AND 'HAPPY' CHICKENS?

What about organic eggs? What if I buy my eggs from a nice farmer? Or I raise my own chickens? Questions abound regarding acceptable conditions for raising laying hens and eating eggs in an ethical way when one is vegetarian or thinking of becoming vegan.

When it comes to buying organic eggs laid by free-range hens, the answer is simple; there is nothing ethical about raising animals, even organically. Young males born on laying hen farms are useless and so are killed at birth, as are laying hens, which become less productive after several years and therefore no longer profitable. Regardless of whether raising livestock is done organically or not, the fate of animals which do not produce enough is the same.

If you think that having your own chickens is a more ethical solution, the first thing to know is that buying hens or chicks to produce your own eggs involves raising them, thus, the exploitation of other hens is the same as the cruel killing of male chicks. In the end, buying chickens to avoid buying eggs is not more ethical, it only shifts the problem (chickens are raised so the young laying hens can be sold instead of selling eggs).

Despite it being accepted that vegans do not eat eggs, there are still many people, even vegans, who ask a very legitimate question: If I find/adopt/rescue chickens and they lay unfertilised eggs in my garden 'is eating them really such an ethical problem, and wouldn't that even be preferable to wasting them?' The issue is far from simple, and as with many matters that divide vegans, there is not necessarily a good answer.

Here are some things to ponder.

Nature can sometimes be very efficient: When an egg is not viable (e.g. a broken egg), it is not uncommon for the hen to eat it and take advantage of its nutrients; taking it away before she has had a chance to eat it, the hen is deprived of a possible source of food.

Would you consider a pigeon's egg or the unfertilised egg of a goose to be a potential source of food that would be a shame to waste if it were abandoned? Yet these eggs are also edible.

Should you really eat those eggs because it would be more ethical to do so, while you manage to cook, sustain yourself, or prepare delicious cakes without them the rest of the time? Would you also eat your hen if she were to die naturally, so as not to let her go to waste? After all, eating this 'happy' chicken meat would also be perfectly ethical.

Doesn't eating the eggs of 'happy' hens contribute to a taste for eggs and the idea that they are a source of acceptable food?

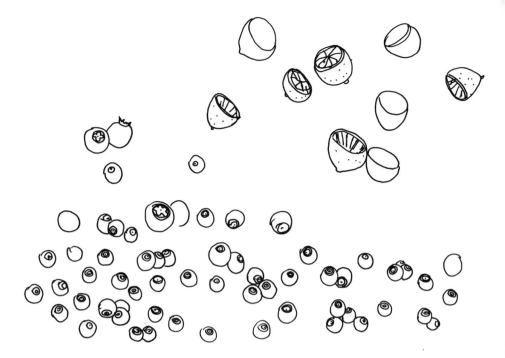

CRÊPES, GALETTES, ETC.

Orange and pecan pancakes

Makes about 12 pancakes

150 g T70 spelt flour
65 g light brown sugar
25 g chestnut flour
1 tbsp cornflour
1 tsp baking powder
½ tsp bicarbonate of soda
350 ml soy milk
2 tbsp neutral vegetable oil
⅛ tsp ground vanilla
4 drops sweet orange oil
25 g pecans, crushed in a mortar
vegetable oil for cooking

Combine all the dry ingredients in a mixing bowl. Whisk in the soy milk. Add the oil and mix well. Add the vanilla, sweet orange oil and the pecans. Lightly oil a frying pan and heat it to medium-high. When the pan is hot pour in half a ladleful of batter. Flip the pancake over when the little bubbles that form on the surface begin to burst. If the underside of the pancake gets too brown, lower the heat a little. Pile the pancakes up to keep them warm and soft.

Delicious with maple syrup.

Banana-blueberry pancakes

Makes about 12 pancakes

150 g T70 spelt flour
70 g light brown sugar
40 g brown rice flour
1 tsp baking powder
1 tsp bicarbonate of soda
⅛ tsp ground vanilla
350 ml rice milk
1 tbsp almond butter
1 tbsp neutral vegetable oil
½ a ripe banana, mashed
30 g blueberries
vegetable oil for cooking

Combine all the dry ingredients In a mixing bowl. Whisk in the rice milk. Add the almond butter, oil and banana. If the batter is not smooth enough, use an immersion blender for a moment. Add the blueberries. Lightly oil a frying pan and heat it to medium-high. When the pan is hot pour in half a ladleful of batter. Flip the pancake over when the little bubbles that form on the surface begin to burst. Pile the pancakes up to keep them warm and soft. They will be a little darker in colour than traditional pancakes.

Korean vegetable pancake

Korean vegetable pancakes

Makes 8 large pancakes

250 g plain flour
1 tsp cornflour
½ tsp baking powder
1 tsp salt
¼ tsp ground turmeric
625 ml cold water
1 small courgette, grated
1 small onion, finely sliced
125 g Chinese cabbage, finely sliced
1 tsp olive oil
1 bunch chives, chopped
1 pinch ground pepper
salt and pepper
vegetable oil for cooking

Combine the flour with the cornflour, baking powder, salt and turmeric in a mixing bowl. Whisk in the water a little at a time. Sauté the vegetables in a large frying pan over high heat in the olive oil for 5-10 minutes. Season and add to the batter. Add the chives and pepper to taste. Lightly oil a frying pan and cook the pancakes for 15 minutes, turning them often until they are golden brown.

Buckwheat galettes

Makes about 10-12 crêpes

300 g buckwheat flour
1 tbsp cornflour
½ tsp salt
900 ml water
2 tbsp vegetable oil, plus a little extra for cooking

Combine the dry ingredients in a mixing bowl and then whisk in the water a little at a time. Add the olive oil. Leave to rest in the fridge for 1 hour. Cook the pancakes in a very lightly-oiled, hot frying pan.

Wheat crêpes from my childhood

Makes 15 crêpes

250 g plain flour
1 tbsp arrowroot
600 ml soy milk
2 tbsp neutral vegetable oil
1 tsp dark rum

Combine the flour and arrowroot in a mixing bowl. Whisk as you pour in the soy milk. Add the oil and rum. Whisk for a few minutes and then leave to rest for 1 hour. Add a little water if the batter is too thick. Cook the pancakes in a hot, oiled frying pan.

Variations: *These pancakes from my childhood were always flavoured with dark rum, but if you're not a fan of its smell or you don't want to use alcohol, substitute it with 1 tsp of vanilla extract or orange blossom water, or with a little cinnamon.*

Reduced sugar wc

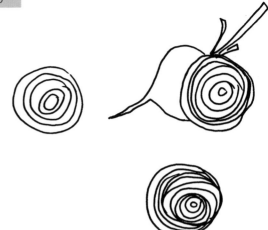

Pink beetroot blinis

Makes about 25 blinis

200 g spelt flour
1 tbsp light brown sugar
2 tsp arrowroot
1½ tsp baking powder
¼ tsp salt
150 ml soy cream
200 ml non-dairy milk
1 small uncooked beetroot, finely diced
2 tbsp olive oil
vegetable oil for cooking

Combine the dry ingredients in a mixing bowl. Whiz the soy cream, non-dairy milk and beetroot in a blender. Whisk into the dry ingredients and then add the oil. Cook the blinis by pouring 1 tbsp of the batter into a frying pan over medium heat. The temperature of the frying pan is very important. The blinis should be just golden and not too brown. Test the heat of the pan with 1 or 2 blinis and adjust it if necessary.

Reduced sugar waffles

Makes 4-6 waffles

60 ml neutral vegetable oil
50 g light brown sugar
200 ml oat milk (or other non-dairy milk)
160 g kamut flour
1½ tsp baking powder
⅛ tsp ground vanilla
oil for the waffle iron
icing sugar for sprinkling

Whisk the oil and sugar together in a mixing bowl. Add the oat milk. Combine the flour with the baking powder and vanilla. Add to the bowl. Whisk well to avoid lumps. Pre-heat a mould or waffle-iron to a fairly high heat. Pour the batter into the waffle plates, close and cook for about 5 minutes. Oil the plates between each batch of waffles. If the waffle-iron has an indicator light, wait for it to turn off before opening to remove the waffles. Serve warm, sprinkled with icing sugar.

Potato and tofu galettes

Makes 8-10 galettes

400 g potatoes, peeled and cut into small dice
125 g firm tofu
125 ml non-dairy cream
2 tbsp spelt flour
2 tbsp chopped parsley
1 tbsp garlic, finely sliced
2 tsp tamari
½ tsp salt
pepper
vegetable oil for cooking

Boil the potatoes until just tender. Drain and put them in a mixing bowl. Add the remaining ingredients and mix with an immersion blender. Stop when the mixture is smooth but still has some texture. Heat a little oil in a frying pan over medium heat. Shape the galettes to the size of a pancake and cook for 3-5 minutes on each side. Wait until the bottom side is fully cooked before flipping over with a spatula.

Serve with vegetables, a green salad, or with soup. These galettes are also good when eaten cold.

QUICHES, TARTS AND PUFF PASTRY PARCELS

Leek quiche

Serves 4-6

3 large leeks, washed and very finely sliced
2 tbsp olive oil
1 tbsp tamari
100 g smoked tofu
200 ml soy cream
1 tbsp tahini
1 tsp cornflour
½ tsp garlic powder
1 quantity shortcrust pastry dough (or see p. 244)
pepper

Sauté the leeks in the olive oil in a pan over medium heat for about 10 minutes. Pepper generously and add the tamari when they are done. Set aside. Blend the tofu with the cream, tahini, cornflour and garlic. Combine this mixture with the leeks. Line a tart tin with the pastry. Bake blind for 5 minutes at 180°C (Gas mark 4), then pour in the quiche filling. Bake at 180°C for 20 minutes.

Shortcrust pastry with olive oil and thyme

Makes 1 tart crust

250 g plain flour
½ tsp salt
2 tsp dried thyme
50 ml olive oil
100 ml water

Combine the flour with the salt and thyme in a mixing bowl. Add the oil, mix with your fingertips and then add the water. Mix well until it forms a smooth dough. (Add a little flour if it is too sticky.) Wrap in cling film and leave to rest in the fridge for 30 minutes. Roll out finely on a floured work surface.

Einkorn shortcrust pastry

Makes 1 tart crust

200 g einkorn flour
½ tsp salt
4 tbsp olive oil
4 tbsp water

Combine the flour and the salt in a mixing bowl. Add the olive oil and mix with a fork. Lastly add the water and mix well to form a smooth dough. Wrap in cling film and leave to rest in the fridge for 30 minutes.

Grilled courgette, pine nut and herb tart

Serves 4-6

3 courgettes, sliced into thin rounds
1 garlic clove, finely sliced
2 tbsp olive oil
2 tbsp pine nuts
1 tbsp freshly squeezed lemon juice
1 sheet organic vegan puff pastry
200 ml soy cream (or other non-dairy cream)
2 tbsp Dijon mustard
1 tsp herbs de Provence, plus a little extra for sprinkling
salt and pepper

Sauté the courgettes and garlic with the olive oil in a large frying pan over medium heat until the courgettes are lightly browned. Mix well with a spatula to avoid them browning too much. Add the pine nuts and lemon juice. Cook for a further 1-2 minutes and remove from the heat. Place the puff pastry (with its parchment paper) in a tart tin and bake blind for 5 minutes at 180°C (Gas mark 4). Mix the cream with the mustard and the herbs de Provence in a bowl. Season to taste. Spread the mixture into the pastry crust. Top with the courgettes and the pine nuts and lightly sprinkle with the extra herbs de Provence. Bake at 180°C (Gas mark 4) for 25 minutes.

Grilled courgette, pine nut and herb tart

Pumpkin and hazelnut pie

Serves 6

1 red kuri squash, cut into small dice
3 tbsp olive oil
2 tbsp chopped parsley
2 tbsp tamari
4 tbsp hazelnut butter
150 g seitan, chopped
2 sheets organic vegan puff pastry

Sauté the red kuri squash in a frying pan over high heat with the oil, stirring often. Add the parsley, tamari and hazelnut butter. Remove from the heat when the red kuri squash is tender. Add the seitan to the mixture. Place one sheet of puff pastry (with its parchment paper) in a pie tin. Pour in the filling and cover with the second sheet of puff pastry. Fold the edges in neatly and bake for 35 minutes at 180°C (Gas mark 4).

Spiced onion puff pastry parcels

Serves 4

3 onions, finely sliced
2 tbsp olive oil
1 tsp ras el hanout
2 tsp ground coriander
2 tsp vegan Worcestershire sauce
2 tbsp maple syrup
2 handfuls of raisins
1 sheet organic vegan puff pastry
salt and pepper

Sauté the vegetables in a frying pan in the olive oil together with the spices over high heat for at least 5 minutes. Add the Worcestershire sauce, maple syrup and raisins and cook for a further 5 minutes over medium heat. Season to taste. Cut the puff pastry into four small squares. Place a little of the spiced onion mixture in the middle. Bring the corners up together to the centre and press to close the parcels. Line a baking tray with parchment paper and bake them for 15 minutes at 180°C (Gas mark 4).

Indian quiche

Serves 4-6

2 peppers, diced
1 onion, diced
1 courgette, diced
2 tbsp olive oil
3 tsp curry powder
125 g firm tofu
50 ml soy cream
100 ml coconut milk
1 tbsp cornflour
1 tsp salt
1 tbsp tahini
1 tbsp chopped fresh coriander
1 quantity shortcrust pastry dough (or see p. 244)

Sauté the vegetables in a frying pan in the olive oil together with the curry powder for 5-10 minutes to brown them. Whiz the tofu with the cream, coconut milk, cornflour, salt and tahini in a blender. Combine the mixture with the vegetables, then add the fresh coriander. Line a tart tin with the pastry and bake blind for 5 minutes at 180°C (Gas mark 4). Pour in the filling and bake at 180°C for about 20 minutes. The quiche should be golden brown.

Petits pois, carrot and coconut muffins

Country-style galette with cherry tomatoes

Serves 4

150 g firm tofu, crumbled
1 tbsp olive oil, plus extra to drizzle
4 tbsp soy cream
2 tbsp capers
1 tsp herbs de Provence
2 tsp Dijon mustard
1 tsp garlic powder
1 quantity shortcrust pastry with olive oil and thyme (see
   p. 154)
300-400 g cherry tomatoes, cut in half
salt and pepper

Mix the tofu with the oil and cream in a bowl. Add the capers and mash well with a fork. Add the herbs de Provence, mustard and garlic. Season and mix well. Roll out the pastry dough onto a baking tray lined with parchment paper. Spread the tofu mixture over it and fold the edges neatly to make a border. Top with the tomatoes, cut side up, placing them closely together. Drizzle with a little olive oil and season lightly with salt and pepper. Bake for 25-30 minutes at 190°C (Gas mark 5).

CAKES AND MUFFINS

Petits pois, carrot and coconut muffins

Makes 12 muffins

100 ml soy milk
2 tsp apple cider vinegar
250 ml coconut milk
100 g fresh or frozen petits pois
2 small carrots, finely grated
<u>Dry ingredients</u>
150 g einkorn flour
50 g plain flour
2 tbsp baking powder
1 tsp bicarbonate of soda
½ tsp salt

Combine the soy milk and vinegar in a mixing bowl. Leave to stand for 5 minutes. Combine all the dry ingredients In a mixing bowl. Mix the coconut milk and the curdled soy milk together and add to the dry ingredients. Add the cooled fresh peas (or the defrosted ones) and the carrots and mix well. Grease a 12-hole muffin tin or line each hole with parchment paper and divide the mixture among them. Bake for 30 minutes at 180°C (Gas mark 4).

- -

Olive and smoked tofu cake

Serves 4-6

200 g plain flour
50 g lupin flour
50 g pre-cooked polenta
1 tsp sea salt
2 tsp herbs de Provence
1 tbsp malted yeast
2 sachets baking powder
400 ml soy cream
70 ml olive oil
3 tsp freshly squeezed lemon juice
100 g smoked tofu, cut into small dice
70 g pitted green olives, roughly chopped

Mix the flours and the polenta in a bowl. Add the salt, herbs de Provence, malted yeast and baking powder. Pour in the soy cream and mix well. Drizzle in the olive oil a little at a time, then add the lemon juice. Add the tofu and olives to the mixture. Line a 25 cm/10 inch cake tin with parchment paper and pour in the batter. Bake for 1 hour at 180°C (Gas mark 4). Leave to cool before unmoulding and cutting into slices.

Potato and herb scones

Makes 6 scones

400 g potatoes, cooked
4 tbsp olive oil
100 ml soy milk
150 g plain flour
1 tsp baking powder
1 tsp salt
1 tbsp chopped basil
1 tbsp chopped parsley

Mash the potatoes with the olive oil and soy milk. Add the flour, baking powder, salt and herbs. Line a baking tray with parchment paper. With floured hands, shape 6 scones and place them on the baking tray. Bake for 35 minutes at 180°C (Gas mark 4).

Mini grilled courgette and non-dairy feta cakes

Serves 4-6

1 courgette
2 garlic cloves
2 tsp olive oil, plus 50 ml extra
1 x 100 g pot soy yoghurt
1 tsp apple cider vinegar
1 sachet baking powder
100 ml almond milk
150 g plain flour
50 g maize flour
80 g homemade feta (see p. 130)
   or tamari-marinated lacto-fermented tofu, cut into
   small dice
1 tsp herbs de Provence
1 tsp each salt and pepper

Cut the courgette into small dice and chop the garlic very fine. Sauté in a frying pan with the 2 tbsp of olive oil over a high heat. Combine the yoghurt and vinegar in a small bowl. Add the baking powder and mix well. Add the 50 ml of olive oil then whisk in the almond milk. Incorporate the flours a little at a time and season. Add the vegetables, non-dairy feta and the herbs de Provence. Oil or line mini cake or muffin moulds. Bake at 180°C (Gas mark 4) for 20-25 minutes. The baking time may vary depending on the size of the moulds.

Buns stuffed with red kuri squash, sesame and miso

Serves 8

200 g red kuri squash, cut into small pieces
1 tbsp olive oil
1 tbsp white miso
100 ml water
2 tbsp tahini
1 tsp tamari
½ tbsp chopped fresh chives
½ tbsp chopped fresh parsley
dough for 8 buns (see p. 37)
soy milk
sesame seeds
pepper

Sauté the red kuri squash over medium heat in the olive oil for 5 minutes. Add the miso, water and tahini. Mix well. Add the tamari, chives and parsley. Season with pepper to taste. Cook for a few minutes and set aside. Prepare the dough for the buns and leave to rise for 2 hours. Divide into 8 portions. Line a baking tray with parchment paper. Flatten each ball of dough and place some filling in the middle. Close, shape into a bun and place on the baking tray. Brush the buns with soy milk and sprinkle with sesame seeds. Bake for 15 minutes at 180°C (Gas mark 4).

s stuffed with red kuri squash, sesame and miso, and potato and herb scones

Broad bean and rocket muffins

Makes about 8 muffins

125 g silken tofu
50 ml olive oil
½ tsp salt
10g sachet baking powder
1 tbsp malted yeast
½ tsp garlic powder
a handful chopped rocket leaves
1½ tbsp freshly squeezed lemon juice
150 ml soy milk
2 tbsp cornflour
250 g wholegrain einkorn flour
100 g maize flour
100 g broad beans, cooked and peeled

Whisk together the silken tofu and the olive oil in a mixing bowl. Add the salt, baking powder, malted yeast, garlic powder, rocket and lemon juice. Whisk in the soy milk a little at a time. Gradually add the cornflour and the other flours. Gently fold in the broad beans. Oil or line the muffin tin with paper cases and fill each hole three quarters of the way up. Bake at 180°C (Gas mark 4) for 25 minutes.

- -

Jerusalem artichoke winter cake

Serves 6-8

200 g Jerusalem artichokes, peeled and cut into small dice
1 tbsp olive oil
50 ml water
6 tbsp olive oil
1 tsp dried wild garlic
125 ml non-dairy milk
3 tsp baking powder
250 g einkorn flour
oil or margarine for the cake tin
salt and pepper

Sauté the Jerusalem artichokes over high heat with the olive oil. Season with salt and pepper. Add the water and turn the heat down to medium. When the Jerusalem artichokes are tender, remove them from the heat and set aside. Combine the olive oil with the dried wild garlic and non-dairy milk in a mixing bowl. Add the baking powder, 1 tsp of salt and some pepper. Mix in the flour. Add the Jerusalem artichokes to the mixture. Oil or line a 22 cm/9 inch cake tin with parchment paper and pour in the batter. Bake for 30 minutes at 180°C (Gas mark 4).

- -

Fruit and nut cake

Serves 6-8

100 g light brown sugar
4 tbsp neutral vegetable oil
2 tbsp cashew butter
3 tsp baking powder
½ tsp ground vanilla
½ tsp salt
200 ml soy cream
100 ml non-dairy milk
300 g type T55 flour
30 g walnuts, chopped
2 dried figs, chopped
30 g raisins

Mix the sugar with the oil and cashew butter in a bowl. Add the baking powder, vanilla, salt, soy cream and non-dairy milk. Whisk everything together well. Add the flour a little at a time. Add the walnuts and the dried fruit to the mixture. Line a 22 cm/9 inch cake tin, pour in the batter and bake for 40 minutes at 180°C (Gas mark 4).

SAUCES

Vegenaise de luxe

Serves 4

100 g raw cashew nuts
120 g silken tofu
5 tbsp mustard
1 tbsp apple cider vinegar
75 g sunflower oil

Soak the cashew nuts in a bowl of water for 2-4 hours. Drain. Whiz the cashew nuts with the silken tofu, mustard and vinegar. Add the oil little by little as you blend. Refrigerate for 1 hour before eating. Keep refrigerated in an airtight container and use within 3 days.

- -

Quick lemon vegenaise

Makes 1 small bowl

3 tbsp Dijon mustard
100 ml soy cream
50 ml sunflower oil (or olive oil)
1 tsp lemon juice
salt

Whisk (or use a fork) the mustard and the soy cream together in a large bowl. Whisk in the oil a little at a time. Add the lemon juice and season with salt to taste. Freeze for 10 minutes, then store in the fridge in an airtight container. Keeps for several days in the fridge.

Tip: Make a more rustic version by using wholegrain mustard, or a chic version adding some finely chopped tarragon leaves.

Tartare sauce

Serves 4

120 g silken tofu
3 tbsp Dijon mustard
4 tbsp olive oil
2 tbsp thick lacto-fermented soy cream
1½ tbsp capers, finely chopped
3 tbsp gherkins, finely chopped
2 tbsp chopped fresh chives
2 tbsp chopped parsley
1 tbsp chopped chervil
1 tbsp chopped tarragon
a few drops chilli sauce
salt and pepper

Whiz the tofu and mustard in a blender. Add the oil and blend again. Transfer to a bowl. Add the thick cream, then the capers, gherkins and herbs. Season with chilli sauce, salt and freshly ground pepper to taste.

- -

Light olive oil béchamel

Serves 4

400 ml boiling water
½ vegetable stock cube
100 ml olive oil
80 g flour
100 ml non-dairy milk
salt, pepper and nutmeg

Make a stock with the water and the ½ vegetable stock cube. Set aside. Heat the olive oil in a saucepan over medium heat and then add the flour. Stir continuously for a few minutes to make a roux. Gradually add the stock, stirring vigorously, until thick and creamy. Add the non-dairy milk and season to taste. Remove from the heat and use at once.

Coconut raita

Serves 2

¼ cucumber, washed and finely sliced with a knife
5 tbsp soy yoghurt
3 tbsp coconut milk
8-10 large mint leaves, finely sliced
½ garlic clove, crushed to a paste
¼ tsp ground cumin
salt and pepper

Combine the cucumber with the soy yoghurt and coconut milk. Add the mint leaves, garlic and cumin. Season with salt and pepper to taste. Refrigerate.

Can be used as a dip, served with a rice dish or as a side dish for an Indian meal.

Cocktail sauce

Serves 4

150 ml vegenaise de luxe (see p. 163)
6 tbsp ketchup
2 tsp bourbon
1 tsp soy sauce
chilli sauce

Whisk the vegenaise and ketchup together in a mixing bowl. Add the bourbon and soy sauce and mix well. Add a few drops of chilli sauce to taste to give it some zing.

Mustard sauce

Serves 2-4

1 tbsp margarine
2 tbsp cornflour
400 ml soy milk
1 tbsp shiro miso
2-4 tbsp Dijon mustard
1 tbsp cashew butter
salt and pepper

Melt the margarine In a saucepan over medium heat. Add the cornflour to make a roux. Whisk in the soy milk a little at a time and mix vigorously until smooth and creamy. Add the miso, mustard and cashew butter. Season with salt and pepper to taste. Serve immediately.

Lemony chive cream

Makes 1 bowl

1 x 100 g pot soy yoghurt
120 g silken tofu
2 tbsp soy cream
2 tbsp freshly squeezed lemon juice
1 tsp olive oil
½ tsp salt
3 tbsp chopped fresh chives
pepper

Whiz the soy yoghurt and silken tofu in a blender and pour in a bowl. Mix in the soy cream with a fork, then the lemon juice and olive oil. Add the chives and season with salt and pepper to taste. Refrigerate and eat within 24 hours.

SCRAMBLES, OMELETTES AND FLANS

Scrambled tofu piperade

Serves 2-4

2 tbsp olive oil
1 onion, cut into medium-sized pieces
1 large red pepper, cut into medium-sized pieces
1 small green pepper, cut into medium-sized pieces
2 tomatoes, cut into small pieces
2 garlic cloves, finely sliced
½ fresh chilli, finely sliced
1 sprig fresh thyme
2 bay leaves
1 tbsp light brown sugar
200 g firm tofu, crumbled
100 ml soy cream
2 tsp mustard
1 pinch ground turmeric
salt and pepper

Heat the olive oil in a frying pan and sauté the onion over high heat for a few minutes to brown it. Add the peppers to the pan and turn down the heat to medium. Add pepper to taste. Cook for 10 minutes, stirring from time to time. Add the tomatoes, garlic and chilli to the pan together with the thyme, the bay leaves, sugar and salt. Cook for 25 minutes over low heat. Mix the crumbled tofu with the soy cream, mustard and turmeric. Season to taste. Remove the thyme and bay leaves from the pan and turn the heat up to high. Add the tofu, stir well and cook for 5 minutes, stirring from time to time. Adjust the seasoning if necessary.

Carrot, thyme and orange flans

Serves 4

300 g carrots, peeled and cut into rounds
120 g silken tofu
100 ml freshly squeezed orange juice
1 tsp agar-agar powder
100 ml water
1½ tsp thyme leaves
¼ tsp garlic powder
salt and pepper

Cook the carrots in boiling water. Whiz them in a blender with the silken tofu and orange juice. Mix the agar-agar and the water in a small saucepan. Bring to the boil and cook for 2 minutes. Add to the tofu and and carrot mixture. Add the thyme and garlic powder and season to taste. Divide the mixture among 4 ramekins. Leave to cool then refrigerate for 1-2 hours before serving.

Scrambled tofu à la forestière

Serves 1

125 g firm tofu, crumbled
100 g silken tofu
1 tbsp non-dairy cream
1 tsp tahini
½ tsp mustard
1 pinch ground turmeric
½ onion, finely sliced
1 small garlic clove, finely sliced
50 g mushrooms, clean the mushrooms and cut into small dice
2 tsp olive oil
1 tsp tamari
salt and pepper

Mix the firm tofu with the silken tofu, soy cream, tahini, mustard and turmeric. Season and set aside. Heat the olive oil in a frying pan and brown the vegetables over high heat, stirring often. When tender and browned, add the tamari and the tofu mixture. Lower the heat a little and cook for 5 minutes, stirring constantly so that the scrambled tofu does not catch on the bottom of the pan. Serve immediately.

This dish goes perfectly with roast potatoes, green beans, or toasted bread. For a brunch, calculate 1 serving for 2 people.

Scrambled tofu with green aspara

Scrambled tofu with green asparagus

Serves 2

200 g firm tofu, crumbled
6 tbsp soy cream
1 pinch ground turmeric
1 tsp dried wild garlic
1 tsp hazelnut oil
10 g hazelnuts, chopped with a knife
150 g green asparagus, washed , hard parts removed
olive oil
balsamic vinegar glaze
salt and pepper

Put the crumbled tofu in a bowl and mix with the soy cream, turmeric, wild garlic and the hazelnut oil. Season to taste. Sauté the whole asparagus in a frying pan with a little olive oil then set aside over a very low heat. Heat a little olive oil in another frying pan and cook the scrambled tofu for a few minutes, stirring continuously. Serve the asparagus and the tofu next to each other on each plate. Drizzle with a little balsamic vinegar glaze, grind a little black pepper over the dish and sprinkle with the chopped hazelnuts.

Little grilled pepper flans

Serves 4

1 large red pepper, sliced
3 tsp olive oil
250 g silken tofu
200 ml oat cream
1 tsp agar-agar powder
½ tsp garlic powder
3 tsp shoyu

Heat 2 tsp of the olive oil in a frying pan and sauté the pepper over high heat. Use an immersion blender and whiz the silken tofu with the oat milk, agar-agar and the remaining 1 tsp of olive oil in a small saucepan. Add the garlic and shoyu and bring to the boil, whisking for 2 minutes. Remove from the heat, combine with the sliced pepper and divide among 4 ramekins. Leave to cool then refrigerate for 2 hours.

Tortilla (Spanish omelette)

Serves 4

600 g potatoes, peeled
2 onions, finely sliced
2 tbsp olive oil, plus a little extra for cooking
330 g silken tofu
150 g firm tofu
3 tbsp oat milk
3 tbsp cornflour
2 tbsp cashew butter
1 tsp tahini
1 tsp shoyu
¼ tsp ground turmeric
salt and pepper

Cut the potatoes into rounds (and into semi-circles if the potatoes are big) about ½ cm thick. Heat the 2 tbsp of olive oil in a medium-sized frying pan and sauté the potatoes over high heat, stirring often, for 5 minutes. Add the onions and cook for a few minutes longer, stirring, until the vegetables begin to brown. Put into a bowl and season with salt and pepper to taste. Set aside. Set the pan aside. Whiz the ingredients for the batter in a blender. Season with a little salt and pepper, and pour over the potato and onion mixture. Mix everything together gently. Oil the frying pan with a little olive oil and pour in the tortilla mixture. Cook for 10 minutes over medium heat. Have a circular plate at least as wide in diameter as the frying pan ready to turn the tortilla. Place the plate over the pan and turn as if unmoulding a cake (use oven gloves or pot holders). Remove the frying pan and then slide the tortilla from the plate back into the pan cooked side up. Cook the tortilla for a further 10 minutes over medium heat. Serve warm or cold.

Tomato, onion and chive frittata

Serves 4

2 onions, sliced

2 tomatoes, cut into thin wedges

1 garlic clove, finely sliced

1 small bunch chives, chopped

1 tbsp olive oil, plus extra for cooking

salt and pepper

Frittata batter

300 g silken tofu

100 g firm tofu

100 ml soy cream

30 g lupin flour

2 tbsp cornflour

1 tbsp olive oil

1 tbsp tahini

1 tbsp malted yeast

2 tsp mustard

salt and pepper

Whiz all the ingredients for the batter in a blender until you have a smooth mixture. Set aside in a bowl. Heat the olive oil in a frying pan and sauté the onions for a few minutes until lightly browned. Add the garlic and tomatoes and cook for 5 minutes over high heat. Season with salt and pepper to taste. Add to the frittata batter together with the chives and mix well. Oil the frying pan with a little olive oil and pour in the mixture. Cook for 30 minutes over low-medium heat (ensure the heat is not too high or the frittata will burn), then place the frying pan under the grill for 10-15 minutes (cover the handle with silver foil to protect it).

Tip: *This Italian frittata -- cut into slices -- goes perfectly with a green salad. The onions and tomatoes can be replaced with other vegetables.*

Fresh herb omelette

Serves 2

240 g silken tofu

150 ml soy cream

40 g chickpea flour

2 tbsp tahini

1 tbsp malted yeast

½ tsp salt

¼ tsp garlic powder

¼ tsp ground turmeric

2 tbsp chopped fresh chives

2 tbsp chopped parsley

2 tbsp chopped basil

pepper

vegetable oil for cooking

Whiz all the ingredients except the herbs in a blender. When the batter is smooth, mix in the herbs with a spoon. You can make one medium-sized omelette for 2 people, or 2 small individual ones. The method is the same: Oil 1 medium-sized or 2 small frying pans and pour in the mixture. Cook over medium heat (never over high heat as this will burn it/them) until the edges and the bottom/s is/ are golden brown. Flip over and cook for a few minutes on the other side. Serve immediately.

Variation: *When the underside of the omelette is cooked, top with a filling of pan-fried vegetables or mushrooms and fold the omelette over. Cook for 1 minute on each side and serve at once.*

mato, onion and chive frittata

COOKING
VEGETABLES

-- LIGHT TERRINES AND DIPS --

-- GOOD-MOOD SOUPS AND PURÉES --

-- GRATINS AND OVEN-BAKED DISHES --

-- SALADS WITH ZING --

-- PIZZAS, TARTS AND VEGETABLE GALETTES --

-- GOURMET VEGETABLES --

-- RAW DISHES --

-- VEGETABLE DISHES FOR CHILDREN --

-- FRUIT IS ALSO WELCOME --

Light summer terrine

Serves 4

1 large courgette, peeled and diced
1 tomato, peeled and diced
½ onion, peeled and diced
1 garlic clove, finely sliced
2 tbsp olive oil
75 ml soy cream
2 tsp tahini
2 tsp white miso
1 tsp agar-agar powder
1 tsp chopped basil
1 tsp chopped fresh mint
salt and pepper

Heat the olive oil in a saucepan and sauté the vegetables over high heat for a few minutes. Lower the heat to medium and cook for 5 minutes, stirring from time to time. Add the soy cream, tahini and miso. Mix well. When the courgette is tender, whiz with an immersion blender. Season with salt and pepper. Stir in the agar-agar and the herbs and turn the heat up. Cook for 1 minute at a gentle boil, stirring continuously. Remove from the heat and pour into a jar, mini-casserole dishes or a metal ring mould on a plate. Leave to set in the fridge for 2 hours.

Aubergine and miso terrine

Serves 4

2 medium aubergines, diced
3 tbsp olive oil
125 g firm tofu, crumbled
300 ml soy milk
1½ tsp agar-agar
5 tbsp white miso
1 tsp tahini
1 tbsp freshly squeezed lemon juice
1 tbsp agave syrup
1 small garlic clove
pepper

Sauté the aubergines in the olive oil in a frying pan over medium heat for 15-20 minutes until very tender. Leave to cool. Combine the aubergines with the tofu. Mix the soy milk and the agar-agar in a small saucepan. Bring to the boil and cook for 2 minutes, stirring continuously. Pour onto the aubergines. Add the remaining ingredients, whiz in a food processor and pour into a terrine dish. Leave to cool and refrigerate for 3 hours before using. Keeps for a few days in an airtight container in the fridge.

bergine and miso terrine

Butternut squash and hazelnut terrine

Serves 2-4

400 g butternut squash, peeled and cut into small dice (do
   not discard the skin)
1 tbsp olive oil
2 garlic cloves, finely sliced
150 g tamari-marinated lacto-fermented tofu
2 tbsp white miso
2 tbsp hazelnut butter
2 tbsp ground flaxseeds
salt and pepper

Sauté the butternut squash and garlic in a frying pan with the
olive oil over high heat for 5 minutes. Season with salt and
pepper. Lower the heat to medium and cook for a further
5-10 minutes. The butternut squash should be tender. Whiz
in a food processor with the remaining ingredients. Adjust
the seasoning if necessary. Press it down well into a small
terrine, a jar or bowl. Refrigerate for 2 hours.

Serve with grilled bread.

Red pepper dip

Serves 2-4

2 large red peppers, cut in half
230 g lacto-fermented soy cream
2 tbsp chopped fresh coriander
1 tbsp arrowroot
½ tsp salt
⅛ tsp red chilli paste

Put the peppers under a hot grill, skin side up, until the skin
is well charred. Peel off the skin and cut the flesh into pieces.
Whiz in a food processor with the remaining ingredients and
pour into a small saucepan. Heat to high and whisk until it
has thickened to the consistency of very thick cream. Put
into a bowl and refrigerate for 1 hour.

*Tip: This cream makes a great alternative to melted
cheese in a burger.*

Summer fruit and orange juice terrine

Serves 4-6

5 apricots, washed and cut into small pieces
4 large red plums, washed and cut into small pieces
500 ml freshly squeezed orange juice
3 g agar-agar powder
4 tbsp light brown sugar
1 pinch ground vanilla
¼ tsp ground cinnamon
½ lemon, zested and squeezed

Combine the cut-up fruit and put in a medium-sized loaf tin.
Pour the orange juice into a saucepan and add the agar-
agar, sugar and spices. Add the lemon zest and juice. Bring
to the boil and cook for 2 minutes, whisking continuously.
Pour the spiced orange juice over the fruit. Leave to cool to
room temperature then freeze for 15 minutes for the jelly
to set well. Leave in the refrigerator for a few hours. Eat
within 48 hours.

Creamed Jerusalem artichoke

Makes 1 bowl

600 g Jerusalem artichokes, peeled and diced
150 ml soy cream
1 tbsp olive oil
1 garlic clove
salt and pepper

Cook the Jerusalem artichokes in simmering water until just tender. Drain and refresh under cold running water. Whiz in a food processor with the remaining ingredients and refrigerate before serving.

Delicious for bruschette topped with grilled vegetables and fresh herbs.

Artichonade

Makes 1 bowl

400 g cooked artichoke hearts
1 garlic clove
3 tbsp olive oil
1 tbsp chopped parsley
1 tbsp chopped basil
salt and pepper

Whiz all the ingredients in a food processor and then refrigerate for 1 hour.

Serve with toasted bread or grissini. Perfect also for stuffing unheated vegetables, as a sandwich filling or to top blinis…

Beetroot and almond dip

Makes 1 bowl

4 cooked beetroot, cut into chunks
3 tbsp white almond butter
1½ tbsp freshly squeezed lemon juice
salt and pepper

Whiz all the ingredients in a food processor until smooth and creamy. Refrigerate.

Fresh tomato and cashew nut dip

Serves 2

150 g raw cashew nuts
2 tomatoes, peeled, cored and quartered
1 garlic clove
2 tbsp freshly squeezed lemon juice
1 tbsp chopped basil
1 pinch Espelette pepper
salt and pepper

Soak the cashew nuts in water for 1 hour. Whiz all the ingredients in a food processor for a few minutes until thick and creamy. Season to taste with the Espelette pepper, salt and pepper. Refrigerate before serving.

Use as a quick and delicious sauce for pasta.

Carrot and sesame terrine

Serves 2-4

200 g peeled carrots, grated
1 garlic clove, sliced
1 onion, sliced
2 tbsp olive oil
125 g firm tofu
2 tbsp tahini
2 tbsp white miso
1 tbsp freshly squeezed lemon juice
¼ tsp ground cumin
salt and pepper

Sauté the carrots, the onion and the garlic in the olive oil over medium heat in a frying pan. Whiz the vegetables in a food processor with the remaining ingredients. Press down well into a small terrine dish or oven-proof dish and bake at 240°C (Gas mark 9) for 20 minutes. Leave to cool. Keeps in the fridge for a few days.

Use as a dip with crudités, for bruschette or as a sandwich filling.

Creamy celeriac purée

Serves 2-4

4 medium potatoes, peeled and cut into large chunks

1 celeriac, peeled and cut into large chunks

5 tbsp thick lacto-fermented soy cream

2 tbsp cashew butter

salt and pepper

Simmer the potatoes and the celeriac for about 40 minutes or until tender. Press them through a potato ricer then whisk in the soy cream and cashew butter. Season and serve.

Red kuri squash and chestnut milk soup

Serves 4

500 g red kuri squash, cut into medium-sized pieces

150 g potatoes, peeled, cut into medium-sized pieces

1 large onion, cut into medium-sized pieces

2 garlic cloves, finely sliced

4 tbsp olive oil

4 bay leaves

300 ml chestnut milk

salt and pepper

Sauté the vegetables and garlic in a saucepan with the olive oil over high heat for 5-10 minutes, stirring often. Add the bay leaves and cover with water. Cook over medium heat for 45 minutes to 1 hour. Remove the bay leaves, pour in the chestnut milk and whiz in a food processor. Season to taste.

Try this soup sprinkled with plain, cooked chestnut pieces just before serving.

Carrot and coconut milk purée

Serves 2

500 g peeled carrots, cut into rounds

90 ml coconut milk

salt and pepper

Simmer the carrots until just tender. Whiz in a food processor with the coconut milk and season to taste.

Miso and coconut vegetable soup

Serves 6

1 tbsp coconut oil

1 green pepper, sliced

1 shallot, sliced

1 garlic clove, sliced

½ leek, sliced

1 tsp finely chopped ginger

2 tsp chopped fresh coriander

2 litres water

5 tbsp white miso

Melt the coconut oil in a large saucepan over high heat and sauté the vegetables and ginger for 2 minutes. Add the fresh coriander and the water and bring to the boil. Put a little of the stock in a bowl and slake the miso. Pour back into the saucepan, turn down the heat to low and cook for 10 minutes.

A great dish as a light first course, and with tofu, noodles or ravioli it makes a delicious meal in itself.

Thai stock with winter vegetab

Thyme-scented parsnip velouté

Serves 4

4 medium parsnips, peeled and roughly chopped
2 small potatoes, peeled and roughly chopped
1 onion, peeled and roughly chopped
2 garlic cloves, peeled and roughly chopped
3 tbsp olive oil
1 tsp dried thyme
salt and pepper

Sauté the vegetables in a large saucepan with the olive oil and thyme for a few minutes. Season and cover with water. Cook for 30 minutes over medium heat then add another 300 ml of water and whiz in a blender. Adjust the seasoning and set aside.

Suggestion: For a more elegant soup, sprinkle with fresh thyme flowers and add homemade croutons by toasting walnut bread in the oven with olive oil, garlic and parsley.

Courgette, petits pois and mint velouté

Serves 2-4

2 tbsp olive oil
1 onion, sliced
1 large potato, peeled and diced
2 courgettes, cut into large dice
150 g fresh or frozen petits pois
1 vegetable stock cube
250 ml rice milk, plus 50 ml extra
1 bunch fresh mint
salt and pepper

Heat the olive oil in a large saucepan over high heat. Sauté the onion, potato and courgettes. Add the petit pois, the stock cube and the 250 ml of rice milk. Cook for 30 minutes. Remove from the heat. Add the 50 ml of rice milk and the mint. Season to taste. Whiz in a blender and serve.

Creamy curried broccoli soup

Serves 2-4

1 broccoli, cut into florets and the stem into dice
1 onion, sliced
1 garlic clove, sliced
1 tbsp olive oil
1½ tsp curry powder
250 ml spelt milk
2 tbsp tahini
salt and pepper

Heat the olive oil in a medium-sized saucepan and add the curry powder, the onion and garlic. Sauté for 1-2 minutes then add the broccoli. Stir for a few minutes and cover with hot water. Bring to the boil and cook for 5 minutes. Pour in the spelt milk then whiz everything in a blender until very smooth. Add the tahini and whiz again. Season to taste and serve.

Thai stock with winter vegetables

Serves 4

2 tbsp coconut oil
125 g butternut squash, diced
1 onion, finely sliced
1 carrot, finely sliced
½ leek, finely sliced
2 tsp chopped fresh ginger
2 tbsp Thai red curry paste
2 tbsp peanut butter
2 tbsp tamari
1 litre water
2 tbsp chopped fresh coriander

Heat the coconut oil in a saucepan and sauté the vegetables over medium heat for 5 minutes. Add the ginger, curry paste and peanut butter and mix well. Cook for 2-3 minutes. Add the tamari and the water and cook for 10 minutes over high heat. Add the fresh coriander and serve.

Tip: For a complete meal, add some diced tofu and previously cooked rice noodles a few minutes before the soup has finished cooking.

Cream of sweetcorn soup

Serves 4

3 sweetcorn cobs, silk removed
3 garlic cloves, sliced
1 large onion, sliced
1 tbsp olive oil
1 vegetable stock cube
1 litre water
2 tbsp cashew butter
salt and pepper

Cut the corn kernels off the cob with a knife. Sauté the sweetcorn, garlic and onion with the olive oil in a large saucepan over high heat for 2-3 minutes. Add the stock cube and cover with water. Cook for 25-30 minutes. Whiz in a blender with the cashew butter. Season to taste and sieve to remove any remaining sweetcorn skins. Serve immediately.

For a little more zing, add some freshly squeezed lime juice, a few fresh coriander leaves and a little finely chopped green chilli.

Cream of grilled tomato soup

Serves 4

10 tomatoes, cut into quarters
5 tbsp olive oil
1 onion, sliced
2 garlic cloves, sliced
1 tbsp cane sugar
200 ml soy cream
1-2 sprigs fresh thyme
salt and pepper

Arrange the pieces of tomato on a baking tray, skin side down. Drizzle with 3 tbsp of the olive oil and season with salt and pepper. Place under a hot grill for about 25 minutes or until the edges of the tomatoes are nicely browned. Remove from the grill and set aside. Brown the onion and garlic in a saucepan with the remaining 2 tbsp of the olive oil over high heat. Add the grilled tomatoes and any juice they have released, the sugar, soy cream and thyme. Season with salt and pepper. Cook for 2 minutes then whiz in a blender.

***Tip:** If your blender is not powerful enough to break up the sprigs of thyme and the tomato skins, sieve the soup after blending to remove them.*

Potato and olive oil purée, pan-fried beetroot and unpeeled garlic

Serves 4

1 kg potatoes, peeled and cut into cubes
2 small beetroot, well scrubbed and sliced
4 tbsp olive oil
10 garlic cloves, skin on
150 ml soy milk (or other non-dairy milk), warmed
2 sprigs fresh thyme
salt and pepper

Steam the potatoes until tender. Heat 2 tbsp of the olive oil in a frying pan and fry the beetroot and garlic for a few minutes over high heat before turning them over and frying them on the other side for a few minutes. Press the potatoes through a potato ricer and then mix with the remaining 2 tbsp of olive oil and the warm soy milk. Season with salt. Put the purée on a serving plate, top with the pan-fried beetroot and garlic. Sprinkle with thyme and a little pepper. Serve immediately.

...tato and olive oil purée, pan-fried beetroot and unpeeled garlic

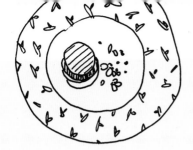

Asparagus clafoutis

Serves 4

250 ml mild-tasting non-dairy milk (soy, oat, etc.)
200 g silken tofu
2 tbsp cashew butter
½ tsp agar-agar
2 tsp cornflour
½ tsp salt
1 bunch asparagus, washed, hard parts removed

Whiz all the ingredients except for the asparagus in a food processor. Cut off the tips of the asparagus and cut the stalks into fine slices lengthwise. Set the tips aside. Combine the slices of asparagus with the clafoutis batter. Pour into an oiled, oven-proof dish and arrange the tips on top. Bake for 30 minutes at 180°C (Gas mark 4). Serve warm or cold.

For a chic first course, put some sprouted seeds on a plate and dress with a drizzle of olive oil and a pinch of fleur de sel. Arrange a slice of clafoutis on top and drizzle with a little balsamic vinegar glaze just before serving.

Tian à la Provençale

Serves 4-6

3 large tomatoes, washed and sliced
2 small aubergines, washed and sliced into rounds
2 medium courgettes, washed and cut into rounds
2 large potatoes, peeled and cut into rounds
5 garlic cloves, finely sliced
2 sprigs fresh thyme
1 tbsp herbs de Provence
4 tbsp olive oil
salt and pepper

Cut the aubergine slices in half. Arrange the vegetables in alternate layers in a large oven-proof dish. Stand some of the vegetables up so that they are well-packed together. (Make sure you choose a dish that is deep enough for this!). Slide the slices of garlic between the vegetables. Add the herbs de Provence, salt and pepper. Drizzle with olive oil. Bake for 1 hour at 150°C (Gas mark 2). The vegetables should be nicely browned on top and tender.

Tomato and parsley crumble

Serves 2-4

5 tomatoes, cut in half, cores removed
1 red onion, finely sliced
1 garlic clove, finely sliced
2 tbsp olive oil
salt and pepper

For the crumble

90 g flour
25 g ground almonds
10 g finely chopped parsley
2 garlic cloves, chopped
3 tbsp olive oil
salt and pepper

Cut each tomato half into 4 pieces. Heat the olive oil in a frying pan over high heat and sauté the vegetables. Season with salt and pepper and cook for a few minutes, stirring often. Place on a large serving dish or 2 individual plates. Prepare the crumble: Put all the crumble ingredients in a deep plate and mix well with your fingertips. Season with salt and pepper. Mix again and sprinkle over the tomatoes. Bake for 15-20 minutes at 200°C (Gas mark 6).

Leek and cream mini-casseroles

Serves 4

6 medium leeks, sliced
2 small onions, sliced
1 garlic clove, sliced
1 tbsp olive oil
100 g smoked tofu, cut into small dice
150 ml soy cream, plus 75 ml extra
1 tbsp cashew butter
1 tbsp malted yeast
breadcrumbs
salt and pepper

Sauté the vegetables in a large frying pan over medium heat in the olive oil for 10 minutes. Add the tofu, the 150 ml of soy cream and the cashew butter. Mix well and cook for 5-10 minutes over low heat. Divide the mixture among 4 mini-casseroles or mini-cocottes. Mix the 75 ml of soy cream with the malted yeast in a bowl. Season to taste and pour over the vegetable mixture. Sprinkle with breadcrumbs. Bake for 10 minutes at 240°C (Gas mark 9).

Jerusalem artichoke gratin

Serves 4

600 g Jerusalem artichokes, finely sliced and rinsed
2 garlic cloves, crushed to a paste
2 tbsp cornflour
2 tbsp white miso
2 tbsp cashew butter
1 tbsp malted yeast
500 ml non-dairy milk
ground nutmeg
oil or margarine for the dish
salt and pepper

Put the garlic, cornflour, miso, cashew butter, malted yeast and a little of the non-dairy milk in a bowl. Whisk everything together and add the remaining milk a little at a time. Season with salt, pepper and nutmeg to taste. Oil an oven-proof dish and arrange the Jerusalem artichoke slices in it. Pour the mixture over and bake for 1 hour and 15 minutes to 1 hour and 30 minutes at 180°C (Gas mark 4).

Hasselback sweet potatoes

Serves 1

2-3 small sweet potatoes, peeled and washed
olive oil
margarine
salt and pepper

Finely slice all along the sweet potatoes but do not cut all the way through. Place in an oven-proof dish and drizzle generously with olive oil. Season with salt and pepper and dot each potato with a few small pieces of margarine. Bake for about 45 minutes at 200°C (Gas mark 6).

Texan-style stuffed peppers

Serves 4

½ onion, sliced
2 garlic cloves, sliced
2 tbsp olive oil
125 g cooked red beans
150 g sweetcorn
1 tsp ground cumin
1 tsp chipotle sauce (or more to taste)
125 g long grain rice
1 tomato, finely diced
2 large red peppers, cut in half and seeded (leave the stem on)
2 tbsp malted yeast
2 tbsp fine breadcrumbs
soy cream
2 tbsp chopped fresh coriander
salt and pepper

Sauté the onions and garlic in the olive oil in a frying pan over high heat. Add the beans and sweetcorn, then the cumin and chilli sauce. Cook for 5 minutes. Season with salt and pepper. Add the rice, mix well and remove from the heat. Add the tomato. Stuff the peppers with the mixture. Sprinkle with the malted yeast and the breadcrumbs. Drizzle with the soy cream and season with salt and pepper. Bake at 180°C (Gas mark 4) for about 45 minutes. Sprinkle with the fresh coriander before serving.

sselback sweet potatoes

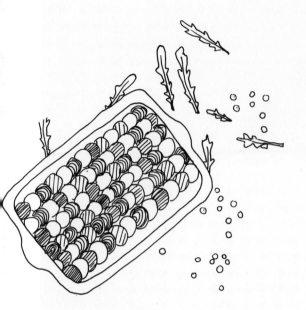

Spaghetti squash au gratin

Serves 2-4

1 spaghetti squash, cut in half lengthwise, seeds removed
150 ml non-dairy cream
4 tsp ground Antilles curry mix
1 tbsp malted yeast, plus 2 tbsp extra
2 tbsp breadcrumbs
1 tsp salt
1 tbsp olive oil
pepper

Cook the squash for 45 minutes in the oven at 220°C (Gas mark 7). Combine the cream with the spices and 1 tbsp of the malted yeast. Scrape the flesh of the squash with a fork to detach it and divide the cream between the two squash halves. Mix the flesh and the cream. Sprinkle with the malted yeast and the breadcrumbs and drizzle with olive oil. Bake for 10 minutes at 200°C (Gas mark 6). Cut each half squash in half and serve.

- -

Sweet potato and lentil Parmentier

Serves 4

200 g green lentils
1 ½ kg sweet potatoes, peeled and cut into chunks
2 tbsp olive oil
2 shallots, sliced
2 garlic cloves, sliced
1 tbsp chopped fresh chives
2 tbsp chopped parsley
1 tbsp tamari
100 ml soy cream
2 tbsp malted yeast
salt and pepper

Cook the lentils in a saucepan with a generous amount of water for 20 minutes. Drain. Cook the sweet potatoes in a saucepan with a generous amount of water. Drain. Heat the olive oil in a frying pan and sauté the shallots and garlic. Add the lentils, herbs and tamari. Cook for 5-10 minutes. Put in the bottom of an oven-proof dish. Press the sweet potatoes through a potato ricer and season to taste. Spread this purée over the lentils and press down well. Spread the cream on top and sprinkle with the malted yeast. Bake for 15 minutes at 180°C (Gas mark 4), then leave under the grill for a few minutes to brown the top.

Butternut pumpkin and chestnut gratin

Serves 4

750 g butternut squash, finely diced
1 onion, finely sliced
2 garlic cloves, finely sliced
400 g fresh chestnuts, roughly chopped
2 tbsp olive oil
300 ml non-dairy cream
ground nutmeg
malted yeast
salt and pepper

Sauté the squash, onion, garlic and chestnuts in the olive oil for a few minutes over high heat. Then, lower the heat to medium and cook until the vegetables are done and lightly browned. Arrange them in an oven-proof dish. In a bowl, season the cream with salt and pepper and add nutmeg to taste. Pour this mixture over the vegetables. Sprinkle with malted yeast and bake for 20 minutes at 180°C (Gas mark 4). The top should be golden brown. Leave under the grill for a few minutes if necessary.

Sweet potato and lentil Parmentier

Thai mango sal

Greek salad

Serves 4

4 tomatoes, cut into large dice
1 green pepper, cut into large dice
½ cucumber, cut into large dice
1 small onion, finely sliced
100 g tamari-marinated lacto-fermented tofu, cut into
  small dice
100 g black olives
3 tbsp olive oil
2 tbsp chopped parsley
1 tbsp capers
1 tsp dried oregano
salt and pepper

Mix all the ingredients together in a large bowl. Season to taste. Refrigerate before serving.

Red cabbage coleslaw

Serves 4-6

½ red cabbage, finely sliced
2 carrots, peeled and grated
1 apple, cut into fine matchsticks
200 g silken tofu
2 tbsp Dijon mustard
3 tbsp olive oil
5 tbsp soy yoghurt
1½ tbsp apple cider vinegar
1 tbsp chopped dill
¾ tsp salt
pepper

Whiz the silken tofu and mustard in a food processor. While you whiz, add the olive oil a little at a time to make a liquid mayonnaise. Add the yoghurt and then the vinegar. Transfer to a bowl and add the chopped dill. Season to taste. Mix the sauce with the raw ingredients and refrigerate.

Thai mango salad

Serves 4

600 g cooked rice noodles
1 red pepper, julienned
1 large carrot, julienned
1 ripe avocado, diced
1 ripe mango, diced
4 tbsp peanut butter
2 limes, juiced
3 tsp tamari
50 ml water
1 tsp lemongrass, very finely sliced
1 tbsp toasted sesame oil
fresh coriander leaves

Keep the cooked noodles in a sieve, submerged in iced water. Use a fork to mix the peanut butter with the lime juice, the tamari and the water in a bowl. Add the lemongrass and the sesame oil. Drain the noodles and combine with the vegetables and the mango in a bowl or on a plate. Serve with the sauce and fresh coriander leaves.

For a very surprising salad, use black rice noodles.

Strawberry and green tomato carpaccio

Serves 4

100 ml balsamic vinegar
4 large green tomatoes
200 g strawberries
4 tbsp olive oil
4 tbsp chopped pistachios
fleur de sel, pepper

Prepare the balsamic reduction: Pour the balsamic vinegar into a small saucepan. Turn the heat to high and stir from time to time until the vinegar becomes thick and coats the back of a spoon. It will still be somewhat liquid, but this is normal. Pour into a small bowl and refrigerate for 10 minutes. Use a well-sharpened knife or a mandolin to very finely slice the tomatoes. Arrange the slices on 4 small plates. Slice the strawberries in the same way and arrange them on the plate as well. Drizzle a little olive oil over each plate. Sprinkle with a pinch of fleur de sel, add pepper to taste, pour a generous drizzle of balsamic reduction over everything and sprinkle with the pistachios.

Dress the dish just before serving and eat at once.

Orange and ginger vinaigrette

Serves 1

2 tbsp freshly squeezed orange juice
1 tbsp sesame oil
1 tsp tamari
1 tsp apple cider vinegar
½ tsp fresh ginger, crushed to a paste

Combine all the ingredients in a vinaigrette shaker or a jar and use.

Fresh herb and lemon salad dressing

Serves 2

1 small pot soy yoghurt
3 tbsp freshly squeezed lemon juice
1 tbsp olive oil
½ tsp each salt and pepper
1 tsp chopped fresh coriander
1 tsp chopped basil
1 tsp chopped curly parsley
1 tsp chopped fresh chives

In a bowl, mix the yoghurt and the lemon juice with a fork. Drizzle in the olive oil a little at a time as you mix, season to taste and add the herbs.

Watermelon panzanella

Serves 2-4

200 g watermelon, rind removed, cut into large dice, seeds removed
2 tomatoes, cut into pieces
1 green pepper, cut into medium-sized pieces
olive oil
¼ country-style baguette, cut into large dice
2 tbsp chopped basil
balsamic vinegar glaze or freshly squeezed lemon juice
salt and pepper

Combine the watermelon and the tomatoes in a bowl. Sauté the pepper in a frying pan with 1 tsp of olive oil for a few minutes. Leave to cool, then add to the bowl. Set aside in the refrigerator. Heat 1 tbsp of olive oil in the frying pan over high heat and brown the bread all over. Season with salt and pepper. Leave to cool. When about to serve, add the basil, drizzle with a little olive oil, add the croutons, season to taste and mix well. Each person can add some balsamic glaze or lemon juice as they wish.

Tamari-caramelised almonds

Serves 4

2 handfuls almonds, roughly chopped
2 tbsp tamari
1 tbsp agave syrup
pepper

Combine the tamari and agave syrup in a frying pan. Add pepper to taste and turn the heat to high. When the sauce is hot add the almonds. Cook for a few minutes, stirring, and remove from the heat when the almonds are nicely caramelised and begin to stick to the pan. Line a plate with parchment paper and spread the almonds on it to cool.

These little delights will give a gourmet touch to any salad!

Hazelnut and shoyu vinaigrette

Serves 2

2 tbsp hazelnut oil
2 tbsp apple cider vinegar
1 tbsp shoyu
salt and pepper

Combine all the ingredients in a vinaigrette shaker or a jar. Correct the seasoning if necessary and serve.

Middle Eastern carrot salad

Serves 2-4

300 g peeled carrots, grated
75 ml freshly squeezed orange juice
250 ml olive oil
½ tsp ground cumin
½ tsp salt
5 dates, pitted and cut into little pieces
1 tbsp fresh coriander leaves
pepper

Combine the grated carrots with the orange juice and olive oil. Add the cumin, dates, and salt and pepper to taste. Leave in the fridge for 1 hour before serving. Sprinkle with the coriander leaves at the last moment.

Roast potato, grilled courgette, Kalamata olive and fresh herb salad

Serves 4

1 kg baby potatoes, washed and cut into medium-sized pieces
3 tbsp olive oil, plus extra for dressing
1 tbsp ground coriander
1 tsp cumin seeds
1 courgette, cut into half-moon slices
200 g Kalamata olives
2 tbsp chopped parsley
2 tbsp chopped fresh coriander
salt and pepper

Brown the potatoes in a frying pan with 2 tbsp of the olive oil and the spices over medium heat for 30-40 minutes. They should be cooked through and well browned. Sauté the courgette slices in a frying pan with 1 tbsp of the olive oil and add salt and pepper to taste. Combine the warm potatoes with the courgette, Kalamata olives, parsley and fresh coriander in a bowl. Season and add a little more olive oil if necessary.

Serve with lemon wedges to squeeze at the table.

Courgette ribbons with mint and lemon pesto

Serves 4

15 g mint leaves
75 ml olive oil
1 lemon, zested
50 g cashew nuts
3 tbsp freshly squeezed lemon juice
2 medium courgettes, washed

Prepare the pesto: Whiz the mint leaves with the olive oil and lemon zest. Add the cashew nuts and whiz well. Add the lemon juice to make the pesto very creamy. Set aside. Cut the courgettes into ribbons with a potato peeler and arrange on a plate. Serve at once with the pesto.

Suggestion: *Great as a first course or as a nice, fresh side dish. Refrigerate the courgettes before cutting them into ribbons for a very cool dish.*

Pizza dough

Makes 2 pizzas for 4 people

600 g plain flour
400 ml warm water
2 tsp salt
1½ sachets dried baker's yeast (approx 14 g)
1 tsp light brown sugar
3 tbsp olive oil

Put the flour in a large mixing bowl. Mix the warm water with the salt, the yeast and the sugar in a bowl. Leave to stand for 10 minutes for the yeast to activate. Mix with the flour and knead for 5 minutes. Add the olive oil and knead for a further 5 minutes. Shape into a large ball and leave to rest in a bowl, covered with a damp tea towel at 20°-25°C for 1-2 hours. Flour the work surface and a rolling pin. Divide the dough into two halves and shape into 2 balls. Roll them out to make the 2 pizza bases.

Pizza dough freezes well. Shape it into a ball and freeze in an airtight freezer bag. Thaw at room temperature.

Calzone stuffed with tapenade

Serves 2

1 quantity pizza dough (see previous recipe)
175 g black olives, pitted
2 garlic cloves
2 tbsp olive oil, plus a little extra
4 tbsp tomato passata
dried oregano
salt and pepper

Roll out the pizza dough and place it on a baking tray lined with parchment paper. Run the olives under water to get rid of any excess brine and drain them. Whiz the olives with the garlic and olive oil in a food processor and season to taste. Spread the tapenade over half of the pizza dough and not quite to the edge. Dampen the edges and fold the dough over itself. Pinch the edges together well. Brush the passata over the top of the calzone, sprinkle with a little oregano, salt and pepper, and drizzle with a little olive oil. Bake at 180°C (Gas mark 4) for 20 minutes.

Chic asparagus and artichoke pizza

Serves 4

5 artichoke hearts, finely sliced
130 g green asparagus, washed and finely sliced
1 garlic clove, finely sliced
olive oil
1 quantity pizza dough (see previous recipe)
150 ml tomato passata
1 tbsp capers
2 tbsp chopped basil
100 g gratable cheese (see p. 135), grated
salt and pepper

Sauté the artichokes, asparagus and garlic in a frying pan with a little olive oil, salt and pepper. Roll out the pizza dough and place it on a baking tray. Spread the tomato passata over it with a spatula or a spoon. Arrange the sautéed vegetables on top. Sprinkle with the capers, basil and grated vegan cheese. Drizzle with a little olive oil and season with salt and pepper to taste. Bake for 15-20 minutes at 200°C (Gas mark 6).

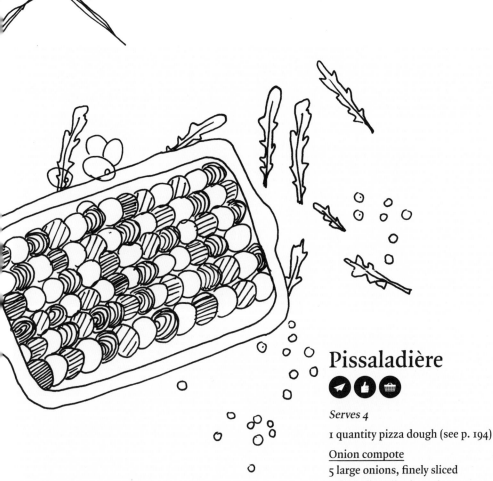

Country-style Jerusalem artichoke galette

Serves 4

1 quantity shortcrust pastry dough (see p.60 or p.244)
225 g Jerusalem artichokes, peeled and finely sliced
olive oil

For the cream

125 g silken tofu
4 tbsp non-dairy cream
3 tbsp yeast flakes
1 tbsp white miso
¼ tsp garlic powder
pepper

Mix all ingredients for the cream together with a fork In a large bowl. Roll the shortcrust dough out on parchment paper, and place it on a baking tray. Spread the cream over the dough but not quite to the edge. Arrange the Jerusalem artichoke slices evenly over the cream. Fold in the edges of the dough, drizzle with a little olive oil and bake at 180°C (Gas mark 4) for about 40 minutes.

Pissaladière

Serves 4

1 quantity pizza dough (see p. 194)

Onion compote

5 large onions, finely sliced
2 tbsp olive oil, plus 1 tbsp extra

Vegetable pissalat

125 g firm tofu
1 sheet yaki nori, crumbled
2 tsp white miso

Filling

50 g black olives
2 sun-dried tomatoes, finely sliced
salt and pepper

Sweat the onions in a saucepan in 2 tbsp of the olive oil over medium-high heat. Stir often and allow to brown nicely. When the onions are well browned, add a little water (enough to cover the bottom of the saucepan) and allow to soften to a compote for 30 minutes over medium-low heat. Season to taste. Set aside. Whiz the tofu, yaki nori, miso and the 1 tbsp of olive oil together. Roll out the pizza dough and place it on a baking tray. Spread the cream over the dough. Cover with the onion compote. Top with the olives and sun-dried tomatoes. Bake for 15-20 minutes at 200°C (Gas mark 6). Serve warm or cold.

FYI: *Pissalat is a very old, traditional Niçoise condiment made with sardines and anchovies. It is an essential ingredient for the famous pissaladière. Here it has been transformed into a delicious vegan version that will no doubt surprise your guests!*

Herb and red pepper pizza spirals

Serves 6

1 quantity pizza dough (see p. 194)
2 tbsp chopped fresh chives
2 tbsp chopped parsley
2 tbsp chopped basil

For the red pepper cream

1½ red peppers
100 ml soy cream
1 tbsp olive oil
2 tsp cornflour
1 garlic clove, finely sliced
1 tsp freshly squeezed lemon juice
½ tsp salt
1 pinch Espelette pepper

Grill (or roast in the oven) the peppers until the skin begins to char. Peel and cut them into pieces. Leave to cool and then whiz with the other ingredients for the red pepper cream in a food processor until smooth. Pour into a small saucepan. Turn the heat to high and cook, stirring continuously, until the cream thickens. Set aside. Roll the pizza dough into a rectangle. Spread the red pepper cream over it with a spoon. Sprinkle with the herbs. Roll the dough up along its length to form a long sausage. Line a baking tray with parchment paper. Cut slices of the dough about 2 cm wide and space them well apart on the baking tray. Bake for 10 minutes at 200°C (Gas mark 6). The pizza spirals should be just golden.

Green pizza

Serves 4-6

100 g Brussels sprouts, cut into quarters
50 g mange-tout, cut into quarters
1 tbsp olive oil
1 quantity pizza dough (see p. 194)
fresh coriander leaves
salt and pepper

For the pesto

60 ml olive oil
50 g pine nuts
20 g basil leaves
20 g raw cashew nuts
2 tsp freshly squeezed lemon juice
½ tsp salt

For the courgette cream

2 courgettes, diced
1 tbsp olive oil
100 ml soy cream
1 garlic clove
2 tbsp fresh coriander leaves
1 tbsp tahini
1 tsp freshly squeezed lemon juice
½ tsp salt
pepper

Whiz all the pesto ingredients together. Set aside. Sauté the courgettes in the olive oil for 5 minutes, then whiz with the other ingredients for the courgette cream. Set aside. Sauté the Brussels sprouts and mange-tout in a frying pan with the olive oil. Season with salt and pepper. Roll out the pizza dough and place on a baking tray. Spread the courgette cream over it and top with the vegetables. Bake for about 20 minutes at 200°C (Gas mark 6). Decorate with dabs of pesto and fresh coriander leaves. Serve.

Mini-pizza spirals, green pizza, and rocket cream and cherry tomato tart (see p.199)

Aubergine, ricotta and mint pesto galett

Rocket cream and cherry tomato tart

Serves 4

1 sheet organic vegan puff pastry

200 g cherry tomatoes, halved

For the rocket cream

60 g rocket leaves

6 tbsp soy cream

2 tbsp cashew butter

1 tbsp olive oil

½ tsp salt

Whiz all the ingredients for the rocket cream together. Line a tart tin with the puff pastry (do no remove the parchment paper it comes with), and pour the rocket cream over it. Arrange the cherry tomatoes over the top, cut side up. Bake for about 25 minutes at 180°C (Gas mark 4).

Creamy carrot tart

Serves 4-6

3 good-sized carrots, peeled and grated with a food processor

125 g curried tofu, crumbled

150 ml non-dairy milk

200 ml oat cream

2 tbsp arrowroot

2 tbsp cashew butter

1 tbsp tahini

1 tsp salt

1 quantity shortcrust pastry dough (see p.60 or p.244)

pepper

Combine the carrots and the tofu in a bowl. Add the non-dairy milk, cream, arrowroot, cashew butter and tahini. Season to taste. Mix well, then whiz briefly with an immersion blender. Line a tart tin with the puff pastry and bake blind for 5 minutes at 180°C (Gas mark 4). Pour the carrot cream into the pastry. Bake for 30 minutes at 180°C. Leave to cool before serving.

Aubergine, ricotta and mint pesto galettes

Makes 8 small galettes

20 mint leaves, plus extra for decorating

15 g pine nuts, plus extra for decorating

2 tbsp olive oil

½ tbsp freshly squeezed lemon juice

1 bowl soy ricotta (see p. 128)

1 small aubergine, sliced into rounds

olive oil

1 sheet organic vegan puff pastry

salt and pepper

Whiz the mint with the pine nuts, olive oil and lemon juice to make a pesto. Mix with the ricotta. Adjust the seasoning if necessary. Sauté the aubergine with a little olive oil in a frying pan for a few minutes on each side. Season with salt and pepper. Cut out discs of puff pastry with a cookie cutter or a small bowl. Arrange the discs on a baking tray. Spread some pesto ricotta over each one. Top with a slice of aubergine. Sprinkle with a few pine nuts. Bake at 180°C (Gas mark 4) for 20 minutes. Decorate with a few mint leaves.

Delicious with a salad.

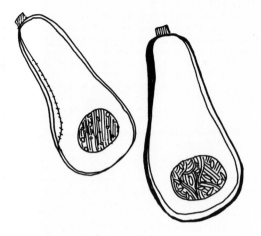

GOURMET VEGETABLES

Stuffed butternut squash

Serves 2-4

1 butternut squash, cut in half
2 tbsp tamari
1 tbsp toasted sesame oil
2 tbsp white miso
1 tsp dried sage
1 tsp garlic powder
250 ml boiling water
40 g textured soy protein
1 onion, sliced
2 garlic cloves, sliced
1 tbsp olive oil
100 ml non-dairy cream
salt and pepper

Remove some of the flesh from the squash and bake for 45 minutes in the oven at 180°C (Gas mark 4). Combine the tamari with the sesame oil, miso, sage and garlic in a large bowl. Season with pepper to taste. Add the boiling water to make a stock. Add the soy protein and leave to hydrate for 30 minutes. Sauté the onions and garlic in the olive oil in a medium-sized frying pan. Brown well. Add the soy protein and its soaking liquid. Cook for 2 minutes then pour in the cream. Correct the seasoning if necessary and fill the butternut halves with the mixture. Bake for 15 minutes at 180°C.

Citrusy pan-fried fennel with black sesame seeds

Serves 2

1 large fennel bulb, sliced
1 orange, supremed
1 tbsp olive oil
1½ tbsp tamari
1 lemon, juiced
1½ tbsp agave syrup
½ tsp black sesame seeds
pepper

Sauté the fennel over high heat with the olive oil. Season with pepper to taste. When the fennel begins to brown, add the tamari and cook for 2-3 minutes. Deglaze with the lemon juice and add the supremed orange segments, agave syrup and black sesame seeds. Cook for a few minutes longer and serve immediately.

Paprika and garlic-scented potatoes

Serves 4

1 kg potatoes, peeled and cut into even-sized pieces
7 garlic cloves, peeled and halved
50 ml olive oil
½ tsp garlic powder
2 tsp paprika
2 tsp salt
pepper

Put the potato pieces in an oven-proof dish with the halved garlic cloves. Drizzle with the olive oil, add the spices and salt. Mix well with your hands. Bake in the oven for 30-45 minutes (depending on the size of the potato pieces) at 200°C (Gas mark 6), turning the potatoes over from time to time.

ffed butternut squash

Banana peppers stuffed with non-dairy che

Banana peppers stuffed with non-dairy cheese

Serves 4

2 banana peppers, cut in half
200 g melty cheese (see p. 135), crumbled
2 tsp cumin seeds
soy cream
salt and pepper

Put the crumbled cheese into the halved peppers. Sprinkle with the cumin seeds and cover with soy cream. Season with salt and pepper and bake for 15-20 minutes at 240°C (Gas mark 9).

Aubergine stuffed with Indian-style rice

Serves 2-4

1 large aubergine or 2 small ones
2 garlic cloves, sliced
1 onion, sliced
1 tbsp vegetable oil
230 g cooked Basmati rice
1 small handful white cashew nuts, chopped
½ tsp ground turmeric
1 tsp ground cardamom
½ tsp ground cumin
200 ml soy cream
2 tsp shoyu
2 tsp chopped fresh coriander
1 tsp chopped basil
salt and pepper

Simmer the aubergine whole for 15 minutes (or 10 minutes if you are using 2 small ones). Sauté the onion and garlic in the vegetable oil over high heat for a few minutes before adding the rice, cashew nuts and spices. Brown for a few minutes over medium heat. Add the soy cream, shoyu and herbs. Mix well, season to taste and remove from the heat. Cut the aubergine/s in half and remove some of the flesh and stuff with the mixture. Bake for 25 minutes at 180°C (Gas mark 4).

Pumpkin roasted with coconut oil

Serves 4

1 kg firm-fleshed pumpkin (butternut or red kuri squash), washed and seeded
60 g coconut oil
2 tbsp fresh coriander leaves
salt and pepper

Cut the pumpkin into 1 cm-thick slices. Preheat the oven to 220°C (Gas mark 7). Put the coconut oil in a large oven-proof dish and put in the oven to melt. Add the pumpkin slices, season with salt and pepper and mix so that the slices are well coated in the oil. Bake for 30 minutes. Sprinkle with the fresh coriander just before serving.

Cauliflower beignets

Serves 2-4

½ cauliflower, cut into medium-sized pieces
1 tbsp cornflour
175 ml water
6 tbsp maize flour
4 tbsp chickpea flour
½ tsp salt
sunflower oil
olive oil
pepper

Combine the cornflour and the water in a bowl to make a batter. In another bowl, combine the maize flour with the chickpea flour and salt. Add pepper to taste. Put an equal quantity of both oils in a saucepan and heat. Dip the cauliflower pieces in the batter and then in the dry mixture. Repeat with all the pieces and set aside. Fry the cauliflower for a few seconds until golden all over. Remove and place on kitchen paper (or a clean tea towel) to absorb the excess oil. Eat at once as the beignets will lose their crispness as they cool.

Snow pea stir-fry

Serves 2

1 onion, sliced
1 courgette, sliced
1 green pepper, sliced
400 g snow peas, stems removed
2 garlic cloves, finely sliced
2 tbsp coconut oil
1 tsp toasted sesame oil
½ tsp ground coriander
200 g firm tofu, diced
1 tbsp tamari
fresh coriander leaves, chopped
freshly ground pepper

Heat the oils in a wok or a large frying pan over high heat. Season generously with pepper and add the ground coriander. Sauté all the vegetables except the garlic. Cook for 5 minutes, stirring often. Add the garlic and tofu and cook for a few minutes. Pour in the tamari and stir for 1 minute. Sprinkle with fresh coriander and serve.

Enjoy it on its own or served with noodles.

- -

Thyme-scented, roasted celeriac medallions

Serves 4

1 large celeriac, peeled and cut into 4 thick slices
olive oil
5-6 sprigs fresh thyme
2 garlic cloves
salt and pepper

Pour enough olive oil to cover the bottom of an oven-proof dish. Place the celeriac slices in the dish and season with salt and pepper. Put the sprigs of thyme in the dish and mix everything with your hands so that the celeriac is well coated. Use the tip of a knife to make a small hole in the middle of each slice and insert half a garlic clove in each one. Bake at 180°C (Gas mark 4) for about 40 minutes, turning the medallions over halfway through cooking.

Stuffed artichokes

Serves 4

2 lemons, cut in half
4 large artichokes
500 ml water
1 vegetable stock cube
6 bay leaves
75 g breadcrumbs
125 g firm tofu, finely crumbled
4 tbsp olive oil
3 tbsp chopped curly parsley
2 garlic cloves, crushed to a paste
salt and pepper

Squeeze half a lemon and pour the juice into a bowl of water. Cut the other lemon into slices. Remove the stalks of the artichokes and then wash them. Remove the outer leaves of the artichokes then cut them in half lengthwise with a large knife. Rub the other half-lemon over the artichokes to stop them from turning black. Use a soup spoon to remove the chokes. Place a slice of lemon on the heart of each artichoke and put into the acidulated water. Prepare the stock: mix the stock cube and the bay leaves with the water. Pour into a large saucepan and put in the artichokes. Cook over medium heat for 35 minutes. Prepare the stuffing: use a fork to mix the breadcrumbs, tofu, olive oil, parsley and garlic. Season with salt and pepper to taste. Remove the slices of lemon and stuff the artichokes. Put into an oven-proof dish and bake for 20 minutes at 180°C (Gas mark 4). The stuffing should brown a little.

Raw, soft fruit tartle

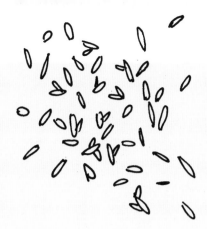

Raw tartlets with berries

Makes 6 tartlets

Approximately 200 g mixed raspberries, blueberries and red currants

For the tartlet bases

70 g ground almonds

50 g dried mulberries

40 g ground hazelnuts

2 tbsp agave syrup

2 tbsp coconut oil

For the strawberry sauce

85 g hulled strawberries

1 tbsp chia seeds

Whiz all the ingredients for the tartlet bases together in a food processor. Line a tray with parchment paper and place a metal ring mould on it. Take one sixth of the dough, press it down firmly in the ring and form even edges with your fingers. Carefully remove the ring and repeat the process until all the dough has been used. Refrigerate for 15-30 minutes. Whiz the strawberries with the chia seeds, then allow the mixture to thicken for 15-30 minutes. Use a spatula to lift the tartlet bases from the tray and then place them on a serving platter or individual plates. Fill them with strawberry sauce and decorate with the fresh fruit.

Carrot and sesame tagliatelle

Serves 2

3 carrots, peeled

2 tsp sesame oil

½ tsp black sesame seeds

½ tsp chopped fresh coriander

1 lemon, juiced and zested

salt and pepper

Cut the carrots into very fine slices lengthwise with a mandolin to make the tagliatelle. Combine the sliced carrots with the remaining ingredients except the salt and pepper. Mix well. Season to taste. Refrigerate for 10 minutes before serving.

'Cheesy' kale chips

For 1 bowl

1 bowlful raw kale, cut into small pieces, removing the thick veins

For the marinade

3 tbsp cashew butter

2 tbsp tahini

2 tbsp tamari

2 tbsp olive oil

2 tbsp malted yeast

2 tbsp gomasio

2 tbsp water

Mix all the marinade ingredients in a large bowl with a fork to form until creamy. Put a handful of kale into the marinade, massage with your hands to soften the leaves then place them on a dehydrator tray (or a baking tray lined with parchment paper). Repeat the process until all the kale has been used. Dehydrate for 12-14 hours (If you don't have a dehydrator, use an oven set on its very lowest setting). Store in an airtight container.

FYI: malted yeast, tamari and gomasio are not raw ingredients. Personally, I don't mind using a few non-raw ingredients in my raw recipes (as do many 'raw' chefs), but they can be replaced with coarsely ground sesame seeds and a little salt.

Raw vegetable and ginger terr

Raw vegetable and ginger terrine

Serves 4

85 g white cashew nuts
2 tomatoes, chopped
1 small carrot, grated
1 tsp finely chopped ginger
1 garlic clove
1 tbsp ground, golden flaxseeds
50 g virgin coconut oil, melted in a bain-marie
½ courgette, grated
salt and pepper

Soak the cashew nuts for 30 minutes to 1 hour in water. Drain. Whiz the first 7 ingredients together in a food processor. Add the grated courgette and season with salt and pepper. Mix well. Pour into a small mould or dish.

Raw banana, blueberry and strawberry ice

Serves 1

1 banana
65 g strawberries
25 g blueberries
1 tsp agave syrup

Chop the fruit into pieces and freeze for a few hours. Whiz the fruit with the agave syrup. Serve immediately.

Cold melon, strawberry and cucumber soup

Serves 4

1 cucumber, peeled, seeded and cut into chunks
½ melon, peeled, seeded and cut into chunks
100 g strawberries, hulled
pepper and chilli sauce

Whiz everything until smooth. Add a little water if necessary. Season with pepper. Serve well chilled with 1-2 drops of chilli sauce if you like, to give it a little extra zing.

Chia seed porridge

Serves 1

15 g walnuts
15 g hazelnuts
2 tbsp chia seeds
200 ml homemade almond (or cashew) milk (see p. 120)
1 tbsp maple (or agave) syrup

Chop the walnuts and hazelnuts in a food processor. Mix them with the chia seeds in a bowl. Mix in the milk. Leave to thicken for 15 minutes. Sweeten with the syrup and serve.

Variation: *Add chopped fresh seasonal fruit (strawberries, mango, pear, etc.), or replace the maple syrup with a handful of raisins.*

Raw cauliflower tabbouleh

Serves 4

1 cauliflower, chopped
2 bunches flat-leaf parsley, finely chopped
2 large tomatoes, finely diced
½ cucumber, finely diced
1 bunch mint, chopped
4 tbsp olive oil
1 lemon, juiced
salt and pepper

Whiz the cauliflower until it is like fine couscous in texture. Combine everything in a bowl with the olive oil and lemon juice. Season with salt and pepper to taste. Refrigerate before serving.

Raw, pizza-flavoured crackers

Makes about 15 crackers

150 g raw cashew nuts
150 ml water
2 tbsp golden flaxseeds
6 sun-dried tomatoes, in oil and herbs
2 tsp oil from the tomatoes
½ clove of garlic
1 tbsp chopped basil
salt and pepper

Soak the cashew nuts in the water for 30 minutes. Drain. Whiz together with the flaxseeds, sun-dried tomatoes, oil, garlic and basil. Season to taste and spread the mixture in a thin layer on a non-stick dehydrator mat. Dehydrate for about 10 hours then cut into small pieces. Return to the dehydrator for about 2 hours or use an oven on its lowest setting. The crackers should be crispy.

Courgette and green olive tartare

Serves 2

1 large courgette
1 handful green olives, pitted and sliced
1 tomato, chopped
1 tbsp capers, chopped
a dozen basil leaves, chopped
olive oil
lemon juice
salt and pepper

Grate the courgette using a large-hole grater. Combine everything in a bowl. Dress with a drizzle of olive oil and lemon juice. Season with salt and pepper. Mix everything again well. Place two metal ring moulds on two plates. Press the tartare well into the rings then remove the moulds.

Courgette spaghetti with a creamy tomato sauce

Serves 2

30 g cashew nuts
2 large ripe tomatoes, cored and cut into large chunks
2 tbsp pine nuts, plus extra to decorate
1 garlic clove
½ tsp fresh (or dried) oregano, plus extra to decorate
½ tbsp lemon juice
Espelette pepper
4 small courgettes
olive oil
salt and pepper

Soak the cashew nuts for 30 minutes. Drain. Whiz the tomatoes with the cashew nuts, pine nuts, garlic, oregano and lemon juice in a food processor. Whiz to a thick sauce. Season to taste with Espelette pepper, salt and pepper. Use a spiral cutter to make courgette spaghetti. Alternatively use a vegetable peeler to make tagliatelle. Divide between 2 plates and cover with the creamy tomato sauce. Drizzle with a little olive oil and decorate with a few pine nuts and oregano leaves.

cauliflower tabbouleh, courgette and green olive tartare, and raw, pizza-flavoured crackers

Raw, sprouted lentil rissoles

Serves 4

200 g sprouted lentils
25 g sunflower seeds
4 sun-dried tomatoes, chopped into small pieces
1 small garlic clove, sliced
20 g walnuts
1 tbsp agave syrup
1 tbsp chopped parsley
60 g ground almonds
salt and pepper

Whiz the sprouted lentils with the sunflower seeds. Add the sun-dried tomatoes, garlic, walnuts and agave nectar. Whiz again. Put the mixture in a bowl and mix in the parsley and ground almonds. Season to taste. Shape into little rissoles and arrange on a plate.

Serve with courgette spaghetti (see p. 210), with a salad, or as you would falafel.

Orange, ginger, carrot and apple smoothie

Makes 1 large glass

juice of 2 oranges
1 apple, peeled and diced
1 carrot, peeled and diced
½ tsp fresh ginger, crushed to a paste
1 tsp agave syrup

Whiz all the ingredients together in a blender. Drink immediately.

Raw coconut, lemon and almond biscuits

Makes about 15 biscuits

85 g dessicated coconut
75 g almonds
50 ml water
4 tbsp agave syrup
1 lemon, juiced
½ lemon, zested

Combine all the ingredients together in a small bowl. Shape the mixture into small balls and flatten them to make round biscuits. Arrange them on a dehydrator tray (or a baking tray with your oven on its lowest setting). Dehydrate for about 12 hours. The biscuits should be dry on the outside and soft inside. Store in an airtight container or jar.

Raw lasagne

Serves 2

1 large courgette, finely sliced
2 tomatoes, chopped
30 g walnuts, chopped
1 garlic clove, sliced
2 tsp olive oil
2 tbsp chopped basil
salt and pepper
For the raw béchamel
100 g cashew nuts
100 ml water
ground nutmeg
salt and pepper

Soak the cashew nuts in water for 1 hour. Slice the courgette thinly. Combine the tomatoes with the walnuts, garlic, olive oil and basil. Season to taste. Drain the cashew nuts then whiz them with the water. Season with salt, pepper and nutmeg. Assemble the lasagne alternating a layer of courgette, a layer of tomato sauce and a layer of raw béchamel.

w lasagne

White and yellow pasta with a creamy avocado and courgette sa

White and yellow pasta with a creamy avocado and courgette sauce

Serves 2-4 children

175 g spaghetti
1 tsp ground turmeric
½ uncooked beetroot
1 avocado, cut into chunks
1 small courgette, cut into chunks
2 tsp olive oil
1 tbsp freshly squeezed lemon juice
1 tbsp cashew butter
1 pinch salt

Cook half of the spaghetti in a saucepan with a generous amount of water and the turmeric. Drain and keep the pasta warm. Cook the other half normally and drain. Whiz the beetroot with 100 ml of water. Strain and pour into a large bowl. Leave the white spaghetti in the beetroot water for a few minutes and then drain. Whiz the avocado and the courgette together with the olive oil, lemon juice and cashew butter. Add the salt. Combine the two spaghetti (optional) and serve with the green sauce.

Carrot and sweet potato mousseline

Serves 4 children

200 g sweet potatoes, peeled and cut into medium-
   sized pieces
200 g carrots, peeled and cut into small pieces
1 tbsp cashew butter
100 ml soy cream
½ tsp salt

Cook the vegetables in simmering water for about 20 minutes until tender. Drain and whiz in a food processor. In a bowl, and using a fork, mix the cashew butter and the soy cream together with the salt. Whisk in the vegetable purée a little at a time.

Cauliflower cream

Makes 1 bowl

½ cauliflower, cut into florets
250 ml soy milk
1 tbsp cashew butter
1 tsp olive oil
1 tsp malted yeast
salt and pepper

Steam the cauliflower florets. Whiz with the soy milk, cashew butter, olive oil and malted yeast. Pour into a saucepan and cook over medium heat to reduce to a smooth, creamy consistency. Season lightly with salt.

This multi-purpose cream is perfect for serving with vegetables, to substitute a béchamel sauce or a creamy cheese sauce, etc.

Courgette beignets

Serves 2-4

75 g plain flour
150 ml soy milk
1 tsp curry powder
2 small courgettes, cut into rounds
vegetable oil for cooking
salt and pepper

Mix the flour and the soy milk to make a batter. Add the curry powder and season to taste. Heat a little oil in a frying pan over high heat. Dip a courgette slice in the batter and then fry for 1-2 minutes each side in the hot oil. Repeat with the remaining slices. Place on a clean tea towel or kitchen paper to absorb any excess oil. Eat them immediately.

Serve with a yoghurt sauce. You simply beat yoghurt with a pinch of salt, ground pepper and a little bit of lemon juice, and can add whatever you want to that base : fresh herbs, spices...

Hummus wraps, chickpea rissoles and vegetable spring

Chickpea and spinach rissoles

Makes about 15 rissoles

300 g cooked chickpeas
75 g whole almonds
1 tbsp almond butter
1 tbsp freshly squeezed lemon juice
3 tbsp water
4 tbsp chopped fresh spinach
1 small bowl breadcrumbs
organic oil for frying
salt and pepper

Whiz half of the chickpeas with the almonds, almond butter, lemon juice and water. Mash the remaining chickpeas with a fork and combine with the above mixture. Add the spinach, season to taste and shape into about 15 rissoles. Roll them in the breadcrumbs and fry for a few minutes until golden brown.

Variation: *Replace the spinach with a mixture of fresh herbs (chives, coriander, parsley and mint). The rissoles can also be baked at 180°C (Gas mark 4) in an oiled oven-proof dish for 20 minutes, but they will be less crispy.*

Curried hummus and crudité wraps

Makes 4 wraps

1 large tomato, sliced
1 avocado, sliced
1 carrot, sliced
lettuce leaves, sliced
4 wheat (or corn) tortillas
seeds of your choice (sunflower, hemp, chia, pumpkin, etc)
For the hummus
200 g cooked chickpeas
2 tbsp tahini
2 tbsp freshly squeezed lemon juice
1 tbsp olive oil
1 tbsp water
1 tsp curry powder
salt

Whiz all the ingredients for the hummus together in a food processor. Heat the tortillas in the oven for a few minutes. Spread some hummus on each tortilla and place some of each of the raw vegetables in the centre. Sprinkle with the seeds, fold the bottom of the tortilla up and then fold in the sides. Serve immediately.

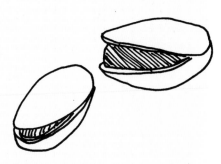

Tofu, basil and tomato croque monsieur

Makes 4

½ tsp mustard
4 tbsp soy cream
¼ tsp herbs de Provence
8 slices wholegrain sandwich bread
200 g basil tofu, finely sliced
1 large tomato, cut into 8 slices
4 sun-dried tomatoes, cut into small pieces
salt and pepper

Mix the mustard together with the soy cream and herbs de Provence. Season to taste. Spread a little of this mixture on each slice of bread. Arrange the tofu on 4 of the slices of bread. Place 2 slices of tomato on top of the tofu. Sprinkle with the sun-dried tomatoes. Top with the other slices of bread. Heat an un-oiled frying pan under the grill and cook the sandwiches for 2-3 minutes each side or use a sandwich maker.

Vegetable and tofu spring rolls

Makes 10 spring rolls

2 carrots, finely grated
1 courgette, finely grated
2 garlic cloves, finely sliced
½ onion, finely sliced
100 g tofu, finely diced
2 tbsp olive oil
1 tsp five-spice powder
1 tbsp tamari
10 rice paper wrappers
vegetable oil for cooking

Sauté the first five ingredients together in a frying pan with the olive oil. Add the spices and cook for a further 5 minutes over high heat. Pour in the tamari, mix well, and cook for 1-2 minutes longer. Set aside. Fill a large shallow dish with hot water. Soak a rice paper wrapper in the water. When it has softened, put it onto a damp tea towel. Place some of the stuffing along the middle. Fold in the sides and then roll the roll up from bottom to top. Repeat the process with the remaining wrappers. Cook the spring rolls in a frying pan with enough oil just to cover the bottom of the pan, or brush them with oil and brown them in the oven at 180°C (Gas mark 4).

Vegetable polenta

Serves 4-6

1 small carrot, grated
1 small courgette, grated
2 tbsp olive oil, plus a little extra for cooking
500 ml non-dairy milk
150 g polenta
salt and pepper

Heat the 2 tbsp of olive oil in a frying pan and sauté the vegetables over medium heat for 5 minutes. Add the milk and season lightly with salt and pepper. When the milk is very hot, sprinkle in the polenta. Cook, stirring continuously, until the mixture is very thick and sticky. Line a baking tray with parchment paper and use a spatula to spread the polenta over the tray. Leave to cool then refrigerate for 1 hour. Cut the polenta (why not use animal-shaped cookie cutters!) and brown the pieces for a few minutes in a hot frying pan with a little olive oil.

Tip: Feel free to use any vegetable you like. If the children you are cooking for aren't fond of the texture of grated vegetables, whiz them with the non-dairy milk before adding them to the polenta. A great dish for little children who are discovering solid food and who love eating with their hands.

Steamed vegetable chips

Serves 6 children

2 large carrots, peeled and cut into chips
2 medium potatoes, peeled and cut into chips
½ butternut squash, peeled and cut into chips
2 tbsp olive oil
salt

Steam the vegetables separately until tender, then gently place them in a large dish and cover with a lid. Drizzle with olive oil and season with a pinch of salt.

Meal ideas: Serve with pink beetroot ketchup (see p. 275), tofu stars with peanut butter (see p. 275), or any other dish with a sauce.

Crudité brochettes and sauce

Makes 6 brochettes

12 cherry tomatoes, halved
¼ cucumber, cut into cubes
1 avocado
½ a lemon, juiced

For the sauce
1 x 100 g pot soy yoghurt
1 tsp mustard
2 tbsp neutral vegetable oil
1 tbsp ketchup
salt and pepper

Combine the soy yoghurt and the mustard in a small bowl. Whisk in the oil with a fork as if making mayonnaise. Add the ketchup and season lightly to taste. Peel the avocado, cut the flesh into cubes and drizzle with lemon juice. Make the brochettes by alternating the tomatoes, cucumber and avocado cubes onto skewers. Serve together with individual bowls of sauce.

Vegetable and non-dairy mozzarella friands

Makes 10 friands

1 courgette, very finely diced
100 g broccoli florets, very finely chopped
1 tbsp olive oil
2 sheets vegan puff pastry
100 g homemade (or shop bought) soy mozzarella
 (see p. 128)

Sauté the vegetables in a frying pan with the olive oil over high heat for 5 minutes. The courgettes should begin to be tender. Roll out a sheet of puff pastry and place small rectangular amounts of the vegetable mixture on it. Top each one with a piece of mozzarella. Roll out the other sheet of puff pastry and place it over the first one. Cut the friands into rectangles around the stuffing. Seal the edges nicely with the tines of a fork. Line a baking tray with parchment paper and bake for 25 minutes at 180°C (Gas mark 4).

Pasta and vegetable 'pizza' gratin

Serves 4-6 children

165 g elbow macaroni
olive oil
250 ml tomato passata
½ courgette, grated
1 tomato, diced
100 g smoked tofu, finely sliced
3 tbsp sweetcorn
fresh herbs (basil, chives, oregano, etc.)
salt and pepper

Cook the pasta and drain it. Oil a tart tin and put in the pasta, pressing well to make a thick base. Cover with the tomato passata. Arrange the grated courgette over the passata. Top with the diced tomato, sliced tofu and sweetcorn. Sprinkle with the fresh herbs and drizzle with a little olive oil. Season lightly with salt and pepper. Bake for about 20 minutes at 180°C (Gas mark 4).

Mini butternut and tofu pies

Makes 6 mini pies

250 g butternut squash, finely diced (do not remove the skin)
1 onion, finely sliced
2 tbsp olive oil, plus a little extra for oiling
100 g firm tofu, crumbled
2 tbsp peanut butter
100 ml oat cream
1 pinch nutmeg
¼ tsp garlic powder
1 quantity shortcrust pastry dough (see p. 244)
salt and pepper

Sauté the butternut squash and the onion with the 2 tbsp of olive oil in a frying pan over medium heat for about 12 minutes. Add the tofu, the peanut butter and the oat cream. Mix well. Add the spices and season lightly. Cut out 6 discs of dough and put them into a lightly oiled muffin tin. The dough should just reach the top of the mould.

Fill each muffin with the vegetable mixture. Cut out 6 smaller discs to make the lids of the mini pies. Seal the edges well and use the tip of a knife to make 4 incisions in the middle of the pies. Bake for about 15 minutes at 190°C (Gas mark 5). The mini pies should be golden brown. Delicious eaten hot, warm, or cold.

Mini vegetable patties to eat with your hands

Makes approximately 12 mini patties

75 g sweet potato, grated
75 g carrot, grated
75 g white cabbage, grated
75 g chickpea flour
2 tbsp arrowroot
100 ml soy milk
50 g maize flour
vegetable oil for cooking
salt and pepper

For the quick sauce
1 x 100 g pot soy yoghurt
2 tsp maple syrup
½ tsp curry powder

Combine the grated ingredients in a bowl. Add the chickpea flour and the arrowroot and mix with your hands. Add the soy milk and mix. Next, add the maize flour, season lightly and mix again. Heat a little olive oil in a small frying pan over medium heat. Shape a little ball of the mixture then flatten a little and put it into the hot pan. Repeat with the rest of the mixture and cook each patty for a few minutes on each side. Immediately place them on kitchen paper and leave to cool. Mix the ingredients for the sauce in a bowl. Serve the patties warm or cold with the sauce.

Tip: This recipe can be adapted to make veggie burgers: just make the patties bigger and cook them longer. Feel free to use other grated vegetables: try leek and potato patties, or combine sweet potato and red kuri squash.

Peach chutney

Makes 1 jar

4 yellow peaches, peeled and diced
1 yellow onion, finely sliced
2 garlic cloves, finely sliced
1 tbsp chopped ginger
2 tsp fresh green chilli pepper, finely chopped
100 ml cider vinegar
5 tbsp cane sugar
½ tsp salt
pepper

Combine the onion and garlic with the ginger and green chilli. Pour the cider vinegar into a saucepan and add the sugar. Bring to the boil and add the onion mixture and the salt. Generously season with pepper. Leave to cook for 1-2 minutes, then add the diced peaches. Lower the heat to medium and cook for 30 minutes.

Cherry tomato chutney

Makes 1 jar

1 onion, finely sliced
4 garlic cloves, finely sliced
500 g cherry tomatoes, quartered
2 tbsp olive oil
2 tsp fresh ginger, peeled and finely chopped
3 tbsp chopped fresh coriander
½ tsp ground cinnamon
½ tsp ground nutmeg
⅛ tsp ground cloves
6 tbsp apple cider vinegar
100 g cane sugar
1 tsp salt

Heat the olive oil in a saucepan and sauté the vegetables. Add the spices. Then, add the vinegar, sugar and salt and cook for 10 minutes over medium heat.

'Cheese' and cherry preserve canapés

Serves 6

200 g stoned cherries, roughly chopped
1 large onion, sliced
1 tbsp olive oil
2 tbsp balsamic vinegar
5 tbsp cane sugar
½ tsp salt
200 g melty vegan cheese of your choice (or see p. 135), finely sliced
6 large slices bread
pepper

Heat the olive oil in a saucepan and sauté the onion and the cherries. Add the vinegar, sugar and salt. Season with pepper to taste. Allow to reduce and cook over medium heat for about 15 minutes. Arrange the slices of cheese on the bread. Grill for about 5 minutes to toast the bread and melt the 'cheese'. Top with the cherry preserve and serve. A sure way to trick the non-initiated into thinking they are eating cheese!

eese' and cherry preserve canapés, and cherry tomato chutney

Avocado and kiwi pudding

Serves 4

2 kiwis, peeled
3 avocados, peeled
½ lemon, juiced
2-3 tbsp agave syrup

Whiz the kiwis and the avocados with the lemon juice. Add the agave syrup and whiz a moment to mix. Divide among 4 ramekins and refrigerate before serving. Eat the same day.

Mango and coconut dessert makis

Makes about 20 makis

200 g short-grain white rice
400 ml coconut milk
200 ml water
75 g light brown sugar
½ mango, peeled and cut into fine strips
1 bowl raspberry coulis (see p. 244)

Cook the rice in the coconut milk with the water and sugar over medium heat for about 30 minutes, stirring continuously. Transfer to a bowl and leave to cool. Cover a bamboo sushi mat with cling film. Spread half of the rice onto the cling film. Place half of the mango in a line on the rice and roll up the maki. Prepare the other roll in the same way. Refrigerate for 30 minutes. Cut the roll into makis and then remove the cling film. Arrange on a serving platter and serve with the raspberry coulis to dip the makis in.

Seitan with pineapple

Serves 4

classic seitan (see p. 96), cut into medium-sized pieces
1 pineapple, peeled and cut into medium-sized pieces
1 small green pepper, diced
1 onion, diced
2 garlic cloves, finely sliced
2 tbsp olive oil
2 tsp toasted sesame oil
4 tbsp vegan Worcestershire sauce
1 tbsp light brown sugar
1 tbsp chopped fresh coriander

Sauté the seitan, pineapple and the vegetables with the olive oil and sesame oil in a large frying pan over high heat for about 5 minutes. Lower the heat to medium, add the Worcestershire sauce and sugar and leave to cook for a few minutes. Add the fresh coriander and serve.

Perfect with fragrant rice or sautéed noodles.

Orange and ginger curd

Makes 1 jar

200 ml freshly squeezed orange juice
1 tbsp arrowroot
2 tsp orange zest
½ tsp fresh ginger, crushed to a paste
4 tbsp cashew butter
125 g light brown sugar
100 ml non-dairy milk

Pour the orange juice into a small saucepan and add the arrowroot, orange zest and ginger. Turn the heat to medium. When the mixture is hot, add the cashew butter and sugar, followed by the non-dairy milk. Whisk everything together well. Turn the heat to high for a few minutes for the mixture to become thick and creamy. Pour into a jar and leave to cool. Put the lid on and refrigerate.

Use as a spread on bread or as a crêpe filling, etc.

Roasted apricot salad

Serves 4

4 apricots, cut into eighths
30 g almonds, roughly chopped
100 g rocket leaves
70 g lamb's lettuce leaves
3 sprigs basil, chopped
olive oil
balsamic vinegar glaze
fleur de sel, pepper

Oil a sheet of parchment paper and place on a baking tray. Place the apricot pieces on the tray. Turn them on the tray so that they are oiled all over and then arrange them, skin side down. Season with pepper and bake for 10 minutes at 200°C (Gas mark 6). Dry-roast the almonds in a frying pan. Wash and spin the salad leaves and put them in a bowl with the basil. Dress with a little olive oil and toss. Arrange a bed of salad leaves on each plate and top with the roasted apricots and almonds. Drizzle with a little balsamic glaze and sprinkle with fleur de sel and freshly ground pepper.

Fig and non-dairy feta sa

Fig and non-dairy feta salad

Serves 6

3 little gem lettuces
6 black figs, quartered
200 g homemade feta (see p. 130) or tamari-marinated
  lacto-fermented tofu, diced
2 tbsp sunflower seeds
olive oil
balsamic vinegar glaze
salt and pepper

Wash the lettuces, remove the bases and detach the leaves. Put them on a plate or in a bowl. Add the figs, feta and sunflower seeds to the salad leaves. Drizzle generously with olive oil and season with salt and pepper. Drizzle with balsamic glaze at the table.

Pan-fried tempeh with mango

Serves 2

200 g tempeh, cut into thick slices
1 mango, diced
2 garlic cloves, finely sliced
2 tbsp olive oil
2 tbsp shoyu
1 tbsp chopped fresh coriander
pepper

Heat the olive oil in a frying pan and sauté the tempeh over high heat for a few minutes to brown it a little. Lower the heat to medium. Add the mango and garlic. Season with pepper and cook for 5 minutes, stirring often. Turn off the heat, but leave the pan on the stove. Stir in the shoyu and leave for 1 minute. Add the fresh coriander off the heat and serve.

GOURMET
RECIPES

Crèmes brûlée with roasted peaches and thyme

Serves 4

For the crème brûlée
400 g silken tofu
150 ml soy cream
3 tbsp cashew butter
3 tbsp light brown sugar
½ tsp agar-agar powder
¼ tsp ground vanilla
For the peaches
2 yellow peaches
½ tbsp non-dairy margarine
1 tbsp light brown sugar, plus extra for caramelising
1 sprig fresh thyme

Put all the ingredients for the crème brûlée in a blender and blend until you have a smooth cream. Peel the peaches and cut them into thin segments. Next, toss them in the margarine in a frying pan over high heat. Add the sugar and the thyme leaves. Cook for a few minutes, stirring well so that the peaches brown but do not catch on the bottom of the pan. When they have browned, divide them among 4 ramekins. Pour the crème brûlée mixture into a saucepan and bring to the boil while mixing with a wooden spoon (the cream tends to catch). When the mixture begins to bubble, stir constantly for 1-2 minutes, then remove from the heat and divide among the ramekins. Leave to come to room temperature then refrigerate for 1-2 hours. Just before serving, sprinkle with cane sugar and caramelise with a blowtorch.

Matcha panna cotta with raspberry coulis

Serves 4

For the panna cotta
250 ml soy cream
250 ml oat milk
3 tbsp light brown sugar
3 tsp matcha tea
½ tbsp cashew butter
½ tsp agar-agar powder
For the raspberry coulis
125 g raspberries
100 ml water
50 g light brown sugar

Whisk all the panna cotta ingredients in a saucepan and bring to the boil. Whisk for 2 minutes. Pour into 4 moulds, ramekins or verrines. Leave to cool then refrigerate for 2 hours. In a small saucepan, combine the raspberries with the water and sugar. Bring to the boil. Cook for 5 minutes, then blend, strain and cook for a further 5 minutes over medium heat. Serve the panna cotta with the cold raspberry coulis.

Earl Grey and spelt pastry cream

Makes 1 tart

1 tbsp Earl Grey tea
500 ml soy milk
10 tbsp light brown sugar
1 tbsp cornflour
4 tbsp spelt flour
3 tbsp cashew butter
3 tbsp water
margarine

Infuse the tea in the milk for 5 minutes in a saucepan over medium heat. In another saucepan, mix the sugar with the cornflour and the spelt flour. Add the cashew butter and water. Mix well to obtain a smooth mixture. Strain the milk through a very fine sieve (lined with a muslin cloth if necessary). Gradually add the hot milk to the other mixture, whisking well. Bring to a simmer over medium heat and whisk for a few minutes until thick and smooth. Pour into a large bowl and rub a little margarine over the top of the custard to avoid a skin forming.

Use to garnish cakes or fruit tarts. Perfect in a pear tart with chocolate curls.

Matcha panna cotta with raspberry coulis

Crème caram

Crème caramel

Serves 4-6

60 g light brown sugar
500 ml soy milk
3 tbsp sugar
1 tbsp cashew butter
1 tsp agar-agar powder
1 tsp arrowroot
¼ tsp vanilla extract

To prepare the caramel, put the sugar in a small saucepan over medium heat. Swirl the saucepan gently but do not stir the sugar. Pour the caramel into mini flan moulds or ramekins. Mix all the other ingredients in a medium-sized saucepan and bring to the boil while whisking. Cook for 2 minutes, then pour into the moulds. Leave to cool, then refrigerate for 2 hours before unmoulding.

Raspberry and vanilla mousse

Serves 4

400 g silken tofu
250 g raspberries (fresh or frozen)
6 tbsp light brown sugar
3-4 drops vanilla extract

Blend all the ingredients in a blender for at least 5 minutes. Divide the mixture among the ramekins and leave to rest in the fridge overnight.

Rose and pistachio puddings

Serves 4

600 ml oat milk
4 tbsp light brown sugar
2 tbsp pistachio butter
2 tsp rosewater
1 tsp agar-agar powder
4 tsp chopped pistachios

In a saucepan, whisk all the ingredients except for the pistachios. Bring to the boil and cook for 2 minutes, whisking constantly. Divide the mixture among 4 ramekins. Leave to cool then refrigerate for 2 hours. Sprinkle with chopped pistachios before serving.

Almond and rhubarb pots de crème

Serves 4

150 g rhubarb
75 g cane sugar
4 tbsp white almond butter
200 ml soy cream (or other non-dairy cream)
a pinch ground cinnamon

In a saucepan, cook the rhubarb and sugar with enough water to cover the base of the saucepan, stirring from time to time. When the rhubarb is very soft, add the almond butter and the soy cream and blend using an immersion blender. Add the cinnamon, mix well and pour into 4 glass yoghurt pots or 4 ramekins.

For an even more gourmet dessert, top the creams with 1 or 2 tbsp of rhubarb compote and sprinkle with toasted, slivered almonds.

Coconut blancmange

Serves 6-8

400 ml coconut milk
250 ml non-dairy milk
175 g light brown sugar
60 g dessicated coconut, plus extra for decorating
zest of 1 lime, plus extra for decorating
1 tsp agar-agar powder
¼ tsp ground vanilla

Combine all the ingredients in a saucepan over medium heat. Make sure the coconut milk and the sugar dissolve completely. Bring to the boil for 2 minutes, whisking constantly. Pour into a fluted flan tin, leave to cool, then refrigerate for 6-8 hours. Unmould onto a round plate then sprinkle with dessicated coconut and lime zest.

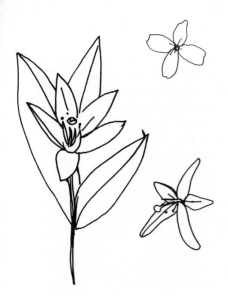

Lemon, almond and vanilla cake

Serves 6-8

150 ml soy yoghurt
170 g sugar
65 g ground almonds (with skin)
zest of 1 lemon
2 tbsp freshly squeezed lemon juice
½ tsp vanilla
4 tbsp neutral vegetable oil
1 sachet (7 g) baking powder
1 tsp bicarbonate of soda
200 g T70 light spelt flour

Whisk the yoghurt and sugar together in a mixing bowl. Add the ground almonds, then the lemon zest, juice and vanilla. Mix well. Add the oil and whisk to incorporate. Add the baking powder and bicarbonate of soda and mix. Sift in the flour a little at a time. Grease a 25 cm/10 inch cake tin with margarine or oil and pour the cake mixture into the tin. Bake at 180°C (Gas mark 4) for 30 minutes.

Hazelnut waffles

Makes 6-8 waffles

3 tbsp neutral vegetable oil
3 tbsp hazelnut butter
60 g light brown sugar
250 ml soy milk (or other non-dairy milk of your choice)
1 sachet (7 g) baking powder
200 g type T55 flour

Whisk the olive oil with the hazelnut butter and sugar in a mixing bowl. Add the soy milk then the baking powder. Finally, mix in the flour. Pre-heat a mould or waffle-iron. Pour the mixture into the waffle plates, close and allow to cook for about 5 minutes. Oil the grill between each batch of waffles. If the waffle-iron has an indicator light, wait for it to turn off before opening to remove the waffles. Serve warm.

Melted chocolate and banana slices go very well with these gourmet waffles.

SNACKS FOR SHARING

Orange blossom milk rolls

Makes 8 rolls

500 g flour
1 tsp salt
60 g light brown sugar
200 ml soy milk, plus 2 tbsp for the glaze
1½ sachets (15 g) baker's yeast
2 tbsp cashew butter
2 tbsp orange blossom water
90 ml olive oil
pearl sugar
1 tbsp agave syrup

In a large mixing bowl, mix the flour with the salt and sugar. Mix the 200 ml of warm soy milk with the yeast and leave to rest for 5 minutes. Pour onto the flour together with the cashew butter, the orange blossom water and olive oil. Mix vigorously with a fork then knead for 10 minutes until you have a smooth and uniform dough. If the dough is too dry, add a little milk; if it is too sticky, add a little flour. Shape the dough into a ball and leave to rise in the mixing bowl, covered with a cloth, for 1 hour at 20-25°C. Line a baking tray with parchment paper. Divide the dough into small balls, form into torpedo shapes, then place them on the prepared tray and leave to rise for 1½ hours in a cold oven. Score with scissors or a knife and sprinkle each roll with a little pearl sugar. Mix the 2 tbsp of soy milk with the agave syrup and brush each roll with the mixture. Bake for 10-15 minutes at 200°C (Gas mark 6).

range blossom milk rolls

Oat, chocolate and pecan cookies

Makes about 15 cookies

200 g plain flour

150 g rolled oats

½ tsp salt

1 tsp baking powder

½ tsp bicarbonate of soda

100 ml neutral vegetable oil

4 tbsp cashew butter

150 g light brown sugar

100 ml oat milk

½ tsp ground vanilla

2 tbsp dark chocolate chips, plus extra for decorating

40 g pecans, chopped, plus extra for decorating

Mix the flour with the oats, salt, baking powder and bicarbonate of soda in a mixing bowl. In a medium bowl, whisk the oil with the cashew butter, sugar, oat milk and vanilla until creamy. Gently fold in the flour-oat mixture with a spoon. Add the chocolate chips and the chopped pecans. Mix together. Line a baking tray with parchment paper. Form small balls with moistened hands (the dough will be very sticky) then flatten them and place them on the prepared tray, leaving plenty of space between them (the cookies will rise and spread). Place a few chocolate chips and pecan pieces on the tops of the cookies. Bake at 180°C (Gas mark 4) for 12-15 minutes. The cookies should be golden brown just at the edges. Remove from the oven, leave to rest for a few minutes, then cool completely on a wire rack. You will probably need to cook them in 2 batches.

Mini strawberry palmiers

Makes about 15 palmiers

1 sheet organic vegan puff pastry

4 tbsp strawberry jam

ground cinnamon

ground vanilla

Unroll the puff pastry and cut into strips about 1 cm wide along the length of the pastry. Spread them with the strawberry jam, sprinkle with a little cinnamon and vanilla, and then roll the strips symmetrically towards the centre from both ends to form palmiers. Line a baking tray with parchment paper. Place them on the prepared tray and bake for 15 minutes at 180°C (Gas mark 4). Use a spatula to loosen the palmiers and leave to cool on a wire rack.

Raspberry and coconut scones

Makes 6 large scones

250 g plain flour

5 tbsp sugar

3 tsp baking powder

¼ tsp salt

50 g coconut oil

175 ml oat milk

1 tbsp dessicated coconut

3 handfuls fresh or frozen raspberries

Combine all the dry ingredients in a mixing bowl. Add the coconut oil and mix with your fingertips, as if making a crumble. Add the oat milk and mix in with a fork. Add the dessicated coconut and raspberries and gently mix. Line a baking tray with parchment paper. With moistened hands, form 5 triangular scones and place on the prepared tray. Bake for 15 minutes at 200°C (Gas mark 6).

...at, chocolate and pecan cookies, mini strawberry palmiers, and raspberry and coconut scones

Strawberries with mint-basil pesto and crea

Banana and speculoos biscuit parfait

Serves 4

3 bananas

100 g speculoos biscuits, crumbled, plus 2 extra, also
  crumbled, to garnish

500 g soy yoghurt

¼ tsp ground vanilla

4 tbsp light brown sugar

Blend the bananas with the crumbled speculoos biscuits.
Beat the soy yoghurt with the vanilla and sugar. In 4 verrine
glasses, alternate 2 tbsp yoghurt with 1 tbsp banana-specu-
loos cream. Sprinkle each with half a crumbled speculoos
biscuit. Refrigerate for 10-30 minutes before serving.

Sweet potato muffins

Makes 6 muffins

100 g light brown sugar

65 ml olive oil

100 ml almond milk

10 g baking powder

½ tsp vanilla

¼ tsp mixed spice or quatre épices

1 pinch salt

200 g plain flour

75 g grated sweet potato

Whisk together the sugar and oil in a mixing bowl. Whisk
in the almond milk then the baking powder. The mixture
should be white and foamy. Add the spices and salt and
whisk well. Fold in the flour a little at a time, then the sweet
potato. Line a muffin tin with paper cases, or oil a tin, and
divide the mixture among them. Bake for 25-30 minutes at
180°C (Gas mark 4).

Strawberries with mint-basil pesto and cream

Serves 4

600 g strawberries

200 ml non-dairy cream

2 tbsp light brown sugar

<u>For the pesto</u>

15 g basil leaves

15 g mint leaves

65 ml olive oil

50 g toasted cashew nuts

juice of 1 lemon

1 tbsp light brown sugar

Wash, hull, and cut up the strawberries and arrange them
on a serving plate. Mix the cream and sugar in a small bowl.
Carefully combine the strawberries and cream. Blend the
basil and mint with the olive oil. Add the cashew nuts, then
the lemon juice and the sugar. Blend well. Store the pesto
in an airtight jar. Serve the strawberries with a spoonful of
pesto.

Tutti-frutti frozen smoothies

Makes 6 ice lollies

200 ml pineapple juice

100 g strawberries

1 Granny Smith apple

2 tbsp agave syrup

Purée all the ingredients in a blender. Pour the mixture into
ice lolly moulds and freeze for 12 hours.

Orange and semolina cake

Serves 6-8

750 ml soy milk
125 g light brown sugar
1 tbsp cashew butter
½ tbsp cornflour
¼ tsp ground vanilla
3 drops sweet orange oil
125 g medium-ground semolina

In a saucepan, whisk all the ingredients except for the semolina. Turn the heat to high. When the first bubbles appear, add the semolina. Mix with a wooden spoon and lower the heat to medium. Cook, stirring constantly for 7-8 minutes, until the mixture is like a thick purée and begins to catch on the bottom of the saucepan. Pour into an oiled 20 cm/8 inch plain or fluted cake tin and bake at 180°C (Gas mark 4) for 30 minutes. Allow to cool completely before removing from the tin.

Serve with caramel or homemade chocolate sauce.

Quick praline creams

Serves 4

400 g silken tofu
4 tbsp agave nectar
3 tbsp hazelnut butter (preferably toasted)

Put all the ingredients in a blender and blend for a few minutes. Divide among 4 ramekins and refrigerate for 1-6 hours.

After trying these delicious homemade desserts you will stop buying the ready-made kind!

Watermelon and coconut salad with mint

Serves 2

300 g watermelon, rind removed
10 mint leaves
1 tbsp coconut flakes
1 tbsp chia seeds
juice of ½ a lemon

Cut the watermelon into chunks. Chop the mint. Put them in a mixing bowl, add the coconut flakes and chia seeds, pour in the lemon juice and mix well. Serve immediately.

A surprising combination of flavours!

Rosewater rice pudding

Serves 2

500 ml non-dairy milk
100 g short-grain white rice
2 tbsp light brown sugar
2 tsp rosewater

Mix all the ingredients in a saucepan and cook over medium heat for 30-40 minutes, stirring often, until the rice is tender and sticky. Divide between 2 ramekins and leave to cool. Refrigerate before eating.

Perfect served with a soft fruit coulis.

nge and semolina cake

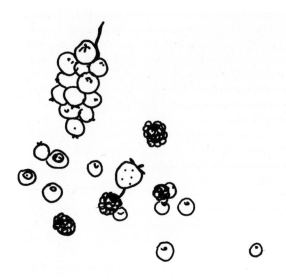

Sweet chestnut verrines

Serves 2

120 g silken tofu

1 x 100 g pot soy yoghurt

9 tbsp sweetened chestnut spread

2 tbsp praline

Blend the tofu with the yoghurt and 3 tbsp of the sweetened chestnut spread. Spoon 3 tbsp of the sweetened chestnut spread into the bottom of 2 verrine glasses. Pour the prepared cream over it and refrigerate for 1 hour. Garnish each verrine with 1 tsp of praline before serving.

Apple and vanilla yoghurt with dried fruit and nut crumble

Serves 4

20 g pecans

20 g dried mulberries

1 tbsp ground almonds

1 tbsp agave syrup

a pinch ground cinnamon

1 Granny Smith apple

500 g soy yoghurt

a pinch of vanilla powder

Chop the pecans and mulberries very finely with a knife, then mix in the ground almonds and agave syrup. Add the cinnamon. Peel and core the apple and cut into dice. Mix the apple and yoghurt with the vanilla, divide among 4 glasses or ramekins and cover with the crumble.

Coconut milk tapioca pudding

Serves 2

150 ml coconut milk

250 ml soy milk

4 tbsp light brown sugar

4 tbsp tapioca

2 tbsp dessicated coconut

Combine the coconut milk with the soy milk and sugar in a saucepan. Turn the heat to medium. When the sugar has dissolved, add the tapioca and coconut and mix. Leave to cook for the tapioca to thicken. Divide between 2 ramekins. Can be eaten warm or cold.

For an extra special dessert, top with a few pieces of fresh fruit (mango, kiwi, orange, Cape gooseberries, etc.) just before serving.

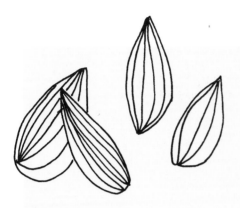

Quick peach crumble

Serves 4

3 tbsp coconut sugar
2 tbsp coconut oil, cut into little pieces
2 tbsp ground almonds
5 tbsp plain flour
a pinch ground vanilla
a pinch ground cinnamon
4 large yellow peaches
1 tbsp margarine (or vegetable oil)

Put the sugar, coconut oil, the ground almonds and the flour in a bowl and mix with your fingertips. Add the spices. Put into a frying pan and cook for a few minutes over high heat, stirring constantly. Set aside in a bowl. Cut the peaches into pieces and toss with the margarine for a few minutes in the pan over high heat. Divide the peaches among 4 ramekins and cover with the crumble. Serve immediately.

Apricot and pistachio tartlets

Makes 8 tartlets

1 quantity biscuit tart dough (see p. 243)
25 g chopped pistachios
100 ml oat cream
2 tbsp light brown sugar
1 tsp cornflour
4 apricots

Line a baking tray with parchment paper or lightly oil 8 tartlet tins. Cut out 8 circles of dough (approximately 15 cm in diameter). Place the pastry circles in/on the prepared tins or tray and fold over the edges to form rustic galettes. Using a mini-chopper or food processor, grind the pistachios to a powder. In a bowl, mix the ground pistachios with the oat cream, the sugar and cornflour. Spread this cream over the tart crusts. Thinly slice the apricots and arrange them on the tarts. Bake for 10-15 minutes at 200°C (Gas mark 6). The edges of the tartlets should be well-browned.

FRUIT TARTS AND CAKES

Rhubarb upside-down cake

Serves 6-8

350 g rhubarb
2 tbsp light brown sugar, plus 200 g, plus extra for the
  cake tin
125 ml grape seed oil
2 x 100 g pots soy yoghurt
2 tsp apple cider vinegar
2 tsp baking powder
½ tsp ground vanilla
350 g plain flour
oil for the cake tin

Trim the rhubarb then cut into approximately 1.5-cm lengths. Place the pieces in a colander, sprinkle with the 2 tbsp of sugar and leave to stand for 30 minutes. In a bowl, mix the oil with the yoghurts and the apple cider vinegar. Add the baking powder and vanilla and mix well. Add the 200 g of sugar then stir in the flour a little at a time, mixing well. Grease a spring form tin (approximately 25 cm in diameter), sprinkle the base with sugar, then arrange the rhubarb pieces side by side (overlapping them to completely cover the bottom of the tin). Pour in the cake batter. Bake at 170°C (Gas mark 3-4) for 1 hour. Allow to cool in the tin. To unmould, slide a knife blade around the edge of the cake and turn the cake out onto a large plate.

Apple, caramel and almond tart

Serves 6-8

550 g apples, peeled
2 tbsp margarine (or vegetable oil)
40 g sugar
1 quantity shortcrust or biscuit tart dough (see p. 243)
25 g ground almonds
For the almond-caramel cream
150 g light brown sugar
3 tbsp water
500 ml soy cream, heated
½ tsp salt
1 tbsp cornflour
100 g ground almonds

Put the sugar and water in a medium-sized saucepan. Turn the heat to high and leave the caramel to form without stirring. When it has reached the desired texture and colour, add the hot cream. Mix well. If the caramel seizes up, melt it again over medium heat, stirring well. Add the salt. Leave the cream to cool, then add the cornflour and ground almonds. Mix well. Set aside. Dice the apples, then toss them with the margarine in a large frying pan. Add the sugar and cook for a few minutes over high heat. Line a tart tin with the pastry. Prick it with a fork and bake blind for 8 minutes at 90°C (Gas mark 3). Sprinkle the bottom of the pastry crust with ground almonds, evenly spread the apples in it then pour the caramel-almond cream over them. Bake for 20 minutes at 190°C (Gas mark 5).

For an even more gourmet tart, prepare a caramel with 75 g sugar and 2 tbsp water. Drizzle a little over each slice of tart just before serving.

Apple and raspberry turnovers

Makes 5 turnovers

1 sheet organic vegan puff pastry
5 tbsp apple compote
1 handful of raspberries
ground cinnamon
cane sugar
soy milk

Using a small bowl as a guide, cut out 4 circles (approximately 10 cm diameter) of puff pastry. Form a ball with the scraps. Roll out and cut out a fifth circle. Place the circles on a baking tray lined with parchment paper. Over half of each circle, put 1 tbsp of compote, a few crushed raspberries, a pinch of cinnamon and a little sugar. Fold the dough over to make turnovers and seal the edges firmly with a fork, pressing the tines all the way along the edge. Brush with soy milk. Bake for 20 minutes at 180°C (Gas mark 4). The turnovers should be well browned.

For an even more divine and gourmet dessert, serve with raspberry coulis.

Biscuit tart pastry dough

Makes 1 tart crust

150 g plain flour
50 g light brown sugar
30 g sifted ground almonds
¼ tsp baking powder
1 pinch salt
3 tbsp grape seed oil
5 tbsp soy milk
a pinch of ground vanilla

Sift the flour into a mixing bowl. Combine with the sugar, ground almonds, baking powder and salt. Add the grape seed oil and mix with a fork. Pour in the soy milk and vanilla and mix well. Knead the dough by hand until uniform and smooth in texture. Roll out on a floured work surface.

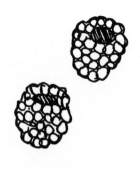

Shortcrust pastry dough

Makes 1 tart crust

250 g plain flour
¼ tsp salt
85 ml vegetable oil
80 ml water

In a small mixing bowl, combine the flour and the salt. Add the oil and mix with a spoon or fork. Pour in the water, mix with a spoon then knead just until the dough comes together. Wrap with cling film or cover and refrigerate for 30 minutes. Roll out on a floured work surface.

Raspberry and rose bavarois

Serves 8

Fresh raspberries for decorating
<u>For the sponge cake</u>
200 g light brown sugar
¼ tsp ground vanilla powder
½ tsp salt
3 tsp baking powder
2 tbsp almond butter
150 ml neutral vegetable oil
250 ml soy milk
50 g cornflour
250 g type T55 flour
<u>For the raspberry and rose mousse</u>
480 g silken tofu
200 ml soy cream
150 g raspberries
100 g light brown sugar
2 tbsp rosewater
2 tsp agar-agar powder
a pinch of ground vanilla
<u>For the jellied fruit coulis</u>
200 ml water
100 g raspberries
35 g sugar
1 tsp agar-agar powder

For the sponge cake: Combine the sugar with the vanilla, salt, baking powder, almond butter and oil in a mixing bowl. Whisk in the soy milk. Add the cornflour, then add the flour in 3 batches. Mix well to avoid lumps. Line a 20 x 30 cm square cake tin and pour in the batter. Bake for 25-30 minutes at 180°C (Gas mark 4). The cake should be nicely browned. Leave to cool. Cut a disc of the sponge cake to the same size as the spring form tin. If the sponge cake is not completely flat or is too thick, even the top with a cake cutting wire or a large chef's knife. It should be 2 cm thick at the most. Cut out a circle of parchment paper of the same size. Place the parchment paper circle in the prepared spring form tin and line the sides with parchment paper as well as this will make it easier to unmould. Place the sponge cake circle in the tin.

For the mousse: Mix all the ingredients in a saucepan. Bring to the boil, whisking constantly. Boil for 2 minutes, stirring vigorously. Leave to cool for a few minutes then pour over the sponge cake. Cool in the fridge or at room temperature for 2-3 hours.

For the coulis: Blend all the ingredients together, then strain through a fine sieve to remove the seeds. Bring to the boil in a small saucepan, stirring constantly. Cook for 1 minute. Pour over the firm mousse and leave to cool in the fridge or at room temperature for about 1 hour.

Remove from the tin by opening the hinge. Place the bavarois on a plate and remove the parchment paper from around the side and from under the sponge cake. Carefully neaten the edges if necessary. Decorate with fresh raspberries.

Totally chocolate muffins, chocolate and berry fondants, and pear, chocolate and almond ta

Chocolate and berry fondants

Serves 4

200 g dark chocolate
100 g cane sugar
200 ml soy cream
50 ml neutral vegetable oil
100 g plain flour
1 punnet raspberries
1 punnet blueberries

Melt the chocolate in a bain-marie, then mix with the sugar, soy cream, oil and flour. Arrange the berries in 4 ramekins then divide the chocolate mixture among them and sprinkle a few berries on top. Bake at 180°C (Gas mark 4) for about 20 minutes. Serve warm.

Totally chocolate muffins

Makes 5 large or 10 small muffins

160 g cane sugar
100 ml vegetable oil
1/8 tsp vanilla extract
125 ml non-dairy milk
3 tsp baking powder
1/4 tsp salt
3 tbsp unsweetened cocoa powder
200 g plain flour
50 g dark chocolate

Combine the sugar with the oil and the vanilla in a mixing bowl. Whisk in the non-dairy milk, baking powder and salt. Add the cocoa, then the flour. Chop the chocolate into small pieces, then fold them into the batter. Line muffin tins with paper cases then fill them with the batter. Bake for about 25 minutes at 180°C (Gas mark 4).

CHOCOLATE!

Pear, chocolate and almond tart

Serves 6

1 quantity shortcrust, biscuit, or sablée/shortbread pastry
  dough (see p. 243)
200 g dark chocolate
200 ml non-dairy cream
35 g ground almonds
65 g cane sugar
75 ml non-dairy milk
2 tbsp cornflour
3 pears
1 large handful slivered almonds

Line a 25 cm/10 inch tart tin with the pastry. Melt the chocolate in a bain-marie, then mix with the cream, ground almonds, sugar, non-dairy milk and the cornflour. Pour over the pastry. Peel the pears, cut them into slices and arrange them over the chocolate cream. Sprinkle with the slivered almonds. Bake at 180°C (Gas mark 4) for 30-40 minutes.

Bergamot and grapefruit chocolate bar

Makes 1 bar

135 g dark chocolate (70 % cocoa solids)
1 bergamot
1 grapefruit

Gently melt the chocolate in a bain-marie. Zest the bergamot and half of the grapefruit. Add 1 tsp of each zest to the chocolate. Mix well. Pour into a chocolate bar mould and sprinkle with another ½ tsp of each zest. Leave to cool to room temperature. Refrigerate for a few minutes if it is too warm for the chocolate to firm up.

***NB:** It is very important to choose organic citrus fruit because in conventional agriculture the skins have been sprayed and are often unfit for consumption.*

Pistachio and praline mendiants

Makes 12 mendiants

150 g dark chocolate
2 tbsp praline
1 tbsp chopped pistachios

Melt the chocolate in a bain-marie. Mix the praline and chopped pistachios together. Line a baking tray with parchment paper. Spoon circles of chocolate onto the prepared tray. Sprinkle with the praline and pistachios. Leave to cool. Refrigerate if necessary.

Banana, hazelnut and chocolate chip muffins

Makes about 12 muffins

2 very ripe bananas
4 tbsp roasted hazelnut butter
150 ml chestnut milk
80 ml neutral vegetable oil
200 g plain flour
150 g light brown sugar
1½ tsp baking powder
¼ tsp salt
½ tsp bicarbonate of soda
4 tbsp dark chocolate chips
1 handful of hazelnuts

Blend the bananas with the hazelnut butter. Add the chestnut milk and oil and blend again. Mix the flour with the sugar, baking powder, salt and bicarbonate of soda in a mixing bowl. Make a well in the centre and pour in the banana mixture. Mix well, add the chocolate chips and fill the muffin tins to three quarters of the way up. Chop the hazelnuts and sprinkle over the muffins. Bake for about 25 minutes (5 minutes more if using large muffin tins) at 180°C (Gas mark 4). Leave to cool on a wire rack before eating.

Orange and pistachio chocolate mousse

Serves 4

400 g tin coconut milk
240 g silken tofu
200 g dark chocolate
60 g icing sugar
2 drops sweet orange oil
4 tsp chopped pistachios
1 tbsp sugar

Refrigerate the coconut milk and tofu until very cold. Melt the chocolate in a bain-marie. Blend the silken tofu with the chocolate and the icing sugar for a few seconds, then pour into a mixing bowl. Open the tin of coconut milk, scoop out the thick cream on top and add it to the mixing bowl. Beat with an electric whisk for 5 minutes. Add the orange oil and beat again until it has the consistency of thick whipped cream. Divide the mixture among 4 verrines or ramekins and refrigerate for 2-6 hours. Put the pistachios and sugar in a small frying pan and heat for a few minutes to caramelise. Sprinkle the pistachios over the chocolate mousses and serve.

Quick chocolate sauce for fresh fruit

Serves 4

200 ml non-dairy milk
3 tbsp light brown sugar
2 tbsp cashew butter
a pinch ground vanilla
8 tbsp cocoa powder

Heat the milk in a small saucepan over low heat. Dissolve the sugar and cashew butter in the milk and then add the vanilla. Next, gradually whisk in the cocoa powder. Cook for a few minutes, add a little water if necessary, and remove from the heat.

Drizzle over fresh fruit or serve as a quick chocolate fondue.

Frozen berry yoghurt

Serves 1

50 g frozen strawberries
10 g frozen blueberries
125 g soy yoghurt
1 tbsp agave syrup

If the strawberries are very big, cut them into pieces. Put all the ingredients in the jar of a blender or bowl of a food processor and blend to a thick, icy cream. Be careful not to blend too long or the mixture will warm up. Serve immediately.

Peach and mango popsicle

Makes 6-8 popsicles

250 g ripe mango (1 large mango)
250 g yellow peaches (2 or 3 peaches)
2 tbsp freshly squeezed lemon juice
3 tbsp agave syrup

Peel the fruit and cut into chunks. Purée the fruit together with the lemon juice and agave syrup. Put into ice lolly moulds and freeze for a few hours.

A simple recipe, but delicious.

Soft fruit and chia seed pudding

Serves 4

100 g strawberries
100 g raspberries
400 ml oat (or almond) milk
4 tbsp agave syrup
8 tbsp chia seeds

Blend the fruit with the milk and the agave syrup. Add the chia seeds and mix in with a spoon. Divide among 4 small bowls and leave to swell for 1 hour before serving.

Add sliced banana and chopped almonds to this pudding for a great breakfast.

Warm pear salad with crystallised ginger and chocolate curls

Serves 4

1.25 litres water
50 g light brown sugar
¼ tsp vanilla extract
4 pears
50 g crystallised ginger
35 g dark chocolate

Bring the water with the sugar and vanilla to the boil in a large saucepan. Peel the pears, leaving the stalk on. Core them from the bottom with a small melon baller. Poach the pears in the liquid for 20-30 minutes. Drain. Cut the pears into thin slices and carefully arrange on 4 small plates. Cut the crystallised ginger into thin slices and alternate them with the slices of pear. Make chocolate curls with a vegetable peeler. Top the pears with the chocolate curls just before serving; they will melt slowly on the slices of warm pear.

ach and mango popsicle

100% apple and raspberry fruit tart

Cold melon and ginger jelly

Serves 4

350 ml water

1 tsp agar-agar powder

500 g melon

½ tsp chopped ginger

3 tbsp agave syrup

Mix the water and the agar-agar in a saucepan. Bring to the boil and cook for 2 minutes. Dice 350 g of the melon. Mix the water with the agar-agar with the diced melon, the ginger and the agave syrup. Divide among 4 verrines and refrigerate for 2 hours. When ready to serve, dice the remaining 150 g of melon and top the jellies with it.

- -

Cold summer fruit and green tea soup

Serves 4-6

700 ml water

1 tbsp sencha green tea

1 mango

80 g strawberries

80 g raspberries

2 tbsp freshly squeezed lemon juice

3 tbsp agave syrup

100 g redcurrants

mint leaves

Heat the water to about 75°C and infuse the tea in it. Strain, leave to cool, then refrigerate. Peel the mango and cut it into pieces. Blend the mango with the strawberries, the raspberries and the cold tea. Add the lemon juice and the agave syrup and mix. Serve in deep dishes sprinkled with the redcurrants and the mint leaves.

Strawberry granita

Serves 6-8

600 ml strawberry juice (or homemade strawberry smoothie)

60 ml agave syrup

juice of 1 lemon

Blend all the ingredients. Pour into an airtight container. Freeze for 1 hour then break it up with a fork. Repeat this process every 30 minutes, scraping the sides well, until the granita is a mass of crystals (about 4-5 hours).

Feel free to add chopped mint leaves to the granita. Or use it as the base for a frozen alcoholic or non-alcoholic cocktail.

- -

100% apple and raspberry fruit tartlets

Makes 6 small tartlets

2 apples

250 ml water

1 tsp agar-agar powder

3 tbsp agave syrup

a pinch ground vanilla

a pinch ground cinnamon

250 g fresh raspberries

1 tbsp agave syrup

Peel and dice the apples. Blend with the water, then pour into a medium saucepan. Whisk in the agar-agar, the agave syrup and the spices. Bring to the boil for 2 minutes, whisking constantly. Divide among 6 small tartlet moulds (or 4 standard-sized ones). Leave to cool to room temperature and refrigerate for 2 hours. Carefully unmould the apple tart bases and arrange on a serving platter. Use a knife tip to make a circle about 5 mm in from the edge of the tartlet. Gently hollow the tartlet base a little with a spoon. Crush 80 g of the raspberries with a fork and mix with the agave syrup. Fill the tartlets with the mixture and top with the remaining fresh raspberries. Serve immediately.

Tip: Use the same method to make tartlets with mango and kiwi, orange and strawberries, etc.

COOKING
FOR EVERY
OCCASION

-- DINNER WITH FRIENDS --

-- BUFFET MEALS --

-- HAVING FAMILY OVER --

-- HAVING A BUNCH OF CHILDREN OVER --

-- HOLIDAY DESSERTS --

-- CELEBRATIONS VEGAN-STYLE --

-- BARBECUES AND PICNICS --

-- VEGAN BRUNCH --

Tofu and avocado California makis

Makes 24 makis

200 g short-grain rice
80 ml rice wine vinegar (or cider)
1 tsp salt
1½ tsp light brown sugar
100 g firm tofu, cut into long slices
1 tsp sesame oil
1 small avocado, sliced
black sesame seeds
1½ sheet yaki nori
1½ bowls vegenaise (see p. 163)

Put the rice in a small bowl, cover with water and mix with your hands to clean it. Throw the water away. Repeat 3 times. Bring the rice and 500 ml of water to the boil in a saucepan, then turn down the heat to medium-low. Cover and cook just until the rice has absorbed all the water. Combine the vinegar with the salt and sugar in a small saucepan and heat. When the salt and sugar have dissolved, remove from the heat and leave to cool. When the rice is done, put it in a bowl and pour the vinegar mixture over it. Cover with a damp tea towel and leave to cool. Brown the tofu in a little frying pan in the sesame oil. Place a piece of cling film on a bamboo mat and sprinkle with black sesame seeds. Spread a third of the rice on the mat. Place ½ a sheet of nori on it and spread a little vegenaise over it. Arrange the tofu and the avocado in two lines along the length of the nori then roll the maki up using the mat to shape it. Wrap in the cling film. Repeat the process with the remaining ingredients. If you are not going to eat them immediately, refrigerate them. Remove the cling film and cut the rolls into makis with a wet knife. If you find it is easier to cut them while wrapped in the cling film, do so and remove it afterwards.

Serve with soy sauce, wasabi and marinated ginger.

Thai vegetable curry

Serves 4-6

2 sweet potatoes, cut into small dice
2 large onions, cut into medium-sized pieces
2 red peppers, cut into medium-sized pieces
2 green peppers, cut into medium-sized pieces
3 garlic cloves, finely sliced
2 tbsp toasted sesame oil
4 tomatoes, peeled and diced
2 tbsp soy sauce
500 ml coconut milk
1 tbsp crunchy peanut butter
2-3 tbsp Thai red curry paste
2 tbsp chopped fresh coriander

Heat the sesame oil in a large, high-sided pan. Sauté the onions, the peppers and the sweet potato over high heat for 10 minutes. Add the tomatoes and garlic to the pan together with the soy sauce. Lower the heat to medium. Cook for 10 minutes. Whisk the coconut milk, peanut butter and curry paste together and add the mixture to the pan. Cook for a further 10 minutes. Sprinkle with the fresh coriander and serve with plain Thai rice.

Cold avocado, sweetcorn and pepper soup

Serves 1-2

150 ml water
125 g sweetcorn
1 avocado
1 small piece green chilli
1 lime, juiced
1 tsp chopped fresh coriander
salt and pepper

Whiz all the ingredients in a blender.

Serve with corn tortillas grilled in the oven for a few minutes or with corn chips.

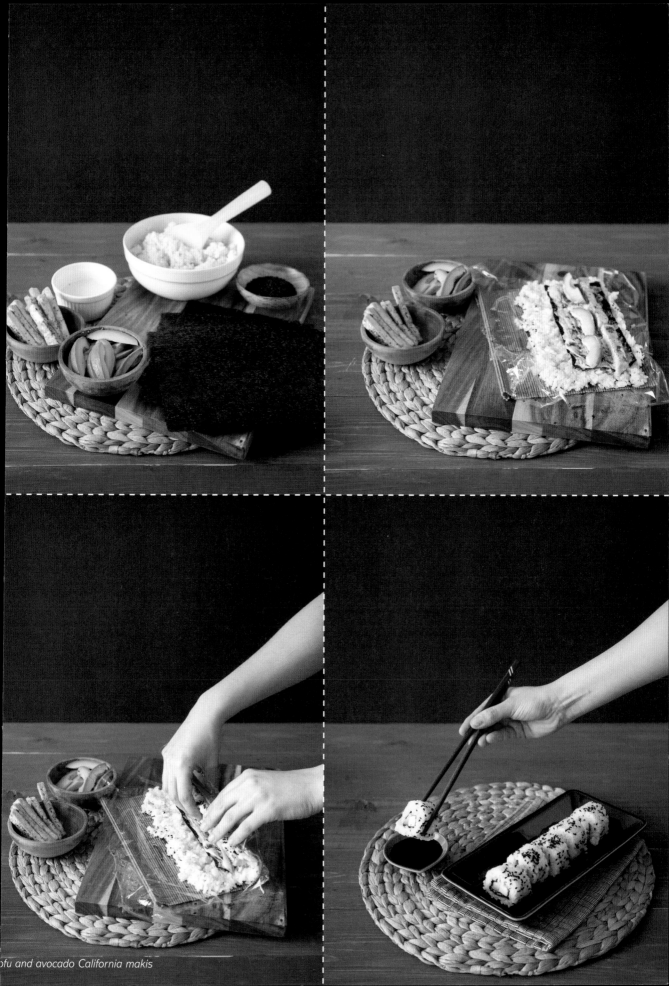

Tofu and avocado California makis

Vitamin-packed sala

Vitamin-packed salad

Serves 4

150 ml balsamic vinegar
150 g baby spinach leaves, washed and dried in a spinner
250 g strawberries, washed, hulled and cut into quarters
1 avocado, diced
2 oranges, 1 zested
olive oil
tamari-caramelised almonds
salt and pepper

Pour the balsamic vinegar into a saucepan and cook over high heat to reduce it. The consistency should be creamy but liquid. Pour into a ramekin and leave to cool. To supreme the oranges, cut along the membranes and remove the segments. Put a handful of spinach leaves on each of the 4 plates. Top with the avocado, the fruit and orange zest. Drizzle with a little olive oil. Sprinkle with the caramelised almonds and drizzle with the balsamic vinegar reduction. Season to taste.

Stuffed courgettes à la Provençale

Serves 2-4

2 large, green courgettes, washed and cut in half
   length wise
150 g firm tofu, crumbled
1 tsp herbs de Provence
1 tbsp olive oil, plus extra for cooking
1 garlic clove, crushed to a paste
8 tsp breadcrumbs
salt and pepper

Use a small spoon to scoop out the courgette flesh. Put the tofu in a bowl with the herbs de Provence, olive oil, garlic, salt and pepper. Mix well. Stuff the courgettes with the tofu mixture. Sprinkle each courgette with 2 tsp of breadcrumbs, drizzle with a little olive oil and bake for about 40 minutes at 200°C (Gas mark 6).

Aubergine pastillas

Serves 4

2 aubergines, cut into small dice
2 small onions, cut into small dice
3 garlic cloves, finely sliced
3 tbsp olive oil, plus extra for the brik sheets
2 tsp ras el hanout
2 tsp ground cumin
150 ml water
2 tbsp tahini
2 tbsp chopped fresh coriander
2 tbsp chopped flat-leaf parsley
8 brik pastry sheets
salt and pepper

Heat the olive oil in a frying pan over high heat and add the spices, aubergines and onions. Mix well and cook for 10 minutes. Add the garlic and cook for a further 5 minutes. Combine the water with the tahini and pour into the pan. Mix well and cook for 30 minutes, still over high heat. Add the herbs and season with salt and pepper to taste. The aubergines should be very tender. Place 1 sheet of brik pastry on a large plate. Lightly brush it with oil and then place a second sheet of pastry over it. Put a quarter of the aubergine stuffing in the middle. Lightly brush the exposed pastry with oil and then neatly fold it over the stuffing with 4 or 5 folds. Turn the pastilla over (the folded side will be underneath) and place on a baking tray lined with parchment paper. Repeat the process with the remaining ingredients. Lightly brush them with olive oil and bake for 15-20 minutes at 180°C (Gas mark 4). The pastillas should be golden brown. When they are done, place them on kitchen paper to remove any excess oil. Serve hot or warm.

Stuffed tomatoes

Serves 4

1 vegetable stock cube
2 tsp barley miso
½ tsp garlic powder
½ tsp liquid smoke
500 ml boiling water
50 g textured soy protein (small pieces)
4 large tomatoes for stuffing, washed
2 garlic cloves
3 tbsp chopped parsley
2 tbsp olive oil
salt and pepper

Combine the vegetable stock cube, miso, garlic powder and the liquid smoke in a bowl. Season with pepper and whisk in the boiling water. Put the textured soy protein into the liquid. Cover and leave to rehydrate for 30 minutes. Cut the tops off the tomatoes and set them aside. Scoop out the flesh and seeds (use to make a coulis or add to a soup) and put the tomatoes in an oven-proof dish. Drain the soy protein and put it back in the bowl. Use a mini-chopper or a food processor and whiz the garlic with the parsley and olive oil. Mix with the soy protein. Season with salt and pepper. Stuff the tomatoes with the mixture, pressing down well. Stand the tomato tops around the edge of the dish. Bake for 15 minutes at 180°C (Gas mark 4). Put the tops on the tomatoes and bake for a further 10 minutes.

Salade Niçoise with broad beans

Serves 4

100 g broad beans, podded
4 good-sized tomatoes, cut into medium-sized dice
1 cucumber, cut into medium-sized dice
1 red pepper, cut into medium-sized dice
1 red onion, sliced
70 g black olives
70 g artichoke hearts, sliced
3 tbsp olive oil
10 basil leaves, chopped
salt and pepper

Cook the broad beans in boiling water for 3 minutes then drain, and peel when cool. Put the tomatoes, cucumber and red pepper in a bowl with the onion. Mix the vegetables together with the olives and artichoke hearts, the olive oil and basil. Season to taste and refrigerate.

Delicious with garlic bread, canapés topped with artichonade (see p. 176) and with my Italian dip (see p. 32) for a complete and flavoursome summer meal.

Savoury basil and lemon cheesecake with a grilled tomato coulis

Serves 4-6

<u>For the base</u>
65 g quinoa crackers
50 g walnuts
1½ tbsp olive oil
1½ tbsp unscented coconut oil

<u>For the filling</u>
240 g cream cheese (see p. 128)
140 g firm tofu
75 g lacto-fermented tofu
4 tbsp cornflour
3 tbsp chopped basil
1 tbsp lemon juice
½ tbsp malted yeast
½ lemon, zested
½ tsp salt
pepper

<u>For the tomato coulis</u>
6 tomatoes, quartered
1 onion, quartered
1 tbsp olive oil
salt and pepper

Whiz the ingredients for the base in a food processor. Spread evenly in a spring form tin about 20 cm in diameter. Use a flat-bottomed tumbler to press down well. Refrigerate for 15 minutes. Whiz the ingredients for the filling together in a food processor. Spread evenly over the chilled base and bake for 30 minutes at 180°C (Gas mark 4). Leave to cool then refrigerate (can be made the day before). Line a baking tray with parchment paper and arrange the tomatoes and onion on it. Drizzle with olive oil and bake for 15-20 minutes under the grill at 275°C. Whiz with salt and pepper. Strain through a fine conical strainer if necessary and leave to cool. Serve the cheesecake cold together with the coulis.

ury basil and lemon cheesecake with a grilled tomato coulis

Pecan brownies

Serves 6-8

125 g dark, baking chocolate, broken into pieces
75 ml rice milk
50 g cocoa powder
85 g margarine, cut into small pieces
¾ tsp salt
½ tsp ground vanilla
100 g apple compote
½ tsp baking powder
200 g light brown sugar
200 g plain flour
45 g pecans, cut into medium-sized pieces

Put the chocolate in a mixing bowl and melt it over a bain-marie. Whisk in the rice milk, then the cocoa powder followed by the margarine. Add the salt, vanilla and apple compote. Mix well and remove from the heat. Off the bain-marie, whisk in the baking powder, sugar and then the flour a little at a time. Stir in the pecans. Mix together with a spatula. Line a square 20 x 20 cm cake tin with parchment paper and pour in the batter. Smooth with a spatula. Bake at 180°C (Gas mark 4) for about 35 minutes. Leave to cool for 1 hour before unmoulding and then cool for 30 minutes on a wire rack. Serve, cut into squares.

BUFFET MEALS

Hummus with coriander

Makes 1 bowl

4 tbsp tahini
250 g cooked chickpeas
4 tbsp olive oil
1 small garlic clove
4 tbsp lemon juice
6 tbsp water
1 tbsp chopped fresh coriander
salt and pepper

Put the tahini, chickpeas, olive oil, garlic, lemon juice and water in the bowl of a food processor. Whiz until thick and creamy. Season with salt and pepper and add the fresh coriander. Whiz again for a few seconds. Put into a bowl and refrigerate. Serve drizzled with a little olive oil.

Guacamole

Serves 4

3 perfectly ripe avocados
2 limes, juiced
½ onion
1 handful fresh coriander leaves
¼ green chilli
1 small tomato, finely diced
salt

Cut the avocados in quarters lengthwise. The skin and stone should come away easily. Put the avocado flesh in a large bowl. Add the juice of 1 lime and mash well with a fork. Use a mini-chopper to finely chop the onion, fresh coriander and chilli. Add to the mashed avocado and season with salt to taste. Add more lime juice if necessary. Stir in the tomato. Serve at once.

Spiced polenta dice

Serves 4

400 ml soy milk
½ tsp vegetable stock paste (½ cube)
½ tsp ground cumin
¼ tsp ground cayenne pepper
1 pinch salt
100 g pre-cooked polenta
2 tsp chopped fresh coriander
olive oil

Combine the soy milk with the stock paste, cumin and cayenne pepper in a saucepan. Bring to the boil and sprinkle in the polenta. Cook over medium heat for 5 minutes, stirring vigorously and continuously with a wooden spoon. Stir in the fresh coriander and remove from the heat. Oil a small square dish or an airtight container and pour in the polenta. Press down well and refrigerate for 1 hour for it to firm up. Cut the polenta into small dice. Oil an oven-proof dish with olive oil and put in the diced polenta. Turn the pieces in the oil so that they are coated all over then bake for 40 minutes at 180°C (Gas mark 4). Serve warm or cold.

Aubergine, tomato and mozzarella bruschetta

Serves 3-6

1 large aubergine
olive oil
½ ball soy mozzarella (see p. 128)
1 tomato, cut into small dice
dried oregano
basil leaves, chopped
salt and pepper

Cut off the cap and stem of the aubergine and cut into 6 slices lengthwise. Line a baking tray with parchment paper and arrange the slices on the tray. Drizzle with olive oil and put under the grill for a few minutes. Turn the slices over and grill again. They should be nicely browned. Cut the mozzarella into thin slices and place on top of the grilled aubergine slices. Top with the diced tomato and sprinkle with the oregano and basil. Drizzle with a little olive oil. Season with salt and pepper and grill again for a few minutes so that the mozzarella melts and the tomato cooks. Serve immediately and enjoy it hot.

Cucumber and mint granita

Serves 4-8

1 cucumber, cut into medium-sized dice
100 ml water
20 mint leaves, finely chopped
3 tbsp agave syrup

Whiz together all the ingredients. Pour into a bowl and freeze for 1 hour. Scrape with a fork to break up the crystals then put it back in the freezer. Repeat every 30 minutes until the granita is a mass of ice crystals. If it has not been eaten within 24 hours, transfer to an airtight container or a freezer bag. Keeps for 3 months in the freezer.

Perfect for a summer aperitif for adults and children alike, or as a cocktail if a little alcohol is added.

Gazpacho verrines with garnish

Serves 6

5 large tomatoes, peeled and roughly chopped
1 large red pepper, roughly chopped
1 small onion, roughly chopped
2 garlic cloves, roughly chopped
½ cucumber, roughly chopped
150 ml water
4 tbsp tomato passata
2 tbsp olive oil
1 tbsp balsamic vinegar
salt and pepper
For the garnish
¼ cucumber, cut into small dice
⅓ baguette, cut into small dice
olive oil
1 tomato, cut into small dice
fresh herbs, chopped
salt and pepper

Make the gazpacho by whizzing the tomatoes with the red pepper, onion, garlic, cucumber and the water. Add the tomato passata, olive oil and vinegar and blend again. Season to taste. Heat a little olive oil in a frying pan and brown the diced bread. Season with salt and pepper to taste. Divide the gazpacho among 6 verrines. Top with the raw vegetables, the croutons and the chopped herbs just before serving.

Cheese, fig and paprika morsels

Serves 4

1 portion melty cheese (see p. 135), cubed
2 black figs, cut into small pieces
sweet paprika
salt and pepper

Put the cheese in a bowl. Mash with a fork until coarse in texture. Add the figs and a little paprika to the cheese. Season lightly with salt. Use your fingers to mix well and then shape into round, bite-sized morsels. Arrange on a serving dish and refrigerate before serving.

Red pesto palmiers

Makes about 20 palmiers

50 g raw cashew nuts
1 tsp malted yeast
½ tsp salt
80 g sun-dried tomatoes in olive oil, drained
5 tbsp oil from the tomatoes
4 tbsp chopped basil
1 sheet vegan puff pastry

Whiz the cashew nuts together with the malted yeast and salt. Add the other pesto ingredients and whiz until very smooth. Unroll the puff pastry, spread the pesto over the entire surface, fold each side towards the centre 3 times and then bring together as if closing a book. Cut into slices 1 cm wide at the most. Line a baking tray with parchment paper and place the palmiers on the tray. Bake at 180°C (Gas mark 4) for 25 minutes.

Grilled courgette spirals

Serves 4

2 courgettes, finely sliced lengthwise
2 tsp olive oil
1 small bowl garlic and herb cheese spread (see p. 133)

Cook the courgette slices in a frying pan with the olive oil. Set aside. Put 1 tsp of the cheese spread at one end of a slice of courgette and roll it up. Repeat the process with the remaining slices. If the spirals unroll, use a toothpick to hold them in place.

Petits pois and coconut samosas

Makes 12 samosas

2 medium potatoes, peeled and cut into small pieces
100 g fresh or frozen petits pois
1 onion, finely sliced
1 garlic clove, finely sliced
1 tbsp vegetable oil, plus extra for cooking
2 tsp curry powder
150 ml coconut milk
150 ml water
3 tbsp plain flour
6 brik pastry sheets

Bring the potatoes to the boil then simmer for 5 minutes. Add the peas to the saucepan and cook for a further 5 minutes. Drain. Brown the onion and garlic in a frying pan with the oil over high heat. Add the curry powder, potatoes and peas. Pour in the coconut milk. Cook over medium heat. Coarsely mash the potatoes and mix well with the other ingredients and reduce. Transfer to a bowl and leave to cool. Whisk the water and flour together in a saucepan then allow it to thicken over high heat until it is like a thick glue. Set aside in a bowl. Cut the brik pastry sheets in half. Make the samosas: Fold the curved side over to form a strip. Place 1 tbsp of the filling in a corner of the strip and fold into a triangle. Brush the end of the pastry with the 'glue' and seal the samosa. Repeat with the remaining ingredients. Make sure that the samosas are well sealed. Heat enough oil to cover the bottom of a frying pan and fry until golden brown. Drain on kitchen paper. Serve hot.

grilled courgette spirals, samosas and cheese morsels

Blueberry panna cotta with saffron-scented lemon jelly

Blueberry panna cotta with saffron-scented lemon jelly

Serves 4

250 g fresh blueberries

For the panna cotta
250 ml soy cream
250 ml soy milk
3 tbsp light brown sugar
¾ tsp agar-agar powder
1 pinch ground vanilla

For the jelly
2 lemons, juiced
1 lemon, zested
3 tbsp cane sugar
¼ tsp agar-agar powder
¼ tsp saffron strands
1 pinch ground turmeric
50 ml water

Whisk all the ingredients for the panna cotta together In a saucepan. Bring to the boil and then simmer for 1-2 minutes, stirring constantly. Put a layer of blueberries in the bottom of 4 verrines. Then add another layer of blueberries. Divide the panna cotta mixture between the verrines. Leave to cool to room temperature then refrigerate for 2 hours. Combine the lemon zest and the juice with the sugar in a small saucepan. Add the agar-agar, saffron and turmeric. Add the water. Bring to the boil and cook for 2 minutes, stirring constantly. Pour over the set mixture and leave to cool. Leave to set in the fridge for 1 hour.

Mini strawberry and rhubarb pies

Serves 6

200 g rhubarb, chopped
170 g strawberry jam
1 pinch ground cinnamon
1 quantity shortcrust pastry dough (see p. 244)

Cook the rhubarb in a little water until soft and jam-like. Add the strawberry jam and cinnamon and reduce over low heat until the mixture is no longer very liquid. Roll out the dough and cut out 6 medium-sized discs and 6 small ones. Line a muffin tin with the large discs. Pour the strawberry-rhubarb mixture into the tin and place a small disc on each pie. Seal them well by folding the edges inwards and pressing lightly with the tines of a fork. Prick the tops 4 times with the tip of a knife. Bake at 180°C (Gas mark 4) for 25 minutes.

Vanilla and chocolate puddings

Serves 4

For the vanilla layer
400 ml soy milk
4 tbsp light brown sugar
1 tbsp cashew butter
½ tsp agar-agar powder
⅛ tsp vanilla extract

For the chocolate layer
100 g dark chocolate
400 ml soy milk
4 tbsp light brown sugar
½ tsp agar-agar powder

Prepare the vanilla layer: Mix all the ingredients and pour into a saucepan. Boil for 1 minute, stirring constantly. Divide among 4 glasses or verrines and leave to cool then refrigerate for 1 hour. Melt the chocolate in a bain-marie then mix with the remaining ingredients for the chocolate layer. Pour the mixture over the vanilla layer in the glasses. Leave to cool then refrigerate for 1 hour.

For a more spectacular dessert, leave the first layer to set at an angle by tilting the glasses and propping them up in a cake mould or bowls.

Green and black tapenade

Serves 4

100 g green olives, pitted
150 g black olives, pitted
2 tbsp capers
3 tbsp olive oil
3 tbsp freshly squeezed lemon juice
1 small garlic clove, finely sliced
pepper

Put the olives in a food processor. Whiz with the capers, olive oil, lemon juice and the garlic to obtain a smooth tapenade. Season with pepper to taste. Refrigerate and eat within 48 hours.

- -

Mini piña colada ice creams

Makes 8 mini ice creams

300 ml pineapple juice
100 ml white rum
100 ml coconut milk

Whiz all the ingredients in a blender and divide among 8 liqueur glasses. Place 2 pieces of Sellotape next to each other across the top of each glass and insert a wooden ice cream stick between them. Freeze for at least for 3-4 hours. Run the glass under hot water to unmould. Serve as an aperitif.

HAVING FAMILY OVER

Gratin dauphinois

Serves 4

900 g firm-fleshed potatoes, peeled, washed and cut into
    slices
300 ml soy milk
500 ml soy cream
3 garlic cloves, 2 crushed to a paste, 1 peeled and cut in half
ground nutmeg
margarine
salt and pepper

Combine the milk and 300 ml of the cream in a large saucepan with the garlic paste and season with salt, pepper and nutmeg to taste. Add the potatoes and turn the heat to medium. Cook for 10 minutes, stirring gently so that the mixture does not catch on the bottom of the pan. Grease an oven-proof dish with the margarine and then rub it with the peeled, cut garlic clove. Use a slotted spoon to gently put the potato slices into the dish then pour the milk mixture over them. Add the remaining 200 ml of cream. Season with salt, pepper and a little nutmeg. Bake at 180°C (Gas mark 4) for 45 minutes to 1 hour. Keep an eye on it as it cooks.

Use a fairly deep dish to avoid the cream boiling over the edge.

Green bean persillade

Serves 4

2 tbsp olive oil
4 garlic cloves, crushed
500 g fresh green beans, steamed
1 bunch curly parsley, finely chopped
salt and pepper

Heat the olive oil in a large frying pan over medium heat and sauté the garlic and the beans. Add the parsley and cook for about 10 minutes. The beans should be firm and just beginning to brown. Season with salt and pepper and serve.

Seitan escalopes with a white wine sauce, tomatoes and olives

Serves 4

350 ml vegetable stock
1 tbsp white miso
150 ml white wine
200 ml soy cream (or oat cream)
1 tbsp cornflour
1 tbsp olive oil
100 ml tomato passata
30 g green olives, pitted
2 tbsp organic vegan margarine
4 escalopes seitanfu (see p. 98)
salt and pepper

Heat the stock in a saucepan. Add the miso and then the wine. Cook over high heat, stirring often for 10 minutes, to reduce. Add the cream and turn down the heat to medium. Whisk in the cornflour. Season and add the olive oil, tomato passata and olives. Cook for a further 5 minutes over low heat. Heat the margarine in a large frying pan and brown the seitan escalopes on both sides. Pour the sauce over the escalopes and serve.

Soy blanquette

Serves 4

50 g textured soy protein (large pieces)
2 tbsp white miso
1 tbsp barley miso
3 tbsp vegetable oil
300 g carrots, peeled and cut into rounds
½ onion, finely sliced
3 tbsp margarine
4 tbsp flour
100 ml soy cream
1 tbsp lemon juice
salt and pepper

For the stock

1 tbsp vegetable oil
½ onion, finely sliced
1 bouquet garni
1 leek, finely sliced
1 vegetable stock cube
1½ litres water

Prepare the stock: Heat the oil in a large saucepan and sauté the onion. Add the bouquet garni, leek, stock cube and the water. Cook over medium heat for 1 hour. Put the soy protein in a bowl with the 2 misos. Cover with boiling water and leave to rehydrate for 30 minutes, then drain. Heat the oil in a saucepan over high heat then add the soy protein, carrots and onion. Lower the heat to medium and sauté for about 10 minutes. Add 1 ladleful of stock and cook for about 20 minutes. Strain the broth. Melt the margarine in a medium-sized saucepan. Stir in the flour to make a roux. Gradually whisk in 750 ml of stock. Add the soy cream and the lemon juice. Season to taste and reduce for 5 minutes. Pour over the blanquette and cook for 5-10 minutes over low heat.

Serve with potatoes.

Pear, mozzarella and rocket salad

Serves 4

125 g rocket leaves, washed and drained
½ ball soy mozzarella (see p. 128), finely sliced
2 large ripe pears, cut into thin wedges
1 handful hazelnuts, roughly chopped
olive oil
white balsamic vinegar
pepper and fleur de sel

Arrange the rocket leaves on a plate. Top with the mozzarella and the pears. Sprinkle with the hazelnuts. Drizzle with a little olive oil and a dash of white balsamic vinegar. Season with salt and pepper to taste. Prepare this salad just before serving it.

Onion, shallot and chive tart

Serves 4-6

5 large onions, sliced
3 shallots, sliced
2 tbsp olive oil
2 tbsp cane sugar
200 ml soy cream
½ tsp salt
1 tbsp cornflour
ground nutmeg
4 tbsp chopped fresh chives
1 sheet vegan puff pastry
pepper

Brown the onions and shallots in the olive oil and the sugar over medium heat. In a bowl, mix the cream with salt and cornflour, add pepper and season to taste with the nutmeg and chives. Line a 25 cm/10 inch tin with the puff pastry (do not remove the parchment paper it comes with), prick the dough, spread the chive cream over it and top with the onions. Neaten the edges of the tart. Bake at 180°C (Gas mark 4) for 30 minutes.

Stuffed potatoes

Serves 4

4 large, firm-fleshed potatoes, washed
2 shallots, sliced
1 tsp olive oil
125 g smoked tofu, crumbled
2 tbsp cashew butter
1 tbsp malted yeast flakes
100 ml non-dairy cream
freshly ground nutmeg
2 tbsp breadcrumbs
margarine or olive oil
salt and pepper

Put the potatoes in a saucepan of water. Cook for 20-30 minutes after the water has come to the boil. The potatoes should not be completely cooked and should still be firm. Hollow the potatoes out but do not remove too much flesh. Brown the shallots in the olive oil. Put a third of the potato flesh in a bowl with the tofu, shallots, cashew butter and the yeast and mix well. Add the non-dairy cream to bind the mixture. Season with salt, pepper and nutmeg to taste. Stuff the potatoes and arrange in an oven-proof dish. Sprinkle with the breadcrumbs. Top each potato with a little piece of margarine or a drizzle of olive oil and bake for about 45 minutes at 180°C (Gas mark 4).

iffed potatoes

Waldorf salad

Serves 4-6

240 g silken tofu
2 tbsp Dijon mustard
4 tbsp neutral vegetable oil
2 Granny Smith apples, cut into matchsticks
250 g celery ribs, finely sliced
100 g walnuts, roughly chopped
50 g raisins
200 g little gem lettuces

Whiz the silken tofu with the mustard and vegetable oil to make a mayonnaise. Pour into a bowl and refrigerate. Combine the apples, celery and walnuts in a bowl. Add the raisins and mayonnaise and refrigerate. Serve on a bed of little gem lettuces on each plate, or combine the leaves with the other ingredients just before serving.

Crème brûlée with raspberries

Makes 4 crème brûlées

400 g silken tofu
200 ml soy cream
50 g light brown sugar, plus 8 tbsp extra for the caramel
2 tsp pistachio butter
½ tsp agar-agar powder
⅛ tsp ground vanilla
1 pinch ground cinnamon
100 g raspberries, halved

Whiz all of the ingredients together except the raspberries. Pour into a saucepan, turn the heat to high and whisk often. When bubbles appear in the mixture, whisk continuously for 2 minutes. Divide between 4 ramekins. Push the halved raspberries into the mixture with a finger or a spoon. Leave to cool then refrigerate for 2 hours. When ready to serve, sprinkle the tops with the sugar and caramelise (use a blow torch for this, do not put them in the oven).

Chocolate mousse à la liégeoise

Serves 4

170 g dark chocolate
1 tbsp coconut oil
50 g icing sugar
400 g silken tofu, very cold
coconut Chantilly cream (see p. 143)

Melt the chocolate in a bain-marie. Remove from the heat, mix with the coconut oil and icing sugar, then with the silken tofu. Whiz with an immersion blender for at least 5 minutes to make the mixture nice and light. Divide among 4 verrines and refrigerate for 4 hours. Top with coconut Chantilly cream before serving.

Decorate with chocolate flakes or, if they are in season, soft fruit.

hocolate mousse à la liégeoise

Tofu stars and pink ketchup

Tomato broth with noodles

Serves 4 children

1½ vegetable stock cubes
5 tbsp tomato double concentrate
1 tsp garlic powder
1 tsp dried basil
1½ litres boiling water
80 g noodles

Put all the ingredients, except the water and noodles in a large saucepan. Slake with a little of the boiling water, then add the rest of the water. Bring to the boil. Add the noodles. Cook until done and serve immediately.

Pink beetroot ketchup

Makes 1 small bottle

135 g cane sugar
60 ml cider vinegar
½ tsp salt
¼ tsp five-spice powder
¼ tsp ground coriander
¼ tsp garlic powder
300 ml tomato passata
1 small beetroot, peeled and chopped

Put the sugar, vinegar, salt and spices in a saucepan. Turn the heat to high. Whiz the passata and the beetroot in a blender. When the mixture in the saucepan comes to the boil, pour in the tomato and beetroot mixture and stir. Lower the heat to medium and cook for 10 minutes. Pour into a small glass bottle and leave to cool. Use as you would shop-bought ketchup. Keeps for 1 week in the fridge.

Mashed potatoes

Serves 6-8 children

1.3 kg potatoes, peeled
300 ml soy milk, warmed
3 tbsp olive oil
ground nutmeg
salt

Bring the potatoes to the boil then simmer until tender. Drain and press through a potato ricer. Vigorously whisk in the soy milk and the olive oil. Season with salt and nutmeg to taste. Serve immediately.

Tofu stars with peanut butter

Serves 4 children

2 x 125 g blocks firm tofu
4 tbsp peanut butter
100 ml water
1 tbsp freshly squeezed lemon juice
1 tsp tamari
¼ tsp ground coriander
¼ tsp ground cardamom
1 tbsp olive oil

Cut the tofu blocks in half along their width and cut out 4 stars using a cookie cutter (keep the scraps for making a stuffing or another dish). Whiz the peanut butter with the water, lemon juice, tamari and spices. Brown the tofu stars in the olive oil in a frying pan then pour in the peanut butter sauce. Cook for a few minutes and serve.

Delicious served with pasta and vegetables.

Tofu Parmentier

Serves 4-6 children

600 g potatoes, peeled and cut into chunks

1 onion, sliced

2 tbsp olive oil

200 g soft, smoked tofu, crumbled

250 ml oat milk, warmed

1 tbsp olive oil

8 tbsp soy cream

4 tbsp malted yeast flakes

Bring the potatoes to the boil then simmer until tender. Drain. Sauté the onions in the olive oil in a frying pan over high heat. Add the tofu and cook for a few minutes. Lower the heat to medium and brown for 5 minutes. Divide among 4 individual moulds and press down well. Press the potatoes through a potato ricer and then mix with the oat milk and olive oil. Divide among the moulds. Top each one with 2 tbsp of cream and 1 tbsp of malted yeast. Bake for 10 minutes at 240°C (Gas mark 9).

Creamy, thyme-scented tomato sauce

Serves 2 children

½ onion

2 tsp olive oil

½ tsp dried thyme

150 ml tomato passata

3 tbsp thick lacto-fermented soy cream

1 tbsp cashew butter

1 tsp tamari

Use a mini-chopper or food processor to whiz the onion to a purée. Sauté the onion with the olive oil in a small saucepan over medium heat for a few minutes, stirring. Add the passata and cook for at least 5 minutes, stirring continuously. Turn off the heat and whisk in the soy cream until well-combined. Add the cashew butter and tamari (optional if preparing this dish for young children) and mix well.

Delicious with pasta, rice, vegetables or tofu...in short, a sauce to turn almost anything into a quick, gourmet dish.

Quick tofu couscous

Serves 4-6 children

1 courgette, sliced

1 small onion, peeled and sliced

1 small potato, peeled and sliced

1 small carrot, peeled and sliced

3 tbsp olive oil

125 g firm tofu, finely diced

1½ tsp ras el hanout

400 ml water

4 tbsp cooked chickpeas

salt

For the couscous

250 g medium-grain semolina

300 ml boiling water

1 tbsp olive oil

Sauté the vegetables in a saucepan with the olive oil over high heat. Add the tofu and the ras el hanout. Sauté for a few minutes, stirring. Add the water and cook for about 15 minutes or until the vegetables are tender. Add the chickpeas and remove from the heat. Season lightly with salt. Put the semolina in a small bowl, pour in the boiling water and cover with a plate. Leave to swell for a few minutes, then add the olive oil and mix with a fork to remove any lumps. Serve the couscous with the vegetable and tofu mixture.

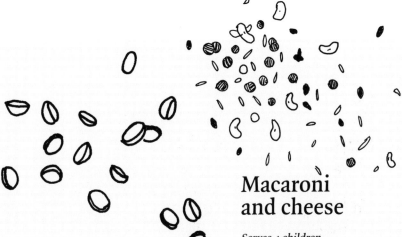

Macaroni and cheese

Serves 4 children

200 g macaroni (or elbow macaroni)

50 g tamari-marinated lacto-fermented tofu, grated on a large-hole grater

300 ml soy cream

3 tbsp cashew butter

2 tbsp yeast flakes

1 tbsp white miso

1 tbsp freshly squeezed lemon juice

½ tsp salt

½ tsp garlic powder

Cook the macaroni in boiling water. Combine the other ingredients in a small saucepan over medium heat for 5 minutes. Drain the pasta and put it back in the saucepan. Pour the sauce over the pasta. Add the grated tofu and mix well. Serve immediately.

Chocolate-coated banana ices

Serves 4 children

50 g dark chocolate

2 bananas, peeled and cut in half

40 g hazelnuts, very finely chopped with a knife

Melt the chocolate in a bain-marie. Stick each banana half on a wooden ice cream stick and dip them in the melted chocolate. Sprinkle with the chopped hazelnuts to completely coat them. Put the bananas on a plate and freeze for 2 hours. Remove from the freezer 15 minutes before eating.

Use 1 banana for very young children but cut each half banana in half again lengthwise.

Peanut butter cups

Makes 10-12 cups

100 g dark chocolate

2 tbsp icing sugar, sifted

2 tbsp peanut butter

Melt the chocolate in a bain-marie, then mix with 1 tbsp of the icing sugar. Mix the peanut butter with the remaining 1 tbsp of icing sugar. Put about 1 tsp of melted chocolate into 10 or 12 little fluted paper cases. Use your fingers to shape little balls of peanut butter and place on the chocolate in the paper cases. Coat with about 1 tsp of chocolate. Refrigerate for 1 hour.

Yoghurt cake

Serves 6

2 x 100 g pots soy yoghurt

2 x pots light brown sugar

3 tsp baking powder

¼ tsp ground vanilla

½ x 125 g yogurt pot olive oil

3 x pots type T55 flour

oil or margarine for the cake tin

In this recipe you use the pots to measure ingredients. Whisk the yoghurt and sugar together in a mixing bowl. Add the baking powder and vanilla. Whisk in the oil and mix well. The mixture should be somewhat foamy. Add the flour a bit at a time. Grease a 22 cm/9 inch spring form cake tin with a little margarine or oil and pour in the cake mixture. Bake for 30 minutes at 180°C (Gas mark 4). Leave to cool before unmoulding.

Fruit jelly trio

Serves 8 children

<u>1st layer</u>
200 ml water
85 g blueberries
3 tbsp cane sugar
1 tsp agar-agar powder
<u>2nd layer</u>
200 ml water
100 g strawberries, hulled
4 tbsp cane sugar
1 tsp agar-agar powder
<u>3rd layer</u>
450 ml freshly squeezed orange juice
5 tbsp cane sugar
1 tsp agar-agar powder

For the first layer: Whiz all the ingredients together and pour into a saucepan. Bring to the boil as you whisk and cook for 2 minutes. Divide the mixture among 8 clear glasses or verrines. Leave to cool until the jelly has just set. Prepare the second layer in the same way as the first. For the third layer, mix the ingredients directly in the saucepan and then prepare in the same way. Leave the jellies to set in the fridge for 2 hours before serving.

For an even more gourmet dessert, decorate with soft fruit and/or chocolate sauce.

Totally chocolate cookies

Makes 12-15 cookies

5 tbsp organic, vegan margarine, softened
100 g light brown sugar
85 g dark chocolate, melted in a bain-marie
½ tsp baking powder
½ tsp bicarbonate of soda
¼ tsp sea salt
¼ tsp ground vanilla
75 ml soy milk
160 g plain flour, sifted
65 g dark chocolate chips

Mix the margarine and sugar together in a bowl. Add the chocolate, baking powder, bicarbonate of soda, salt and vanilla. Fold in well with a spatula. Add the soy milk. Add the flour to the mixture. Add the chocolate chips. Line a baking tray with parchment paper. With moistened hands, shape little balls of dough and place them on the tray, spaced well apart. Flatten them slightly. Bake for 12-15 minutes at 180°C (Gas mark 4). Leave to cool on a wire rack.

Chocolate whoopie pies

Makes 12 whoopie pies

90 ml neutral vegetable oil
200 g light brown sugar
⅛ tsp vanilla extract
250 ml almond milk (see p. 120)
175 g plain flour
50 g low-fat cocoa powder
40 g cornflour
1 tsp baking powder
½ tsp bicarbonate of soda
¼ tsp salt
<u>For the ganache</u>
200 g dark chocolate
50 g icing sugar, sifted
5 tbsp non-dairy cream

Mix the oil with the sugar, vanilla and almond milk in a bowl. Mix the dry ingredients in another bowl and then combine with the liquid ingredients. Whisk together well and pour into a piping bag. Line 2 baking trays with parchment paper and pipe 6 discs of dough onto each. Bake for 10 minutes at 180°C (Gas mark 4). For the ganache: Melt the chocolate in a bain-marie, then mix it with the icing sugar and cream. Leave to cool then put into a piping bag with a star nozzle. Pipe a little ganache onto 6 of the cookies and sandwich together with the remaining 6.

Chocolate whoopie pies

Chocolate and soft fruit pizzas

Makes 8 portions

1 quantity pizza dough (see p. 194)
200 g dark chocolate
5 tbsp non-dairy cream
250 g soft fruit of your choice (strawberries, raspberries, redcurrants, blueberries, blackberries, etc.), washed and cut up if necessary

Roll out the dough on parchment paper. Prick the surface with a fork. Bake blind for 10 minutes at 180°C (Gas mark 4), uncovered and without 'baking beans'. Leave to cool. Melt the chocolate in a bain-marie and then add the cream, a spoonful at a time, to make the ganache. Turn the pizza over and spread the ganache over it. Cut into 8 portions. Arrange the fruit on the pizza portions.

Idea: *This fun and easy recipe is great for teaching children to cook. You can make mini pizzas in the same way, or change the topping and make a pizza with yellow fruit (peaches, mango, apricots, etc.) or winter fruit (oranges, bananas, kiwi, etc.).*

colate and soft fruit pizzas

Pink velvet cheesecake

Serves 8

For the biscuit base
200 g totally chocolate cookies (see p. 278), crushed
3 tbsp melted coconut oil

For the filling
125 g hulled strawberries
125 g raspberries
4 tbsp oat cream
1 uncooked beetroot, roughly chopped
400 g firm tofu, roughly chopped
150 g silken tofu
90 g light brown sugar
6 tbsp cashew butter
6 tbsp cornflour
For the jellied coulis
250 g hulled strawberries
100 ml water
½ tsp agar-agar powder
3 tbsp light brown sugar

For the biscuit base: Use a fork to combine the crushed cookies with the coconut oil. Spread evenly in a spring form tin about 25 cm in diameter and use a flat-bottomed tumbler to press down well. Refrigerate for 15 minutes.

For the filling: Whiz the strawberries and raspberries with the oat cream, then strain through a sieve to remove the seeds. Whiz the beetroot with a little water to obtain its juice. Set 8 tbsp of it aside. Whiz all the remaining ingredients together. Pour onto the biscuit base and bake for about 45 minutes at 180°C (Gas mark 4). The top of the cheesecake should be firm. Leave to cool to room temperature.

For the coulis: Whiz the strawberries and the water, then strain through a sieve to remove the seeds. Pour into a small saucepan and add the agar-agar and sugar. Mix well. Bring to the boil and stir for 2 minutes. Pour over the cheesecake. Leave to cool and refrigerate for 2 hours. Carefully unmould just before serving. Keeps well for two days in the fridge.

My advice: Make this cheesecake the day before to save work on the 'big day'.

Pear and chocolate cupcakes

Makes 12 cupcakes

100 g light brown sugar
4 tbsp neutral vegetable oil
2 tbsp almond butter
2½ tsp baking powder
¼ tsp salt
6 tbsp soy cream
4 tbsp ground almonds
200 ml almond milk
⅛ tsp ground tonka beans
200 g type T55 flour
1 pear, peeled and finely diced
For the ganache
400 g chocolate
2 tbsp margarine
200 ml soy cream

In a mixing bowl, whisk together the sugar and oil. Add the other ingredients, one at a time, mixing well after each addition. Add the flour in 2 batches. Line a 12-hole muffin tin with paper cases and divide the mixture among them. Put some diced pear on each one and gently push the pieces in with a knife so that they are mixed in and submerged. Bake for 25 minutes at 180°C (Gas mark 4). For the ganache: Melt the chocolate over a bain marie. Add the margarine and then the soy cream. Leave to cool. Whisk the ganache for a few seconds then put into a piping bag with a very large star nozzle. Pipe the ganache onto the cupcakes when they have cooled completely. Do not refrigerate.

Chocolate and speculoos layer cake

Serves 10-12

For each layer of the cake
75 g dark chocolate
80 g light brown sugar
50 g neutral vegetable oil
75 ml soy milk
1 pinch ground vanilla
1 tsp baking powder
100 g plain flour
For the speculoos cream
200 g vegan speculoos biscuits
200 ml soy cream
3 tbsp virgin coconut oil
For the decoration
pieces of speculoos biscuits
chocolate shavings

Melt the chocolate in a bain-marie. Mix the sugar and oil together, then add to the melted chocolate. Add the soy milk, vanilla and baking powder. Whisk everything together well. Mix in the flour. Cut out a 25 cm/10 inch disc of parchment paper and put it in the base of a spring form tin of the same diameter. Pour in the mixture and bake for 25 minutes at 180°C (Gas mark 4). Leave to cool. Open the tin, turn the cake out onto a plate and remove the parchment paper. Prepare the other 2 cakes in the same way. Leave them to cool. Mix all the ingredients for the cream (do not melt the coconut oil). Assemble the layer cake: spread a third of the cream on one cake and top with another one. Spread another third of the cream onto the second cake and place the third one on it. Spread the remaining cream on top of the third layer. Decorate with pieces of speculoos biscuits and chocolate shavings.

Coconut and mango shard ice cream

Serves 4

250 ml coconut milk
200 ml soy milk
100 ml soy cream
60 ml agave syrup

70 g fine, dessicated coconut
50 g light brown sugar
1 mango, cut into small pieces

Whiz all the ingredients except for the mango and put into an ice-cream maker. When the mixture has thickened, add the mango. Make sure it is well mixed in, then transfer it to an airtight container and freeze. If you don't have an ice-cream maker, pour the mixture (without the mango) into an airtight container, put on the lid and freeze. After 1 hour, take the container out and mix with a fork to break up the crystals. Add the cut-up mango pieces. Return to the freezer. Take it out again after 1 hour and mix again with a fork. Repeat the process for the next 2-3 hours.

Orange blossom-scented iced nougat

Serves 6-8

250 ml soy milk
200 ml soy cream
2 sachets organic whipped cream stabiliser
150 g cane sugar
50 g ground almonds
2 tbsp orange blossom water
30 g chopped pistachios, plus extra for decorating
30 g praline, plus extra for decorating
30 g almonds, skin on, chopped with a knife

Whisk the soy milk and cream together in a bowl. Add the whipped cream stabiliser and whisk vigorously for 2 minutes. Add the sugar and whisk for a few minutes. Add the ground almonds and orange blossom water. Now whisk very gently: the mixture should be very light and foamy. Add the chopped pistachios and keep whisking. Add the praline and whisk again. Lastly, gently whisk in the almonds. Sprinkle some of the extra praline and chopped pistachios in the bottom of a loaf tin. Carefully pour in the mixture. Freeze overnight. Remove from the freezer 5 minutes before serving. Unmould if possible and serve on a platter, perhaps with a raspberry coulis.

Chocolate, praline and coconut l

Chocolate, praline and coconut log

Serves 8

60 ml neutral vegetable oil
100 g light brown sugar
200 ml non-dairy cream
50 g ground hazelnuts
¼ tsp ground vanilla
1½ tsp baking powder
¼ tsp salt
160 g type T55 flour
200 g dark chocolate
2 tbsp coconut oil
3 tbsp hazelnut butter
50 g icing sugar
400 g silken tofu
60 g praline
20 g dessicated coconut

Combine the oil and sugar. Add the non-dairy cream, ground hazelnuts and vanilla and then the baking powder and salt. Mix in the flour. Line a tray with parchment paper and spread the cake mixture over it. Bake at 180°C (Gas mark 4) for 15 minutes. Leave to cool completely. For the cream: melt the chocolate in a bain-marie, then add the coconut oil and hazelnut butter. Fold in the icing sugar. Add the silken tofu. Whiz with an immersion blender and freeze for 15 minutes. Cut 3 rectangles of the same size from the cake. Assemble the log: spread a little of the cold cream on a serving platter. Place a rectangle of cake on it, cover it with cream and sprinkle with praline. Place another layer of cake, cream and praline over it and top with the last rectangle of cake. Lastly, cover the whole log with cream. Mix the remaining praline with the dessicated coconut and cover the log with it. Refrigerate before serving.

Chocolate and chestnut tiramisù verrines

Serves 4

cocoa powder
For the sponge cake
1 tbsp almond butter
60 ml olive oil
100 g light brown sugar
¼ tsp ground vanilla
1½ tsp baking powder
250 ml soy milk
75 g type T55 flour
50 g chestnut flour
For the cream
250 ml vegan Chantilly cream (see p.144)
8 tbsp unsweetened chestnut purée
1-2 tbsp agave syrup (optional)

Mix the ingredients for the cake in a bowl in the order given. Grease or oil a 22 cm/9 inch cake tin and pour in the batter. Bake for 30 minutes at 180°C (Gas mark 4). Leave to cool. Make the cream by whisking the chestnut pureé into the Chantilly cream a little at a time. Next, whisk in the agave syrup. Unmould the sponge cake and cut it into wide strips. Mix 1 tsp of cocoa powder with 150 ml of boiling water in a deep plate. Quickly dip the sponge cake pieces in it and remove them immediately. Carefully place them on a flat plate. Put a layer of sponge cake in the bottom of the verrines. Cover with cream, another layer of sponge cake and another layer of cream. Refrigerate. Sprinkle with cocoa just before serving.

Tip: Use a fine sieve or tea-strainer to sprinkle the cocoa to ensure it is fine and lump-free.

Chestnut and crystallised orange log

Serves 8

35 g crystallised orange peel

<u>For the chestnut cream filling</u>

125 g chestnut cream

2 tsp agar-agar powder

150 ml water

<u>For the sponge cake</u>

70 ml vegetable oil

100 g light brown sugar

¼ tsp vanilla extract

¼ tsp salt

1 tbsp cashew butter

125 ml soy milk

1½ tsp baking powder

50 g cornflour

125 g type T55 flour

<u>For the chestnut cream</u>

250 g chestnut cream

240 g silken tofu

200 ml non-dairy cream

100 ml non-dairy milk

2 tsp agar-agar powder

Prepare the filling: whisk the chestnut cream with the agar-agar and the water in a small saucepan. Bring to the boil, whisking continuously for 1 minute. Line a loaf tin with parchment paper. Pour in the chestnut mixture, leave to cool then refrigerate for 30 minutes. Gently unmould it and cut a strip 5 cm wide and set it aside.

Prepare the sponge cake: mix the oil with the sugar, vanilla and salt. Add the cashew butter, soy milk and baking powder. Whisk in the flour a bit at a time. Line a baking tray with parchment paper. Spread the cake mixture on it and bake for 15 minutes at 180°C (Gas mark 4). Leave to cool.

Whiz the ingredients for the cream together and pour into a small saucepan. Boil for 1 minute, whisking continuously. Pour the cream into a log mould (lined with cling film or rhodoid to unmould it easily) and leave to set until it is firm enough to be able to withstand the weight of the filling. If it is too set the remaining cream will not bind and stick to it. Place the filling along the centre of the cream. Bring the remaining cream to the boil and pour it into the log mould. Arrange the crystallised orange peel on the cream. Cut a piece of sponge cake the same size as the base of the mould and lay it on top. Press it down gently. Leave the log to cool for 1 hour. Refrigerate before unmoulding and serving.

Decorate the log by sprinkling it with cocoa or icing sugar and placing small pieces of chestnut or crystallised orange along the top.

Kings' cake

Serves 6-8

130 g ground almonds

100 g cane sugar

85 g margarine

2 tbsp white almond butter

2 sheets vegan puff pastry

2 tbsp soy cream

½ tbsp neutral vegetable oil

½ tbsp agave syrup

Use a fork to combine the ground almonds, sugar, margarine and almond butter. Roll out 1 sheet of puff pastry onto a baking tray, without removing its parchment paper. Spread the frangipane mixture over it and place the other sheet of puff pastry on top. Seal the edges with the tines of a fork and draw a pattern on the pastry with the tip of a knife. Mix the soy cream with the oil and agave syrup and brush it over the cake. Bake for 40 minutes at 180°C (Gas mark 4).

Chestnut and crystallised orange log

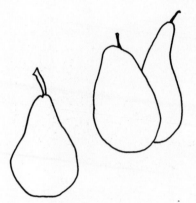

Poached pears and oat praline crumble

Serves 4-8

1 litre water
225 g sugar
¼ tsp ground vanilla
1 tbsp freshly squeezed lemon juice
4 pears, peeled, stem left on
50 g dark chocolate

For the crumble

40 g rolled oats
40 g cane sugar
40 g margarine
1 tbsp praline

Pour the water into a saucepan. Add the sugar, vanilla and lemon juice and turn the heat to medium. Use a melon baller to remove the seeds from the pears, scooping out the flesh from the base of the fruit. Cook the pears in the syrup for 40 minutes over medium heat then leave them in the cooking liquid until ready to serve so that they remain tender. Prepare the crumble: with your fingertips, rub the rolled oats together with the sugar, margarine and praline. Line a baking tray with parchment paper and spread the crumble on it. Bake for 10 minutes at 180°C (Gas mark 4): the crumble should be a nice gold colour; not too pale nor too dark. Leave to cool. Melt the chocolate in a bain-marie. Place half a pear or a whole one on each plate. Use a spoon to drizzle a little of the melted chocolate over the fruit. Sprinkle with the crumble and serve.

Praline truffles

Makes about 15 truffles

200 g dark chocolate
2 tbsp hazelnut oil
2 tbsp oat milk
1 tbsp hazelnut butter
2 tbsp icing sugar
30 g hazelnuts, finely chopped

Melt the chocolate in a bain-marie. Stir in the hazelnut oil, then the oat milk. Leave the ganache to cool so that it is solid enough to work with without it melting (leave in the fridge for a few minutes if necessary). Mix the hazelnut butter with the icing sugar in a ramekin. Spread the chopped hazelnuts on a plate. Shape the truffles by making a small ball of ganache. Press a finger into it to make a hole and fill it with a little hazelnut butter. Cover over the hole with the ganache, then roll each ball in the chopped hazelnuts. Place each truffle in a little paper case.

CELEBRATIONS VEGAN-STYLE

Chestnut flour and crystallised orange peel spiced bread

Makes 1 spiced bread

175 g einkorn flour
75 g chestnut flour
50 g cane sugar
7 tsp spice mix for spiced bread
1 tsp baking powder
1 tsp bicarbonate of soda
200 ml non-dairy milk
200 ml liquid sweetener (agave syrup, rice syrup, liquid sugar cane, etc.)
1 tbsp dark molasses
40 g crystallised orange peel, finely diced

Combine the dry ingredients, except for the orange peel, in a bowl. Whisk the liquid ingredients together and then combine them with the dry ingredients. Fold in the crystallised orange peel with a spoon. Grease a loaf tin with margarine or oil, or line it with parchment paper. Pour in the cake mixture and bake for 30 minutes at 180°C (Gas mark 4).

Puff pastry parcel of a thousand flavours

Serves 8

30 g textured soy protein
2 tbsp miso
2 tbsp tamari
1 tsp dried thyme
½ tsp garlic powder
150 g red kuri squash, cut into small dice
100 g sweet potato, peeled and cut into small dice
100 g fresh chestnuts, chopped
2 garlic cloves, sliced
1 onion, sliced
2 tbsp olive oil
2 tsp five-spice powder
125 g smoked tofu, crumbled
1 tbsp hazelnut butter
2 sheets vegan puff pastry
soy milk
vegetable oil
pepper

Put the soy protein in a bowl with the miso, tamari, thyme and garlic powder. Cover with boiling water. Generously season with pepper. Mix well and leave to swell for about 20 minutes. Heat the olive oil in a large frying pan over high heat and sauté the vegetables with the five-spice powder, stirring often, for 5 minutes. Drain the soy protein (keeping the soaking liquid) and add it to the vegetables together with the tofu. Lower the heat to medium and cook for a few minutes, stirring continuously. Slake the hazelnut butter with the soaking liquid and add to the pan. Turn the heat right down and mix well. Leave to cook for a few minutes. Roll out 1 sheet of puff pastry onto a baking tray, without removing its parchment paper. Fold in one third of the pastry and fold the other third over it to make creases and reopen. Cut the two outer sides into fringes, about 1 cm wide (see p.108). Place half of the stuffing along the central third of the pastry. Fold in the top and bottom of the dough, then fold the fringes towards the middle, alternating left and right, as if making a plait, until the parcel is closed: the stuffing should not be visible. Mix a small amount of soy milk with a little vegetable oil and brush the parcel all over with it. Prepare the other parcel in the same way. Bake for 20-25 minutes at 180°C (Gas mark 4).

Apple and onion chutney

Makes 1 small jar

3 medium onions, sliced
3 garlic cloves, sliced
3 small apples, sliced
1 tbsp vegetable oil
1 tsp five-spice powder
1 tsp coriander seeds
1 tsp fennel seeds
½ tsp salt
125 ml cider vinegar
8 tbsp cane sugar
black pepper

Sauté the onions in a frying pan with the oil over high heat for a few minutes. Add the spices, season, and mix well. Pour in the vinegar, add the apples, garlic and sugar. Cover. Cook for 10 minutes over medium heat. Remove the lid and leave to reduce for 5-10 minutes. Add a little water if necessary. Pour into a jar and leave to cool. Keeps for 1 week in the fridge.

Roast seitan stuffed with chestnuts

Serves 6-8

miso gravy sauce (see p. 103)

miso gravy sauce (see p. 103)

For the stuffing
1 tbsp olive oil
2 shallots, sliced
200 g cooked chestnuts, chopped
1 tsp dried sage
1 tsp dried wild garlic
½ tsp ground coriander
100 ml water
1 tbsp tamari

For the seitan
175 g gluten
75 g maize (or rice) flour
1 tsp garlic powder
¼ tsp freshly ground black pepper
250 ml vegetable stock
5 tbsp tamari

For the cooking stock
3 litres water
3 vegetable stock cubes
2 tbsp brown miso

Prepare the stuffing: heat the olive oil in a frying pan and sauté the shallots. Add the chestnuts, dried herbs and coriander. Cook for a few minutes. Add the water and tamari and leave to reduce. Set aside. Prepare the seitan: combine the gluten with the flour, garlic powder and pepper to taste. Pour in the vegetable stock and tamari and knead. Lay a piece of cheesecloth or cotton material on a flat surface. Spread the seitan on it, and the stuffing along the middle of the seitan. Roll the seitan up to enclose the stuffing completely. Roll the roast seitan in cheesecloth and tie with string as you would a salami. Do not tie it up too tightly as the seitan will swell as it cooks. Prepare the cooking stock and put the tied-up seitan in it. Cook for 40 minutes. Remove the string and cheesecloth. Place the seitan in an oven-proof dish and cover with the gravy. Roast for 10 minutes at 180°C (Gas mark 4). Serve with the remaining sauce.

Truffle risotto

Serves 2-4

2 tbsp olive oil
1 onion, sliced
200 g short-grain white rice
200 ml white wine
½ vegetable stock cube
2 tbsp white miso
1 litre boiling water
1 x 80 g jar sliced black summer truffles in oil
black pepper

Heat the olive oil in a large frying pan. Sauté the onion over high heat, then add the rice. When the rice is translucent, pour in the white wine and allow it to be absorbed. Slake the ½ vegetable stock cube and the miso in the boiling water. When the wine has been absorbed by the rice, cover with the stock. When that has been absorbed, cover with stock again. Remove the truffle slices from the jar. Set aside 8 thin slices and chop the rest with a knife. Cover the rice with stock again and add the chopped truffles. Add the rest of the stock and the oil from the jar. Season with pepper. Mix well and cook for a few minutes longer. Serve, topped with the slices of truffle.

FYI : *Black truffles from Périgord are unfortunately not in season at Christmas time, so I suggest you use summer truffles that are sold in jars for this recipe. They can be easily found during the holiday season (at about €30 a jar...yes, this is a luxurious recipe!). The flavour of summer truffles is similar, but less pronounced. Of course, this recipe can be prepared with fresh truffles when they are available: use 40-50 g for this recipe.*

Roast seitan stuffed with chestnuts

Vegetable caviar on buckwheat blin

Buckwheat blinis

Serves 4

100 g wholegrain buckwheat flour
50 g plain flour
1 tbsp light brown sugar
1 tsp arrowroot
1 tsp baking powder
½ tsp dried baker's yeast
⅛ tsp salt
150 ml soy cream
100 ml soy milk
1 tbsp olive oil

Combine all the dry ingredients in a mixing bowl. Whisk in the cream and then the milk. Lastly, whisk in the oil. Leave to stand for 30 minutes. Oil a frying pan and turn the heat to medium. Place 1 tbsp of the batter in the pan and let it cook for about 1 minute. Flip the blini over when little bubbles form. Cook the other side for about 1 minute. Repeat the process with the remaining batter. The blinis should be just golden.

Vegetable caviar

Serves 2-4

5 g kombu seaweed
5 g wakame seaweed
250 ml water, plus 150 ml extra
1 sheet yaki nori, cut into little pieces
1 tbsp tamari
250 g rapeseed oil
2 g agar-agar powder

Prepare the seaweed stock: wash the seaweeds and put them in a saucepan with 250 ml of water. Bring to the boil and cook for 2 minutes. Strain and leave to cool. Whiz the yaki nori with the 150 ml of water, the tamari and 1 tbsp of the seaweed stock. Strain to obtain the liquid. Pour the oil into a large glass and refrigerate for 1 hour. Combine the yaki nori liquid with the agar-agar in a small saucepan. Bring to the boil and cook for 2 minutes, stirring continuously. Whiz with an immersion blender until smooth and then pour into a syringe. Take the jar of oil out of the fridge. Use the syringe to push little drops of the mixture into the oil bath to form tiny spheres. Leave to cool for 15 minutes then remove the spheres with a slotted spoon and put them in a water bath. The oil will float to the surface: pour the liquid through a small sieve or colander to retrieve the spheres and then put them in a small jar or container. Serve with buckwheat blinis (see next recipe), homemade soy crème fraîche (see p. 143) and lemon.

A very simple but spectacular recipe that requires speed and precision as the spheres must be made before the agar-agar thickens as it cools in the saucepan or in the syringe.

Roasted potatoes with sage and Espelette pepper

Serves 6

800 g potatoes, peeled and cut into medium-sized pieces
1 onion, cut into medium-sized pieces
4 tbsp neutral vegetable oil
2 tbsp chopped fresh chives
1 tbsp dried sage
1½ tsp garlic powder
¼ tsp Espelette pepper
fleur de sel, pepper

Arrange the pieces of potato in an oven-proof dish. Separate the onion layers. Put the onion into the dish together with the oil, herbs, garlic powder and Espelette pepper. Mix well. Bake at 180°C (Gas mark 4) for 1 hour and 15 minutes, turning everything over every 10 minutes. Season with fleur de sel and pepper when about to serve.

Marinated tofu brochettes

Serves 4

250 g firm tofu, cut into cubes
1 red pepper, cut into medium-sized pieces
1 onion, quartered
For the marinade
10 g fresh ginger, finely diced
1 lemon, quartered
4 tbsp shoyu
4 tbsp maple syrup
1 tbsp sunflower oil
ground cayenne pepper
pepper

Combine all the marinade ingredients (add cayenne and pepper to taste). Add the tofu and leave to marinate in the fridge for 12 hours. Separate the onion layers. Assemble the brochettes, alternating pieces of pepper, tofu and onion as you thread them onto the skewers. Grill them for a few minutes each side on a barbecue.

Vegetable yakitori

Makes 6 brochettes

5 tbsp tamari
2 tbsp agave syrup
½ courgette, thickly sliced
1 small onion, thickly sliced
3 large button mushrooms, thickly sliced

Combine the tamari and agave syrup in a large bowl. Put in the vegetables and marinate for 30 minutes to 1 hour. Assemble the brochettes alternating the vegetables as you thread them onto the skewers. Grill them on a barbecue for a few minutes each side.

Penne and pistou salad

Serves 4-6

250 g penne rigate
2 tbsp olive oil, plus extra for the cooking water
1 large tomato, finely diced
½ red pepper, finely diced
20 g rocket leaves, chopped
2 tbsp sunflower seeds
salt and pepper
For the pistou
2 bunches basil
50 ml olive oil
50 g white cashew nuts
1 tbsp freshly squeezed lemon juice

Cook the penne in a large saucepan of boiling water with a drizzle of olive oil and a large pinch of salt. Drain and refresh under cold running water. Whiz all the ingredients for the pistou together. Combine the pasta and the pistou in a large bowl. Add the olive oil. Toss the pasta with the tomato, red pepper, rocket leaves amd sunflower seeds. Season to taste and mix well. Refrigerate.

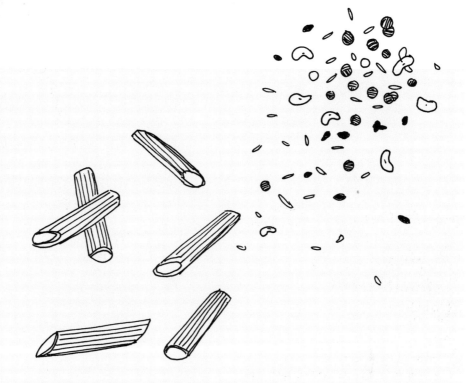

Indian-style rice salad

Serves 2

1 tbsp olive oil
½ tsp ground turmeric
½ tsp ground cardamom
½ tsp ground fenugreek
200 g Basmati rice
50 g cooked petit pois
1 red pepper, diced
1 handful raisins
1 handful cashew nuts, roughly chopped
salt and pepper

Heat the olive oil in a large saucepan over high heat and put in the spices. Add the rice and stir to mix well. When the rice is transparent, add 400 ml of water and cook over medium heat until the water has been completely absorbed. Put into a fine sieve and quickly rinse so that the rice grains do not stick together. Drain and leave to cool. Combine the rice with the petit pois, red pepper, raisins and cashew nuts. Season with salt and pepper to taste.

Delicious with coconut raita (see p. 164).

Summer wraps

Serves 4

250 g firm tofu, cut into 1 cm wide strips
1 courgette, cut into 1 cm wide strips
1 onion, cut into thick slices
olive oil
herbes de Provence
4 lettuce leaves
4 wheat wraps
1 x 200 g tub aubergine caviar or homemade
salt and pepper

Place the tofu and vegetables in a dish and baste with olive oil. Sprinkle with herbes de Provence and season with salt and pepper. Grill on a barbecue. Put a lettuce leaf on each wrap, cover with aubergine caviar and top with grilled tofu, courgette and onion. Fold in the base of the wraps, and then fold in from the sides.

***Picnic version:** Grill the vegetables and the tofu in a frying pan. Leave to cool before stuffing the wraps. Put kitchen paper and then silver foil around each wrap.*

Seitan brochettes cooked like spare-ribs

Serves 4-8

<u>Dry ingredients</u>
230 g wheat gluten
80 g lupin flour
1½ tsp garlic powder
1 tsp paprika
pepper

<u>For the stock</u>
1 tbsp barley miso
1 tbsp vegetable stock paste (or 2 cubes)
1 tbsp shoyu
1 tbsp balsamic vinegar
½ tsp liquid smoke
1 litre boiling water

<u>For the marinade</u>
1 onion
2 garlic cloves
4 tbsp BBQ sauce (see p. 300)
3 tbsp maple syrup
3 tbsp tomato passata
2 tbsp soy sauce
2 tsp ground coriander
1 tsp mustard
1 tsp balsamic vinegar
pepper

Combine the dry ingredients in a bowl. Mix the stock ingredients in a jug to make a paste. Slake with a little of the boiling water, then add the rest and mix well. Take 450 ml of the stock and add to the dry ingredients. Mix and shape into a ball. Flatten it with your hands on a floured worktop. Flour the seitan. Pour the rest of the stock into a dish and gently place the seitan into it (be very careful as it is very delicate). Pour in water to cover as necessary. Bake for 45 minutes at 180°C (Gas mark 4). Remove the stock and cover the seitan with parchment paper to avoid it drying out and put it back in the oven for 20 minutes. Cut the seitan into 4 thick slices. Store overnight in the fridge in an airtight container. The next day, prepare the marinade: whiz the onion and the garlic to a purée and then mix with the other ingredients. Marinate the seitan for 4-6 hours. Put a skewer lengthwise through each slice of the seitan and grill them for a few minutes each side on the barbecue.

Herb and spice marinated corn cobs

Serves 4-8

4 fresh or vacuum-packed cobs of corn
<u>For the marinade</u>
5 tbsp sunflower oil
2 tbsp chopped fresh coriander
2 tbsp chopped fresh chives
2 tsp dried onion
1 tsp ground cumin
1 tsp ground coriander
1 tsp paprika
1 tsp garlic powder
½ tsp salt
a few drops chilli sauce

Cut the corn cobs in half. Mix all the marinade ingredients together and brush the corn cobs with it. Leave for 1 hour. Barbecue for 10 minutes, turning the cobs often.

seitan brochettes and corn cobs

Grilled aubergines with curried miso cream

Serves 4

2 large aubergines, cut in half lengthwise

for the curried miso cream

100 ml soy cream

1 tbsp barley miso

1 tsp curry powder

1 tsp soy sauce

Put all the ingredients for the curried miso cream in a bowl and mix with a fork. Score the cut surface of the aubergines deeply in one direction and then in the other to make a criss-cross pattern. Grill the aubergines on the barbecue, cut side down, for 3-5 minutes to brown them nicely. Turn the aubergines over and spread with the curried miso cream. Leave to cook for 10 minutes. Serve hot.

Vanilla-scented strawberry and melon salad

Serves 4

1 large melon, cut into cubes

250 g strawberries, washed and hulled

1 lemon, juiced and half the lemon zested

2 tsp agave syrup

⅛ tsp ground vanilla

Cut the strawberries into quarters. Combine the lemon zest and juice, the agave syrup and vanilla in a ramekin. Pour this syrup over the fruit. Serve chilled.

Iced watermelon

Serves 8

1 medium watermelon

Cut 2 round slices of watermelon, and then cut each one into quarters. Use a knife to cut a slit in the rind of each slice and then slide in a wooden ice cream stick. Put the slices of watermelon in a large container or on a plate and freeze for at least 2 hours. Eat like an ice lolly.

BBQ sauce

Makes 1 bowl

1 onion, sliced

2 tbsp olive oil

1 garlic clove sliced

2 tbsp balsamic vinegar

4 tbsp muscovado sugar

2 tbsp vegan Worcestershire sauce

2 tbsp tamari

250 ml tomato passata

6 tbsp ketchup

1 tsp liquid smoke

Sweat the onion in a small saucepan with the olive oil for 5 minutes. Lower the heat to medium and add the garlic. Cook for a few minutes. Add the vinegar and sugar. Mix well. Add the Worcestershire sauce and tamari, then the passata, ketchup and lastly the liquid smoke. Mix well and turn the heat to low. Cook for 30 minutes, stirring often.

Tomatoes
à la Provençale

Serves 4-8

4 tomatoes, washed and cut in half lengthwise
3 garlic cloves, finely chopped
1 bunch curly parsley, finely chopped
50 g fine breadcrumbs
2 tbsp olive oil, plus a little extra
salt and pepper

Place the tomatoes in an oven-proof dish, cut side up. Combine the garlic and parsley in a bowl with the breadcrumbs. Add the 2 tbsp of olive oil and season with salt and pepper. Top the tomatoes with this mixture, drizzle with a little olive oil and bake for 20 minutes at 180°C (Gas mark 4) for 5-10 minutes.

- -

Herb marinade for
barbecuing

4 tbsp olive oil
2 tbsp balsamic vinegar
2 tbsp shoyu
1 tbsp herbes de Provence
1-2 tsp mustard
pepper

Combine all the ingredients in an airtight container. Leave to marinate 2-24 hours depending on the ingredient (2 hours for mushrooms, 4-6 hours for vegetables, 12 hours for tofu, 24 hours for seitan). Shake the container regularly to mix the ingredients well.

This quantity of marinade is for 250 g of tofu, tempeh or seitan; or for 2 courgettes, 1 aubergine or 1 punnet of mushrooms.

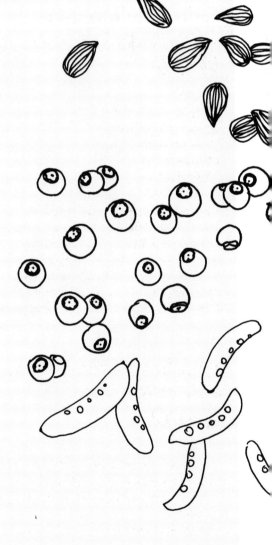

Tomato and basil muf

Tomato and basil muffins

Makes about 8 muffins

175 g spelt flour
2 tbsp cornflour
2 tsp dried onion
1½ tsp baking powder
½ tsp salt
freshly ground pepper
250 ml soy milk
1 tsp apple cider vinegar
50 ml olive oil
50 g sun-dried tomatoes in olive oil, drained and finely
  diced
2 tbsp chopped basil
1 tbsp tomato passata

Combine all the dry ingredients in a bowl. In another bowl, mix the soy milk and vinegar together. Leave to stand for a few minutes. Whisk in the olive oil until the mixture is nice and foamy. To avoid a lumpy mixture, first whisk in half of the dry ingredients. Whisk in the remaining dry ingredients. Add the sun-dried tomatoes, basil and tomato passata. Mix together with a spoon. Line muffin tins with paper cases then fill them three-quarters of the way up with the batter. Bake for 25 minutes at 180°C (gas mark 4).

Strawberry lemonade

Serves 4

2 lemons, juiced
4 strawberries, washed, hulled and cut into little pieces
3 tbsp agave syrup
1 litre sparkling water

Combine the strawberries with the lemon juice. Add the agave syrup. Mix well. Strain through a fine sieve. Pour the sparkling water into a jug and then add the fruit juice. Mix briefly if necessary. Store in an airtight container. Keeps for 24 hours in the fridge.

Peach and jasmine-scented iced green tea

Serves 4

1 tbsp (or 2 sachets) jasmine-scented green tea
1 litre cold water
1 white peach, peeled and cut into pieces
2 tbsp agave syrup

Steep the tea in the water and leave in the fridge for 3 hours. Remove the sachets or strain the iced tea. Whiz the peach, a little of the iced tea and the agave syrup in a blender. Pour into the jug containing the iced tea. Mix well. Refrigerate. Add some ice cubes to the jug or directly into the glasses when about to serve.

Chocolate and hazelnut milk spread

Makes 1 pot

1 litre hazelnut milk
250 g light brown sugar
1½ tbsp cocoa powder

Whisk all the ingredients together in a large saucepan. Bring to the boil, then cook over medium heat until the mixture has reduced considerably and small bubbles begin to appear (this may take 1-2 hours). It is important to stir often and and keep a close eye on it to prevent a skin forming on top and the mixture catching on the bottom of the pan. The spread is done when it is thick enough to coat the back of a spoon. Pour into a glass jar and put on the lid. Leave to cool before refrigerating. Keeps for 1 month in the fridge.

Rose-scented pancakes

Makes 10 pancakes

150 g plain flour
60 g light brown sugar
2 tsp cornflour
1 tsp baking powder
½ tsp bicarbonate of soda
300 ml non-dairy milk
2 tbsp neutral vegetable oil
1 tbsp rosewater
vegetable oil for cooking

Combine the dry ingredients in a bowl. Whisk the non-dairy milk into the dry ingredients and then add the oil and rosewater. Cook the pancakes in a lightly oiled frying pan over medium heat. Flip them over when little bubbles form and burst, and the surface is almost dry.

Chocolate and speculoos spread

Makes 1 pot

100 g dark chocolate
100 g speculoos biscuits, crumbled
6 tbsp non-dairy milk
4 tbsp agave syrup
3 tbsp cashew butter

Melt the chocolate in a bain-marie. Whiz the speculoos biscuits to a fine powder. Add the melted chocolate together with the remaining ingredients and whiz until very smooth. Pour into a glass jar. Do not store in the fridge. Use within 2 weeks.

Banana bread

Serves 6

2 very ripe bananas, peeled and cut into pieces
80 ml neutral vegetable oil
200 g light brown sugar
2 tsp baking powder
½ tsp bicarbonate of soda
½ tsp salt
250 g plain flour

Whiz the bananas in a food processor. Mix the oil and sugar together and then add the banana purée. In another bowl, combine the baking powder and bicarbonate of soda, salt and flour. Stir in the banana mixture a little at a time. The mixture will be quite thick, so stir vigorously. Oil a medium-sized loaf tin and pour in the mixture. Bake for 40-45 minutes at 180°C (Gas mark 4). Leave to cool before unmoulding.

Blueberry and chocolate chip scones

Makes 12 scones

150 g plain flour
150 g spelt flour
80 g light brown sugar, plus extra for sprinkling
½ tsp baking powder
½ tsp bicarbonate of soda
½ tsp ground vanilla
80 ml soy milk
1 tsp apple cider vinegar
50 g vegan margarine
2 tbsp cashew butter
35 g chocolate chips
50 g blueberries

Combine the dry ingredients in a bowl. Mix the soy milk and vinegar in a bowl. Rub the margarine and the cashew butter into the dry ingredients with your fingertips as if you were making a crumble. Mix the soy milk in with a fork. Add the chocolate chips and the blueberries. Mix well. Line a baking tray with parchment paper. Shape a dozen scones on the prepared tray. Space them well apart as they will spread as they cook. Bake for 20-25 minutes at 180°C (Gas mark 4). The scones should be golden brown.

Savoury polenta madeleines

Makes 10 madeleines

80 g plain flour
75 g pre-cooked polenta
½ tsp baking powder
½ tsp salt
120 g silken tofu
2 tbsp olive oil
1 tbsp cashew butter

Combine the dry ingredients in a bowl. Add the liquid ingredients and mix well with a fork. Oil the madeleine moulds then fill each one right to the top with the mixture. Press gently and smooth them with the back of a wet spoon. Bake for 15 minutes at 200°C (Gas mark 6-7). Leave to coo.

For an elegant presentation, serve topped with a spread and finely diced vegetables.

Savoury Tex-Mex cupcakes

Makes 12 cupcakes

150 g T70 spelt flour
100 g maize flour
55 g pre-cooked polenta
2 tsp baking powder
½ tsp salt
350 ml soy milk
½ tbsp apple cider vinegar
70 ml olive oil
For the topping
400 g cooked red beans
2 tbsp olive oil
2 tbsp freshly squeezed lemon juice
1 tbsp cashew butter
4 tsp chilli spice mix
½ tsp salt
pepper

Combine all the dry ingredients in a bowl. In another bowl, mix the soy milk and vinegar and leave to curdle for 5 minutes. Whisk in the oil to mix well. Add the liquid ingredients to the dry ones and mix. Divide the mixture among a 12-hole muffin tin lined with paper cases. Bake for 25 minutes at 180°C (Gas mark 4). Leave to cool completely before decorating. Whiz all the ingredients for the topping together. Fit a pastry bag with a large star nozzle, fill with the topping and refrigerate. Pipe the topping onto the cupcakes just before serving to avoid them becoming dry.

Savoury thyme and lemon muffins

Makes 9 muffins

250 ml soy milk
1 tsp apple cider vinegar
200 g plain flour
75 g rolled oats
1½ tsp baking powder
½ tsp bicarbonate of soda
1 tsp salt
6 tbsp olive oil
2 tsp dried thyme

1 lemon, zested
1 tbsp freshly squeezed lemon juice

Mix the soy milk and vinegar together in a bowl and leave to curdle for 5-10 minutes. In another bowl, combine the flour with the rolled oats, baking powder, bicarbonate of soda and salt. Whisk the oil vigorously into the curdled soy milk to make it foamy. Add the thyme, lemon zest and juice and whisk again. Use a fork to incorporate the flour a little at a time. Line 9 holes of a muffin tin with paper cases then fill them with the mixture. Bake for 25 minutes at 180°C (Gas mark 4).

Chocolate marble waffles

Makes 8 waffles

75 g light brown sugar
3 tbsp vegetable oil
3 tbsp cashew butter
1 sachet (10 g) baking powder
75 ml soy cream
250 ml non-dairy milk
225 g type T45 flour
⅛ tsp ground tonka beans
⅛ tsp vanilla extract
⅛ tsp ground cinnamon
2 tbsp cocoa powder

Mix the sugar with the oil and cashew butter in a bowl. Add the baking powder, soy cream and non-dairy milk. Lastly, mix in the flour. Pour half of the mixture into another bowl. Mix the ground tonka beans into one half of the mixture. Mix the vanilla extract, cinnamon and cocoa powder into the other half. Heat a waffle iron. Spoon a little of the chocolate mixture into the waffle iron, making sure not to fill every hole. Immediately spoon in the white mixture to fill the empty holes. Mix gently to swirl and create a marbled effect. Cook like regular waffles.

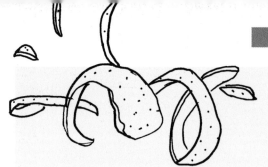

Seitan 'bacon'

Serves 4

150 g gourmet shop-bought or homemade seitan
(see p. 96), finely sliced
<u>For the marinade</u>
3 tbsp tamari
2 tsp agave syrup
2 tsp tomato passata
1 tsp liquid smoke

Mix the ingredients for the marinade in a dish. Marinate the seitan slices for 30 minutes to 2 hours. Cook the seitan slices in a frying pan over medium-high heat to brown both sides.

Delicious with scrambled tofu and potatoes.

Crystallised orange peel and chocolate chip brioche

Makes 1 medium brioche

250 g type T55 flour
30 g light brown sugar
½ tsp salt
125 ml soy milk, warmed, plus extra for glazing
½ sachet dried baker's yeast
40 g neutral vegetable oil
3 tbsp dark chocolate chips
2 tbsp crystallised orange peel, chopped

Mix the flour with the sugar and salt in a bowl. Mix the warm soy milk with the yeast and leave to stand for a few minutes. Pour it onto the flour and mix in with a spoon. Mix in the oil. Knead well for 5-10 minutes by hand, folding the dough over and over itself. The idea is to incorporate as much air as possible into the dough. The dough should be supple and smooth, and not sticky. Leave to rise in a bowl covered with a clean tea towel for 1 hour, ideally at 25°C. Knead again for 1 minute and add the chocolate chips and the orange peel. Knead again to incorporate them well. Shape the dough as desired: for a classic brioche, shape the dough into medium-sized balls and place side by side in a loaf tin or spring form cake tin. Leave to rise for 2 hours in a turned-off oven with the door closed. Brush with soy milk and bake for about 30 minutes at 180° (Gas mark 4). Keep the brioche wrapped in a tea towel as it tends to dry out quickly.

Sweet potato rosti

Serves 4-6

125 g potato, peeled
200 g sweet potato, peeled
1 onion, finely sliced
vegetable oil for cooking
salt and pepper

Grate the potato and sweet potato in a food processor and then spread out on a tea towel. Roll the tea towel up tightly to absorb the excess moisture of the vegetables. Mix in a bowl with the onion. Season with salt and pepper. Place a metal ring mould (6-8 cm diameter) in a lightly oiled pan and press a little of the mixture in it to form a thin layer. Cook a few minutes over medium-high heat for the bottom of the rosti to become nicely brown. Then, using a spatula, turn the ring over and gently press the edges of the rosti so it drops down onto the pan. Cook again for a few minutes. Remove the ring mould and set the rosti aside on a plate. Cook the remaining mixture in the same way.

A few rosti can be cooked at the same time in a large frying pan using as many ring moulds as will fit.

Bagels

Makes 8 bagels

550 g type T55 flour

10 g sachet dried baker's yeast

3 tbsp cane sugar

2 tsp salt

1 tbsp olive oil

300 ml warm water

2 tbsp seeds of your choice (sesame, poppy, caraway, cumin, nigella, etc)

<u>For the cooking water</u>

2 litres water

1 tsp bicarbonate of soda

1 tsp salt

2 tbsp agave syrup

Combine all the dry ingredients in a bowl. Mix in the olive oil and water with a wooden spoon until it all comes together into a ball. Knead by hand on a worktop for at least 5 minutes. Leave the dough to rise for 1 hour in a bowl covered with a clean tea towel. Make 8 balls of dough making sure the joins are underneath. Using both thumbs, make a hole in each ball, then rotate the ball around your thumbs to enlarge the hole to about 5 cm in diameter and form a ring. Line a baking tray with parchment paper and place the dough rings on the tray. Cover with a tea towel and leave to rise again for 1 hour. Bring the cooking water to the boil in a large saucepan with the bicarbonate, salt and agave syrup. Poach the bagels in the water one or two at a time for 1 minute, then turn them over and poach for another 30 seconds. Dry them gently with a tea towel and put them back on the parchment paper-lined baking tray. Sprinkle with the seeds and bake at 220°C (Gas mark 7-8) for 15-25 minutes. The bagels should be lightly golden.

Slice in half and fill with cream spread with fresh herbs, salad leaves, slices of avocado, vegan cheese, basically anything you like!

Strawberry, banana and blueberry oatshake

Serves 1

1 banana

45 g strawberries

15 g blueberries

300 ml oat milk

agave syrup to taste

Leave the fruit in the freezer for a few hours so that they become icy. Whiz with the oat milk and agave syrup. Serve immediately.

Green olive and onion spelt rolls

Serves 4-8

500 g spelt flour, plus extra for dusting

1 tsp salt

10 g sachet dried baker's yeast

300 ml water, heated to 50°C

1 large onion, sliced

1 tbsp olive oil

75 g pitted green olives, sliced into rounds

Combine the flour and salt in a bowl. Mix the yeast with the water and leave to stand for 5 minutes. Pour the water onto the flour. Mix well then knead for 5 minutes on a floured worktop. Leave to rise in a bowl, covered with a damp tea towel, for 2 hours at about 25°C (near a radiator, in a turned-off oven, etc). Sauté the onion in the olive oil with the olives for 5 minutes until tender and just browned. Add to the dough and mix in well with your hands. Shape into 4 balls. Place on a baking tray lined with parchment paper. Bake at 200°C (Gas mark 6) for 25 minutes.

Alphabetical index

Ingredients index

Agar-agar
Apple and raspberry fruit tartlets 253
Asparagus clafoutis 183
Aubergine and miso terrine 172
Bergamot puddings 123
Blueberry panna cotta 267
Carrot, thyme and orange flans 165
Chestnut and crystallised orange log 288
Coconut blancmange 231
Cold melon and ginger jelly 253
Cream cheese 128
Cream cheese with grilled peppers 138
Crème brûlée with raspberries 272
Crème brûlée with roasted peaches
    and thyme 228
Crème caramel 231
Fruit jelly trio 278
Light summer terrine 172
Little grilled pepper flans 167
Matcha panna cotta with raspberry coulis
    228
Melty cheese 135
Pink velvet cheesecake 282
Raspberry and rose bavarois 244
Rose and pistachio puddings 231
Seitan rillettes 102
Sliceable cheese with cumin 136
Soy mozzarella 128
Summer fruit and orange juice terrine 175
Vanilla and chocolate puddings 267
Vegetable caviar 295
Winter lentil pâté 30

Amaranth
Amaranth and raisin cookies 46
Amaranth tabbouleh with grilled peppers
    56
Provençale galettes 44

Apples
Apple and cinnamon rice pudding with
    maple syrup 127
Apple and raspberry fruit tartlets 253
Apple and onion chutney 291
Apple and raspberry turnovers 243
Apple and vanilla yoghurt with dried fruit
    and nut crumble 240
Apple, caramel and almond tart 243
Orange, ginger, carrot and apple smoothie
    212
Tutti-frutti frozen smoothies 237
Waldorf salad 272

Apricots
Apricot and pistachio tartlets 242
Roasted apricot salad 223
Summer fruit and orange juice terrine 175

Artichokes
Artichonade 176
Chic asparagus and artichoke pizza 194
Country-style Jerusalem artichoke galette
    195
Creamed Jerusalem artichoke 176
Jerusalem artichoke gratin 184
Jerusalem artichoke winter cake 162
Paella 116
Salade Niçoise with broad beans 260
Stuffed artichokes 204

Asparagus
Asparagus clafoutis 183
Chic asparagus and artichoke pizza 194
Sautéed quinoa and green asparagus
    salad 75
Scrambled tofu with green asparagus 167

Aubergine
Aubergine and miso terrine 172
Aubergine and ricotta and mint pesto
    galettes 199
Aubergine pastillas 259
Aubergines stuffed with Indian-style rice
    203
Aubergine, tomato and mozzarella
    bruschetta 263
Grilled aubergines with curried miso cream
    300
Grilled einkorn with aubergine 43
Lasagne with summer vegetables, ricotta
    and pesto 51
Lebanese-style sautéed bulgur 46
Tempeh tagine with aubergines and
    olives 86
Tian à la Provençale 183
Vegetable and quinoa Antilles curry 74
Vegetable moussaka 95

Avocado
Avocado and kiwi pudding 222
Cold avocado, sweetcorn and pepper soup
    256
Crudité brochettes and sauce 218
Curried hummus and crudité wraps 217
Guacamole 262
Thai mango salad 189
Tofu and avocado California makis 256
Vitamin-packed salad 259
White and yellow pasta with a creamy
    avocado and courgette sauce 215

Barley
Pan-fried barley and fennel with mint 47
Pan-fried Brussels sprouts and pearl barley
    salad 44

Beans
Azuki bean and brown rice galettes 36
Black bean burritos 62
Black bean hummus 32
Chilli sin carne 66
Green bean persillade 269
'Hot' dip 30
Italian dip 32
Lisbon-style black-eyed bean salad 65
Lupin bean gratable cheese 135
Red seitan 101
Savoury Tex-Mex cupcakes 306
Sea-flavoured rillettes 113
Sweet, azuki bean paste 62
Texan-style stuffed peppers 184
Tex-Mex burgers 38
Two-bean rillettes 69
White bean, fresh coriander and lemon
    dip 30
White bean rissoles with tomato and
    basil 37

Beetroot
Beetroot and almond dip 176
Pink beetroot blinis 153
Pink beetroot ketchup 275
Pink velvet cheesecake 282
Potato and olive oil purée, pan-fried
    beetroot and unpeeled garlic 180
White and yellow pasta with a creamy
    avocado and courgette sauce 215

Blueberries
Banana-blueberry pancakes 149
Blueberry and chocolate
    chip scones 305
Blueberry panna cotta 267
Chocolate and berry fondants 247
Frozen berry yoghurt 250
Fruit jelly trio 278
Raw tartlets with berries 207
Raw, banana, blueberry and strawberry
    ice 209
Strawberry, banana and blueberry
    oatshake 311

Brik pastry
Aubergine pastillas 259
Middle Eastern briks 90
Petits pois and coconut samosas 264
Tofu and vegetable pastilla 81

Broad beans
Broad bean and rocket muffins 162
Broad bean falafel 40
Broad bean risotto 65
Salade Niçoise with broad beans 260
Warm broad bean and rocket salad 66